My War Diary

THE CHURCH AND SCHOOL AT LES AULNEAUX

My War Diary
A Lady's Experience of the Great War in Europe
1914-1918

Mary King Waddington

LEONAUR

My War Diary
A Lady's Experience of the Great War in Europe 1914-1918
by Mary King Waddington

First published under the title
My War Diary

Leonaur is an imprint of Oakpast Ltd

ISBN: 978-1-78282-024-6 (hardcover)
ISBN: 978-1-78282-025-3 (softcover)

http://www.leonaur.com

Publisher's Notes

Contents

Preface

This simple, every-day record of the experiences through which one French family has lived since August, 1914, may seem at first sight a charming, but not very important contribution to the literature of the war. But if we accept Henry Cabot Lodge's *dictum* that "one fact is gossip, and that two related facts are history," we shall realise in closing the bode how much history we have absorbed in a Jourdainesque kind of ignorance.

The *cure* at Mareuil, the little grandsons finding a German skull, the lawn sacrificed to potatoes, the roses rising triumphant over utilitarianism, the goodbyes at the railroad-stations, the Christmas tree, the friendly talks all these may be trifles in one way; but they are making history. After all, we know more about the Lilliputians than about the Brobdingnagians, and they are more illustrative of Swift.

This story of the past war months is like a rich fabric so cunningly woven that the rare and restrained touches of emotion stand out in brilliant relief against the neutral—no, that word has fallen into disrepute—against the sober tones of the daily background. And it is only in certain lights that one catches the gleam of the discreetly hidden threads of gold and silver which indicate the heroism of mother and wife. Ah, they are beautiful and sublime, these lives of French women! Son or husband at the front, while the children at home are cared for, the wounded, poor, and wandering helped, fields tilled, shops kept open, and everything done cheerfully, "all in the day's work," with no posing, no assumption of being above the ordinary. To those of us honoured by the author's friendship this book means a great deal. We have seen her brilliant in the world, tender and gay at home, helpful and widely charitable in her many duties, while all the time we divine that the mother's heart holds always the pride and the ache of which she writes so seldom.   Helen Choate Prince.

Mobilisation—First Days of the War

Mareuil, Saturday, August 1st, '14.

I will try and write regularly, dear, but this iniquitous war has come so suddenly that we are all bewildered. Even my journey down here seems a horrible dream, the Gare de l'Est crowded with troops of all grades, reservists joining their corps, soldiers guarding the line, a strong detachment at every bridge and tunnel. When I think that on Thursday, when Francis lunched, he said the state of things was serious, that many men had been sent off to join their corps, but merely as a matter of precaution, but that the two emperors, German and Russian, were still "talking," and everyone hoped there would be no general war! He thought I could perfectly start for Cowes on Monday, and it was agreed that I should come down here for the day, Saturday, to say goodbye to them all. However, I must say that on Wednesday night, when Ambassador Herrick and Sir Austin Lee of the British Embassy had dined with us, they were pretty blue. Mr. Herrick thought a general war was inevitable; it would be impossible to keep it between Austria and Servia; that Russia would surely interfere if Servia was attacked, and then France must fight.

Friday afternoon we drove about Paris in all directions. Here in our part of the town and in the Champs Elysées, all was quiet enough, but the boulevards were crowded. In front of the office of the *Matin* that issued an extra about 7 o'clock, a long line of people stretched halfway across the *boulevard*. All threw themselves on the paper, those who could not get one reading over the shoulders of those who had one. A perfectly quiet, well-dressed crowd, a great many women, a great many Americans, all most eager for news. Austria's declaration of war to Russia, the only news—speculations of all kind in the crowd; "Austria has gone mad," we heard an Englishman say; everybody wondering what France would do; all the men looked grave, but there was no excitement. The *Petit Temps*, which comes about 9 o'clock, didn't give anything more, so I decided to come down here, as we had agreed.

As soon as I got into the Gare de l'Est this morning, I realised how serious the state of affairs was. The station was crowded with officers, soldiers, recruits, and baggage. They gave me a return ticket, as I had told Henrietta [1] I would take the afternoon train back and get home for late dinner. I asked an officer what it all meant: Merely a measure of precaution, he told me—all the men, officers, soldiers, and recruits joining their corps. There was perfect order, the trains starting at their regular hours, but anxiety was in the air. At every station there were soldiers.

On getting here, I found only the gardener to receive me. He told me Francis [2] had received his convocation this morning, and had gone to Paris with Charlotte, but would be back for dinner. It was extraordinary to see soldiers at our little station. I lunched quietly with Madeleine Sallandrouze and the children. We walked about the garden, the boys showing me their *potager* with much pride, and then settled ourselves under the trees, discussing the situation and trying to persuade ourselves that there would be no war.

Suddenly, about 4 o'clock, we heard the drum, an ominous sound in these days. In all the big towns, the mobilisation, or a great fire, or accident, is announced by the bells—a "tocsin;" in the villages by a drum. We all rushed to the gate. The men came running in from the fields (we are in full harvest time), leaving their horses and placid white oxen on the road, anywhere. Women ran out of the cottages, their babies in their arms, and children tugging at their skirts, and the drummer, escorted by the whole population, us also, put up his *affiches* at the *mairie* and the station, for instant mobilisation.

The whole village was in a turmoil. Some of the men were to start at once—at 9 that night. The *chef de gare* had his orders; nothing but military trains were to pass—you will remember that we are in the direct line to Germany, five hours' rail from the frontier. He told me it was impossible for me to get back to Paris tonight; the train would probably not start, might wait on a siding all night, or perhaps arrive in the middle of the night. It would be most imprudent for me to risk it alone. I tried to telephone—already cut; sent a telegram which never arrived, and Henrietta went nearly mad with anxiety waiting for me and imagining every possible misfortune.

1. Madame Waddington's sister.
2. Madame Waddington's son.

Mme. Sallandrouze came down at 6 o'clock alone. Francis and Charlotte [3] had breakfasted with her and promised to meet her at the *gare*, but they didn't appear. I suppose he had too much to do, as he had to buy all sorts of things, army shoes and flannel shirts, knapsack, flask, etc. Hers was the last passenger-train that left the Gare de l'Est. She thought Francis must start tomorrow morning.

All the evening from 6 o'clock, military trains passed; mostly cavalry—horses and men in the trains, all cheering and singing. Our boys were wild with excitement, but we finally got them to bed. When I went upstairs to say goodnight to them, they were saying their prayers, kneeling before a little shrine with a statue of the virgin and some flowers—Mme. S. and Madeleine kneeling just behind them. When they had finished little childish prayer, "*Bon Dieu, bénissez Papa, Maman, Bonne Maman, Danny, tout ceux que nous aimons*," there was a pause, and then: "*Bon Dieu, préservez la France*." I think, perhaps, that simple baby prayer will be listened to as much as the superb proclamations of the *Kaiser* to the "God of our fathers, who is always with us!"

All night the trains passed. About 9.30 we heard the sound of cheering, and ran down to the edge of the garden to see the soldiers. We thought the boys were sound asleep in their beds, but we suddenly saw two little figures in their white nightgowns, running over the lawn and the tennis, barefoot, waving their flags and shouting: "*Vive l'armée! Vive la France!*" at the top of their voices. They climbed upon the wall and no one had the heart to send them away. I have sent again to the last train, which did not come, and the *chef de gare* assures me there is no chance of our getting away tomorrow. I am perfectly miserable. I must see Francis before he goes. I may never see him again. I don't think anyone is sleeping much tonight, in this house or in the village.

Paris, Sunday, August 2nd.

Have arrived, but such a journey. I was up at 6 this morning, as the *chef de gare* sent me word a train might perhaps come at 7 o'clock, and I had better come at once to the station and wait for it, but that everything was very uncertain; he could not guarantee that it would reach Paris. I went as soon as I could get ready, and waited at the station until the train arrived about 8—a very long one, almost entirely military, only one or two passenger carriages, which were crowded.

We were fourteen in our carriage (which in ordinary times seats eight), ten seated, four standing, and three children. We stopped at

---

3. Madame, Waddington's daughter-in-law.

every station, soldiers on our train, and all the trains we passed, singing and cheering. At one of the small stations, many of the soldiers got out and were transferred to the Château-Thierry line, and from there, directly to the front. A pretty girl was saying goodbye to her soldier and crying. She was instantly taken to task by one of his comrades on our train. "*Voyons, petite, du courage; ne pleure pas; nous reviendrons!*" She looked up at me through her tears, saying: "*Tous ne reviendront pas, Madame.*" And that is what we all are saying in these awful days. Who will be missing at the final roll-call? However, all the men are going off cheerfully, and sure that they are going to win this time.

We had a nice family in the compartment, a refined, clever-looking young man, a professor from Alençon, with his wife and two babies. They had been travelling since 5 o'clock yesterday afternoon, and the poor little things were so hot and tired, but wonderfully good. They had been at Verdun, close to the frontier, for their holidays, and took the last train that left, as the professor had to start instantly with his regiment. He said the mobilisation was being wonderfully carried out. One hour after the order was posted, trains were leaving every half-hour—men and horses in perfect condition, and the spirit of the men excellent.

I am frightened at the superiority in numbers of the Germans. They say they have three men to one over us. *One* man, however good he may be, cannot hold his own against *three*.

They had left in such a hurry that they had no baggage. Couldn't have taken it if they had had it. All their belongings were tied up in a nice clean linen sheet. When we got to Paris I said to her: "I hope you and your babies will get safely to Alençon, and that happier days are in store for you."

Then she broke down, kissed me, and said: "Ah, *Madame*, my troubles are only beginning. At Alençon my husband leaves at once for his regiment at the frontier!"

I said to him: "I mustn't say '*bonne chance*,' but I can say '*courage*.'This wicked war has been so forced upon us that we must win."

He answered: "I hope and believe it, *Madame*, but how much blood must flow, how many lives be sacrificed before we get to the end of our struggle!" He did not look as if he could stand much, a slight, delicate figure, but his fighting blood was up, as it is in every man in France today.

We had to wait a few minutes in the train, when we got to Paris, to let a military train pass. It was pathetic to see the young soldiers, some of them looked mere boys—all were brave and gay, trying to keep up. One nice fair-headed child (for that is what he looked like) was saying goodbye to his mother and sisters. The women were smiling and talking until the last moment, when the train started, and the young fellow jumped onto his carriage. Then the poor mother broke down and sobbed. The girls patted her back,, saying: "Don't let him see you cry; wave your handkerchief!"

The whole aspect of the place was changed since I left yesterday morning. Then all the trains and autobuses were running as usual; nor were there many people outside the station; it was only when I got inside and saw the crowd of soldiers and reservists that I had realised that war was not only possible, but probable. This morning it is absolutely deserted—no tramways, no autobus. They were all taken off at 10 o'clock last night, and utilised at once for the army. Very few cabs, and they were instantly taken by officers. I had to walk to the church of St. Augustin before I got one; such a broken-down old nag, he could hardly get along. The coachman told me that all the good horses had been taken at once for the army.

I was completely exhausted, body and mind, when I got to the house, and poor H. was almost as tired. She had waited dinner until nearly 10 o'clock, imagining all sorts of things. Francis and Charlotte had been to see her, saying they were going down to Mareuil at 4 o'clock. Then came the news of the mobilisation, and all the people who came in to see her, told her there was no chance of any train leaving Mareuil that night. The whole "*ligne de l'Est*" was taken for the military. I found nothing from Francis; but a telegram came later from him, asking me to meet him at the Gare de l'Est tomorrow morning at 9 o'clock. He was to join his regiment at Caen, that afternoon.

The M.'s and De C. F. dined, all saying that the spirit and attitude of the French were splendid. No declaration of war yet from Germany. I wonder what she is waiting for. We are still doubtful about England. If she comes with us, I think Germany is finished—but will she?

Monday, August 3rd.

I was at the Gare de l'Est at 9, getting there with difficulty with Arsène, who still has his horses. He asked me to bring my *coupe-file*,[4] as he had been stopped once or twice the other day by officers who wanted his horses. I waited until 11 for Francis, sitting in the carriage—I didn't dare get out for fear someone would take it.

---

4. Police-pass.

The street was most interesting, crowded with, people, soldiers, army wagons, every now and then a squad of recruits passing with their sacks on their backs, the crowd following and carrying their bundles. Two *équipes d'infirmière de la Croix Rouge* in uniform, in private autos, driven by their owners and going at full speed. Their Red Cross flag gave them the right to pass everything, like the *pompiers*. They were, of course, wildly cheered: "*Vivent les Femmes de France!*" There was a great demand for conveyances, and I suppose the *cochers de fiacre* asked exorbitant prices, as we heard a row going on between an officer and a coachman, who evidently had refused to take him. (Officers and *Croix Rouge* nurses needn't pay if they haven't the money.)

However, the crowd would have settled that matter by breaking the carriage to pieces. They were beginning to demolish it when he gave in. As they passed us, he was scowling and muttering to himself, the officer standing up in the carriage, his sword out of the scabbard, unpleasantly near the back of the coachman's neck. One of the young reservists stopped alongside of my carriage, saying civilly enough: "*C'est mal, Madame, de rester assise seule dans votre voiture; vous devriez la donner aux militaires!*" "*Que voulez-vous, mon ami, j'attends mon militaire; je l'emmène à la gare pour partir rejoindre son régiment.*"

He appeared at 11 o'clock, my *militaire*, looking very well and fit; his hair cut short, a sack on his back, another in his hand, good stout shoes, and a flannel shirt. He was rather blue, having left his wife and children at Mareuil—had put his house on a war footing. There are only maids in the house, and two boys of eighteen, a young footman, and gardener. Mme. Sallandrouze and Madeleine stay with Charlotte. He gave his wife a Browning and revolver, showed her and the English nurse how to use them; gave strict orders that the house should be shut and barred every night at 8 o'clock, and should show as little light as possible. The farmer next door promised to come in every day and look after them. The miller, also a friend of the family, promised sacks of flour. Francis was not afraid of Germans getting anywhere near this time, but of tramps or a wandering population who might get roused if we should have a reverse at first, which is quite possible.

He came up to breakfast with us, and then I went to the station. They would not let me go in; no women were allowed inside, but a great many had come with their men, and the leave-takings were trying—though I must say, as a rule, the women behaved beautifully. I was glad when it was over and my boy with his bright smile had disappeared under the *voûte*. Still he was not going directly to the front as so many of his cousins are—Walter and John Waddington, Pierre Guérard, all cavalrymen, who will bear the first brunt—but such partings leave their mark. Two women in a shop looked at me so sympathetically, saying: "*Pauvre dame, c'est son fils qui parti!*" There were quantities of people in the place, but perfect order. Not a cry of "*A Berlin!*" or of "*A bas les Allemands!*" merely "*Vive l'Armée!*" as the train steamed out of the station.

We had visitors all the afternoon, all sorts of rumours flying about. There are thousands of Americans stranded here, without money, and without any means of getting home! The ambassador has his hands full. The embassy and *chancellerie* are besieged. Schön, the German ambassador, is still here and very blue. Germany has not yet declared war on France; wants to provoke France into declaring it first, but she won't move—only mobilised as a measure of prudence, as other nations were doing the same.

Tuesday, August 4th.

The declaration of war from Germany came this morning. Such a trivial, lying message, given verbally by Schön, the ambassador, to Viviani, Foreign Minister—in substance that French troops had invaded German soil, and that aeroplanes had dropped bombs in Germany—which they knew was perfectly untrue. Viviani listened in perfect silence, merely saying the accusations were quite false, and that preparations would be made at once for the ambassador's departure. He left this evening in a special train, with all his staff, without a hostile demonstration of any kind—absolute silence when he made his way to his carriage. Mr. Martin, *Directeur du Protocole*, was on the platform to see that all the arrangements were well carried out. Mr. Herrick takes over the German interests, and I think will have plenty to do, as there are many women, wives of workmen and employees, who could not get away with their men.

The headquarters of the *Croix Rouge* is almost next door to us in the rue Francois Ier, and the activity there is wonderful, autos, carriages, camions all day at the door. Officers and nurses in uniform, coming and going, and boy scouts starting off in all directions, carrying messages. I rather protested at the boys being enrolled, but some of our men friends explained that they could do an excellent service; a strong, intelligent boy of twelve or fourteen years could carry verbal messages perfectly well, and also get in and out of places where a full-grown man couldn't pass; also that they are so eager to go and be of some use. I suppose we ought not to hold them back. At an open window of the *rez-de-chaussée*, two ladies are taking down the names and addresses of the scores of girls and women who stand all day in a long line, asking to be employed in some way.

While I was standing outside, waiting to speak to Henry Outrey, I met my niece Marguerite Delmas—one married daughter, whose husband is with the army, and her son with her. She had come up from the country where she is installing an ambulance in her *château*, and was waiting in hopes of getting a nurse whom she would take down with her. Her auto has been *réquisitionné*, but she had managed to find another, and was anxious to get away as soon as possible. I brought them all back to breakfast. The husbands of both her daughters are gone, but the girls are very brave, going back with their mother to do hospital work. They started at 3 o'clock with the nurse.

The *séance* in the *Chambre des Députés* was splendid today—all the *députés* standing when Deschanel, the President of the Chamber, made a panegyric of Jaurès. After all, according to his lights and conscience he was a patriot, was dead, assassinated, and all party feeling should be stilled before his tragic end. The President's proclamation and Viviani's statement, showing how France had been forced into the war, were enthusiastically received, all the deputies standing and cheering, and turning to the diplomatic tribune, where were the British and Russian ambassadors.

I went late to the U. S. Embassy. Quantities of people were waiting in the anterooms and gallery. The ambassador and Mrs. Herrick were in his library, with several American women and his secretaries coming and going all the time with despatches, telegrams, and cards of people who wanted to see the ambassador. He had seen Schön before he went. Someone of the Germans had suggested that Herrick should put up the German flag at the American Embassy—a most brilliant idea, but not very practical—which, naturally, was immediately rejected. The American Embassy would have been demolished at once. The French are behaving wonderfully well, so calm and dignified, but one must not ask too much of them, and the sight of the German flag floating amicably alongside of the Stars and Stripes would have been too much for their nerves.

Various men came in this afternoon. The principal news that Germany has violated Belgian territory—her troops having invaded Belgium. I don't think England will stand that; still she has not moved yet, except to say that she would protect the French seacoast.

Wednesday, August 5th.

Great news this morning! Hurrah for old England! She declared war on Germany at 12 o'clock last night. She had waited until then for an answer to her ultimatum saying Germany must respect the treaty and not invade Belgium. The answer was perfectly unsatisfactory when it came, and war was declared at once—instant mobilisation of army and navy ordered. It is an immense relief to us, as now Great Britain can blockade Germany's ports and not only take her ships and stop her commerce, but eventually starve her, if the war lasts long. This will be a great blow to the German emperor, who never believed that Britain would go against him; that the two great Protestant powers would fight each other.

Accounts from Berlin say the *Kaiser* is quite demoralised, shut up in his palace, not showing himself, the triumphant "War-Lord," to his people. De Courcy told us today that he heard from friends in Berlin that there had been very stormy scenes between the *Kaiser* and the crown prince before the declaration of war, the crown prince insisting that war was necessary, the *Kaiser* resisting.

Finally the son said: "You must fight; if not, it is the end of the Hohenzollerns!"

After a few moments' hesitation, the *Kaiser* answered: "We will fight; but it will be the end of Germany!"

I passed the *Croix Rouge* on my way downtown. Still the same crowd, autos filled with bags and bundles, and the long file of women waiting patiently at the window. I talked to a nice-looking country-woman of uncertain age, who wanted to speak to someone in authority. I said to her: "What do you want? You are too old to start as a nurse."

"Not me, *Madame*, but my daughter, who is young and strong; there must be work for women."

I talked to the girl, a nice, healthy-looking young peasant, with good, honest blue eyes—evidently very poor, almost in rags. "Do you know anything about nursing?"

"No, *Madame*."

"Can you sew?"

"No, *Madame*; but do help me to get to the front."

I read her from the notices posted up that the *Croix Rouge* had so many offers of service they couldn't even answer them. They would only take doctors, surgeons, or medical students of both sexes. It didn't make the least difference; she remained standing in the file, saying:

"There must be something for me to do as I am young and strong. I can scrub floors, make beds, lift heavy things, run messages. Oh, *Madame*, do help me to go!"

I had not then seen Viviani's proclamation to the women of France, calling upon all those who were young and strong to replace the men in the fields, insure this year's harvest, and prepare the next.

There were a great many people and great confusion inside the *Croix Rouge*. I wanted to see the Comtesse d'Haussonville, the *Présidente*. She is indefatigable, there all day, from 8 in the morning till 8 at night, attending to everything, sending off bands of nurses (her own daughter with one group at Rethel on the frontier), stores of all kinds, and organising work in all the *arrondissements* of Paris. She looks very tired, and yet this is only the beginning of the war.

I wanted to speak to her about starting an *ouvroir* with one of my friends, Mrs. Mygatt, who has lived a great deal in Paris, and is very anxious to give some help to the poor women of France. Mr. Mygatt will give us rooms in his office in the Boulevard Haussmann, and we can dispose of one or two competent maids, sewing women, and sewing-machines; but we must find out what are the things most needed, and get patterns of shirts, *caleçons*, bandages, etc. I waited some time, but couldn't see Mme. d'Haussonville; shall try another day.

People are in and out of our house all day, and we hear all sorts of rumours. The papers are sensible; don't have so many foolish stories, and the minimum of war news. The Germans have had a good repulse in Belgium. They believed with their usual arrogance that they could march straight through Belgium directly to Paris, make a great *coup* at once, knock Paris to pieces, get large sums of money, then turn their attention to the Russians, who are slow in moving and have great distances to cover and few railways. They never dreamed that Belgium would resist, or that Great Britain would fight against them. The defence of Liège has been heroic, their forts holding out splendidly.

I have a letter from Charlotte this morning; all well, and living as quietly as possible. They have suppressed all luxuries in their daily life: black coffee, afternoon tea, cakes, etc. If anyone is hungry in the afternoon, they can have dry bread and cheese; but they only have two good meals a day, not always meat. All day long military trains pass, soldiers always gay and cheering. As soon as they will give me a pass I will try and get down there and take them some provisions, but as one can only take a hand-bag I couldn't carry much.

There is a certain *détente* in the air since Britain's attitude. At some of the *cafés* in the Champs Elysées people were sitting outside taking their *apéritifs* and reading the papers. The city is *pavoisé*; flags are flying everywhere, quite a number of British flags with the Tricolour, a few Russian. Gery Cullum walks about the streets all day with a Tricolour cockade and a small British flag pinned on his coat. He says lots of people come up to him and shake hands violently—one man saying to him the other day: "*C'est beau, mon vieux, la France et l'Angleterre ensemble; rien ne tiendra contre nous!*" *Dieu le veuille!* It is such an iniquitous war, has been so forced upon us that I can't think we can be beaten. Even for Germany's masses of troops, the coalition of France, Great Britain, and Russia must be a formidable one.

Friday, 7th August .

The Belgians are fighting splendidly. Their great forts at Liège, with the guns encased in steel turrets as on battleships, are making havoc with the Germans, who didn't expect any resistance. The French have not taken any part as yet, but troops are being hurried to the Belgian frontier.

I have a telegram from Francis this morning, from Octeville, a suburb of Cherbourg. He says he is well and busy.

Daisy Cameron came in before breakfast, and we went to the *Affaires Etrangères* to see if we could get any news of her niece Mary whom she had left at Heidelberg with a German governess. We saw the *chef de cabinet*, who told us no communication was possible with Berlin. I thought that as the American ambassador there, Mr. Gerard, had taken on the French interests, he would probably have means of communication with Paris; but he said there was no way of getting at Berlin. She might get information, perhaps, through Rome. If Mr. Herrick would telegraph the United States ambassador in Rome, he could communicate with his colleague in Berlin, but that France could do nothing. Daisy was very worried as she was afraid the child with her governess might have left Heidelberg, trying to join her in Paris; and of course a German would never have been allowed to enter France.

Saturday, August 8th.

I went to the bank yesterday, which was crowded with Americans, all wanting money, and the bank giving very little. They did give me some, but no gold. Then I went to the annex of the *Croix Rouge* in the rue Charron, to see about starting an *ouvroir*, giving work to the hundreds of women who are utterly destitute—but I don't find any one very competent. I will try another day.

Daisy came in late and we walked down to the American Embassy, where the American committees. Repatriation and Ambulance, seem to be sitting in permanence. The ambassador told me the news was excellent: the French had advanced in Alsace and had taken Mülhausen. He thinks the Germans are going to be badly beaten.

Sunday, 9th August

Good news this morning. French at Mülhausen enthusiastically received by the entire population. Germans driven off at the point of the bayonet, and pursued by French cavalry. No names given of killed and wounded. The loss of life must have been terrific. I went to the American church, which was crowded. They sang splendidly the hymn "O God of Battles!" which rather upset me. Of course all one's nerves are on end.

I went to breakfast with the Carrolls. It was so cool and peaceful sitting on their terrace opening on the garden, with birds singing, and the scent of flowers all around us, that it was hard to believe a fierce battle was raging just over the frontier. They live in an old-fashioned part of Paris in the Faubourg St. Germain, a quiet street, few houses and big gardens, very little passing at any time—nothing today. Charlie Carroll is very busy on the Repatriation Committee sending Americans home, and she is on the Executive Committee for the buying of material for the American Ambulance.

The ambassador, in the name of his compatriots in Paris, has offered to the French Government an ambulance entirely equipped with a competent staff of surgeons, doctors, and nurses, and sufficient funds to run the whole thing. They have taken the Lycée Pasteur, a large new building at Neuilly, near the American hospital, under whose supervision the ambulance is put. The building is enormous, high, large rooms and courts, plenty of air and space. They can put in two thousand beds, but are beginning with five hundred. It is a most generous contribution, and is much appreciated by the French.

I stayed at home all the afternoon as it was very hot. We had a great many people at teatime. They only got tea and *pain de ménage*—no such luxuries as cakes in wartime. There is little news. Very angry letters from Americans and English stranded in Germany, who are being outrageously treated. Jusserand, who is here on leave, wants to get back to America. He and his wife, Joe Stevens and other friends are at Havre, hoping to sail on the *France*. They have been there for several days, but the steamer does not dare venture out, as German battleships are still cruising in the Atlantic

Jusserand was afraid the enormous German population in America would create a hostile feeling toward France; but I don't think he need worry himself on that score. The Germans themselves are rapidly alienating all sympathy from the United States. Everyone is speculating and commenting on the attitude of the Austrian Ambassador, Count Szecsen, who still remains here, must, I suppose, until Austria declares war upon France, or sends troops to reinforce the Germans before Liège, which apparently she is doing quietly, without saying anything. He doesn't seem to realise his position.

He went to dine at the Union Club the other night and asked Lahovary, the Roumanian minister to dine with him. They had just sat down when a message came to Lahovary saying someone wanted to speak to him upon urgent business. When he got out of the dining-room, he found several of the clubmen who told him he must tell the ambassador to go. They didn't want to be rude to him, or make a scandal, but they would certainly turn their backs on him, and not speak to him. Lahovary went back to the ambassador, saying, "I have a disagreeable communication to make to you," and gave his message.

Szecsen was furious, said: "I thought I was with gentlemen!"

"So you are," said Lahovary, "but with French gentlemen who are unwilling to meet you at present, and would prefer you should leave the club quietly and not make a scandal."

He was most unwilling to go—wanted Lahovary still to dine with him, which he absolutely refused to do. He departed at last in a rage, saying: "Where can I get my dinner? I can't run the risk of being insulted in a restaurant!"

He is still here; wants to oblige France to give him his passports, as that would force Italy to move, France being the aggressor. But France will not be quite so foolish as that. I think when the Italians move, which they must do eventually, it will not be against us. They are most outspoken, even the Embassy men. In their hearts all Italians must hate Austria; her rule in Italy was so cruel.

Loubat came to see us late before dinner, and was very interesting. He was here in 1870, saw all the troops go off, many of them already hostile to the emperor before starting, and even those who were not, so nervous and excited and doubtful of their generals—soldiers as well as officers— and the talk at all the clubs so violent and wild. Now the whole of France marches like one man. No excitement, no cries of

"*A Berlin!*" the men grave, but cheerful, the women splendid, saying goodbye to their men, without a tear, and encouraging them to the last moment; but all feel what a terrible struggle is before us.

Monday, August 10th.

It has been frightfully hot all day. There was very little war news this morning. All the movements of troops have been kept very quiet. It is awful to wake up every morning with such a weight on one's heart. The stillness of the city, too, is so awful, so unlike Paris. Very little passing, no loud talking or laughing, not a sound of singing or whistling since the declaration of war. I would give anything to hear the workmen singing and chaffing in the big house they are building opposite to us, but there are none left; all have gone to the front. The only note of gaiety are the boy scouts attached to the "Red Cross," who breakfast every morning at the *café* on the corner; they range from twelve to sixteen, look as lively as possible, such eager young faces and so important. I often stop and talk to them and ask for news.

I tried again today at the annex of the Red Cross to get some models of garments for the sick and wounded, and to know what were the things most needed, but no one seemed to know anything. They sent me from one room to another. Everywhere ladies were working, rolling bandages and hemming handkerchiefs. They asked me if I had come to work, and would I hem handkerchiefs; that I declined absolutely. Really not worthwhile to waste my time that way. Any schoolchild would have been delighted to earn a few *sous* and hem all they wanted.

When I was finally told I had better see the mayor of my *arrondissement* and ask for permission, my temper and patience gave way, and I expressed myself vigorously to the very mild old gentleman—a *tapissier* in ordinary times, who was the last person I was sent to. It is really too bad, at such a time, the amount of talking and writing and red tape generally one must go through before accomplishing anything. I wanted their *models*, because some of the shirts that have been sent to the hospitals could never have been put on any human figure—the neck so small that the head of a newborn babe could hardly pass, and long, narrow sleeves that hung like strings from the shoulders.

However, one must not criticise, for the Red Cross is doing splendid work, and they must be driven crazy with all the inane offers of service they receive.

We had a good many visits this afternoon—some of the ladies

connected with the American ambulance. Forty ladies meet at the embassy every day. Mrs. Herrick is president, and she will certainly get all the money she wants. People are all so fond of her. She came in late, looking rather exhausted, but revived with a cup of tea; said the meetings were very tiring, so many suggestions and opinions, and forty women all talking at once.

Charlie Forbes and Gery Cullum dined with us. We warned them they would have a very frugal repast. No one has anything else these days—but they didn't mind. They had dined last night at one of the big *cafés* on the *boulevards*—dinner very good, a great many people; diplomatists and strangers. At 9 o'clock two policemen appeared, saying the doors must be closed. No one made any objection; all trooped out into the street and walked about a little. At 10 o'clock the *boulevard* was as deserted and quiet as any provincial town.

The troops have been sent off very quietly, either at night or by the underground railway. We have seen no regiments marching through the streets, flags flying, music playing, followed by an enthusiastic, excited crowd. I have never seen Paris so calm.

Tuesday, August 11th.

Another very warm day—no particular news in the paper. The allied armies seem to have joined forces, but no big battle has taken place yet. It is awful to think of these two great armies facing each other, and of the terrific loss of life there will be when the fighting really begins. I don't know how the German Emperor dared take such a responsibility.

The Austrian ambassador has finally departed. It seems the Austrian explanations were vague when our Foreign Office asked if Austrian troops were moving quickly to Alsace to reinforce the Germans. War is not declared between the two countries, but there is a diplomatic rupture. Both ambassadors in Paris and Vienna recalled. I imagine Szecsen was glad to go. His position cannot have been very agreeable these last days. Mr. Herrick takes over the Austrian interests. He will have his hands full, as he already has the Germans and all his own people. He is quite equal to the task, is perfectly quiet and prudent, and is winning golden opinions. America is lucky to have had such a man here at this time.

It is extraordinary how the Germans have managed to put everyone against them. I fancy the sympathy for France in the United States has been a disagreeable surprise for them.

I have no further news of Francis, merely his first telegram from Octeville; if he had been moved I think he would have told us. Charlotte's letters come pretty regularly. She writes they are all well but a little short of provisions. I hope I shall be able to get down to Mareuil for two days, now that the mobilisation is nearly over.

Wednesday, August 12th.

Another very hot day; still no fighting. I don't know if the delay is good. It gives the French more time to concentrate their forces, and also for Russia to advance.

I made another attempt to get patterns this morning, and finally succeeded. I went to the principal office of the *Croix Rouge* and saw D'Haussonville who did all I wanted, and sent Henry Outrey (who is working at the Red Cross until he is called to the colours) with me to the "lingerie." There I found the Duchesse de Trévise and some ladies whom I knew, and got all sorts of patterns and measures, carrying off a shirt which I promised to send back at once, as they had very few. They told me they particularly wanted old linen sheets for bandages and compresses, also new cotton sheets and pillow-cases. H. had some old sheets and we sent them off at once.

I went about 5 to the embassy to pick up Daisy Cameron, who has just taken charge of the *ouvroir* for the American Ambulance. Baronne Castelli—an American born—has put her apartment in the Champs Elysées at the disposal of the American Ambulance; and Daisy is going to organise her work-rooms. The embassy gates and doors were open. Quantities of people about inside and outside. I waited in the gallery as Daisy was still in the committee-room. I saw George Munroe and Fred Allen, both of whom are working hard at the relief fund to send back Americans. Herman Hayes, too, I saw in the distance. The bankers are doing all they can to relieve the money pressure, and have a hard time, as of course everyone is short of funds.

The war came so suddenly. George Munroe has his son at the front. Daisy and I walked down-town late. Everything quiet; almost all the shops shut; on many of them a notice posted up: "*Fermée le propriétaire est sous les drapeaux.*" We went as far as Colombin's, where we had a cup of tea, cakes, and sandwiches as usual. There were quite a number of people—almost all Americans. The *caissière* told us they had several tables taken every day for luncheon. I was astonished to see cakes. Our baker and others in our quarter since four or five days make no more cakes, nor even rolls and croissants. We have *pain de manage*, which is a little tough but more healthy, I fancy, than finer bread. We don't mind it; one gets accustomed to everything.

"*Les journées passent et se ressemblent.*" The heat is awful, but they say it is better for the soldiers than rain or damp. Great heat dries up the microbes. We have got our work-room started, and it will be a great help to us to feel we are doing something. Nothing but occupation of some kind can keep up the courage of the women who sit at home and wait. Mrs. Mygatt and I went to the *Croix Rouge* and had a long wait at the lingerie, carrying off a bundle of shirts, belts, bandages of every possible shape.

I had a letter from Francis this morning from Octeville. His regiment is doing *garde-côte*, and he is *secrétaire-cycliste* to the colonel; carries despatches. He says he has a very good room and bureau. As soon as the mayor heard his name, he put himself at his disposal and does all he can to make him comfortable. They are on a hill with a splendid view of the port and sea, and delightful sea air. They have a very good mess (the *sous-officiers*). A chef from Paris, from the Cercle Volney, looks after them. He says their journey from Caen was one long *marche triomphale*; they were showered with fruit, wine, flowers, and cigarettes all along the route.

Saturday, August 15th,
Assumption Day.

It is generally such a gay day here; bells ringing, churches open, everybody out in holiday attire. This morning it is quiet enough. No one feels very cheerful with this awful war-cloud hanging over us, and the dread of what the morrow may bring, when those two great armies meet. I enclose a scathing sonnet to the *Kaiser*, published by the *Times*.

I have been all the afternoon at the *ouvroir*. We are beginning very modestly, but hope to get more funds as we go on. We have two capable women, Mrs. G.'s maid and a dressmaker, out of work now, who buys our stuff much cheaper than we can, and cuts out shirts and dresses; also two sewing-machines. There is quite a pile of flannel, cotton, coarse linen, and old shirts on the tables. I worked all the afternoon basting hems of shirt-tails for the machine. I certainly have not done anything of that kind for thirty-eight years, and I was quite tired when I got home.

They asked me at the *Croix Rouge* what I wanted to do: had I any aptitude *médicale*, or any experience of nursing? I answered promptly:

"None whatever;" knew nothing about sickness, and hated a sickroom, but of course I would do what I could, and offered to start an *ouvroir* with my friends, which they accepted with joy.

We had an interesting woman this afternoon, an Alsatian, a trained nurse, who will come and work with us until she is ordered off to some hospital; she looks tired to death, has already been nursing, but won't hear of resting; also a Belgian couple, who will work regularly with us. They are so proud of their country, as they well may be, and France should be eternally grateful to the Belgians, as that first repulse of the Germans at Liège has given them time to get up their troops, and has also made a moral effect which has been splendid for us. If we had had a first defeat at the frontier (which we all expected), there might have been a panic in the country.

They read us interesting letters from their parents who are in the country in Belgium, about three miles from Liège. Their three children are with them, all wildly excited about the war and against the Germans. They write they will certainly have the Germans at their place, if they advance at all into the country, and that his father was exhorting the children and servants to be perfectly civil to them when they came. They can't help having them, and any rudeness might make serious complications for them, and end in his being shot, as those barbarians make short work of any who stand in their way. What a wicked war in these days of education and Christianity!

Charlie Forbes came to tea with us. Mrs. Mygatt gives us tea always, and the slices of bread and butter made of the perfectly plain *pain de manage* (which some of our pampered servants don't eat in ordinary times) were very good. Charlie was most amiable—let us try all our shirts, hospital and convalescent, on him. We were particularly asked to make the armholes wide, and the sleeves loose. He is such a big man that what went on easily over his coat was quite large enough for anyone.

One of the party read aloud the curious prophecy of Madame de Thèbes, that appeared in her calendar at the beginning of this year, and Annunzio's splendid *Ode pour la Résurrection Latine*. I wonder if Italy will move.

I went to see Mrs. Herrick after leaving the work-room, and happily found her alone, not surrounded by her forty women of the American Ambulance Committee. She says her ambassador is very well, very busy, and very tired, but very pleased with the way in which all his American friends have stood by him and helped him.

Daisy Cameron came in before dinner, much relieved at having had news of Mary, who is safe in Berlin with the Gerards at the embassy. I didn't go out this morning except for a few minutes to the *Croix Rouge*, to ask if we must do anything about putting their flag on our building, but I found no one who could tell me. They are overwhelmed with business, one hardly likes to ask a question.

I went to the *ouvroir* about 2.30 and met Olive Tiffany coming in. She is a capital worker; said she would do anything that was wanted, so she was instantly given a pile of shirts and asked to make buttonholes, three in each. They suggested I should sew on buttons, which I quite refused to do. After all, people must work according to their limitations, and I preferred basting hems. I think I must have basted miles of shirt-tails so far.

Comtesse de Franqueville (*née* Lady Sophia Palmer) came in at tea-time; so pleased that France and England were fighting together. She had been standing in the crowd near the British Embassy to see Sir John French arrive; said he was most enthusiastically received, and looked very well and soldierly in his *tenue de campagne*. They are going to have ten thousand sheep in the park of their Château de la Muette, just at the entrance of the Bois; and a large flock has just been put on the race-course at Longchamp, cows on the Auteuil course, and an immense enclosure in the Bois, railed off for oxen. I suppose these are necessary precautions, but at the present moment we are feeling not the slightest inconvenience from the state of siege. The markets are supplied as usual, and no increase of prices. One day chickens were dear—a very small one, *frs.* 14—just double the ordinary cost. We declined it, and I fancy everybody else did the same, as they have returned now to their normal price.

Monday, August 17th.

We are still living our quiet life in a dead city. News this morning of fresh French successes. Germany repulsed on the Meuse, many drowned in the river, and we hope it is true, and wish there are many more Meuses and many more Germans drowned in them—which is an awful state of mind to be in for a Christian woman. But the sooner the war is over and the more Germans disappear from the face of the earth, the better for civilisation and the whole of Europe.

I walked about the Trocadéro and near the Tour Eiffel this morning, and there one realises that the situation is serious. There are cannon and soldiers in the Trocadéro grounds, and a strong guard and *mitrailleuses* at the Tour Eiffel. All the sentries with fixed bayonets and looking very grim. I went as usual to the *ouvroir*, which begins to look very businesslike. One of our workers, a small dressmaker, had been applying to various maids and small people she knew, and had got a pile of fairly good linen sheets for one franc apiece.

Of course they ought to be given at such a time, but everyone is glad to earn a little money. There are so many women and girls thrown out of employment by all the big shops shutting, and business generally stopped, that there is great misery already, and the war not really begun. The wives and mothers of men *sous les drapeaux* are being looked after by the government, but it is only private initiative that can help the others.

It is pathetic to see the little *midinettes*, generally so smiling and well-dressed, often with a little bunch of violets on their coats, looking so sad and pale and hungry. And one knows that they are hungry, but they don't complain.

The Americans living in Paris are most generous, but they all have to look first after their own compatriots stranded here with no money and no shelter—and have organised besides their ambulance on a grand scale.

Our teas are rather amusing; every one contributes something. Mme. del M., our Belgian friend, brought a pot of strawberry jam today, I a plain cake made at home, someone else a loaf of English bread, which makes better *tartines* than thick *pain de manage*. Everyone else does the same thing.

Henry O., who is working at the War Office, dines often with the Jean Sallandrouzes and brings a ham or a round of cold beef with him. Palma Ruspoli brought a rumour which she said, however, was not confirmed at the embassy, that there had been an awful naval battle in the North Sea. Eight British battleships sunk, twenty-eight Germans, and a great number of the merchant ships sunk. There is no mention of it in tonight's papers.

I am writing late, 11 o'clock. The street is perfectly quiet, not a sound nor a light; I should not think there was anybody left in the street except on the entresol opposite, where we see a light every night, which looks friendly. There are, however, many people in town. Quite a number of autos were running up and down the Champs Elysées yesterday when I came home at 7 o'clock.

Wednesday, August 19th.

We lose almost the count of the days, they go on so monotonously.

We pore over the papers, but they give so little news. The weather is enchanting, bright, beautiful summer days; rather cooler this morning. Report says that the German crown prince charged with the Imperial Guard at Dinant and was badly wounded, but it was not confirmed in the official *communiqué* this afternoon. The War Office issues a bulletin every afternoon at 5 o'clock, and somebody always comes in to tell us the last news.

Mr. Herrick and Austin Lee dined this evening. Both men are most interesting. Our repast was frugal—war rations, a soup, piece of beef, salad, a vegetable and a compote—not exactly an ambassadorial banquet. Fruit is plentiful and cheap. Mr. Herrick said the young American army men who were out here, either for the manoeuvres or instruction in some of the French *corps d'armée*, were astounded at the order and quickness with which the mobilisation was carried out—also that they had been very intelligent and useful in helping him handle the mass of Americans who congregate every day at the *chancellerie*, begging to be sent home. The American Ambulance is going splendidly; they get all the money they want.

I had a long letter from Charlotte this evening, the first in many days. Of course, being on the line of the Est, she sees a great deal of the movement of troops, and writes:

> Tuesday, we went to La Ferté-Milon to give the soldiers flowers. They love it, and all the carriages are covered with branches and flowers given to them. The soldier Madeleine gave the bouquet to, kissed her, then me, and then my mother on both cheeks. I gave my bouquet to a nice little young soldier who was quite touched by it, so much so that when the train started, he called an *employé* of the station and asked him to give me '*de sa part sa médaille de la Sainte Vierge*,' a very pretty one in silver. I think it was so sweet of that young man, and so delicately done. I shall keep it as a souvenir '*d'un inconnu.*'
>
> I gave my *cotisation* (subscription) for the drinks of the soldiers; they made a collection in the town to buy absinthe. They put a litre of absinthe into thirty litres of water, and the young women and girls of La Ferté-Milon give it to the soldiers in their tin cups when the train stops. As they passed every twenty minutes for eight days, we were very busy. The men are delighted to drink something cool. Some of them had travelled twenty-four hours in those horse-vans, poor creatures. One lot of prisoners

has already passed here. Uhlans.

We have very little news from the war, the *Petit Journal* being the only paper we receive. It is quite difficult to get about, no trains, no carriages, as all the horses have been taken, and we have to have a *laissez-passer* every time we stir out of Mareuil. We cannot even go on the Meaux or Fleury roads. They are very severe because of the railway-line, as *espions* have already tried several times to blow up bridges and tunnels.

We work hard for the *Croix Rouge*—shirts, bandages, sheets, etc. I have organized a '*garderie d'enfants*' to allow the mothers to go to the fields for the harvest; and we have in the courtyard every day, from 8 to 10, and from 1 to 6, fifty or sixty children. I assure you it is a piece of work, and I hope it counts as charity. '*Monsieur le Curé*' rings every night at 8 o'clock the special prayers for time of war, and we all go.

The boys are flourishing—much excited when the trains pass. I put the newspaper every day on the garden wall, near the gate, so that people who have no paper can read the news. Ever so many have thanked me.

Friday, August 21st.

I went this morning to the service of the English church for their naval and military forces now engaged in war. It was very solemn, almost all women, some oldish men. Two boy scouts distributed the leaflets with the special forms. Mr. Cardew asked everyone to think of the sailors when singing the hymn "For those in peril on the sea."

The papers are always interesting with all the various letters and experiences of unfortunate travellers—British or Americans trying to get home. It is lucky that the French are a non-travelling race. I don't know what would have happened if four or five thousand French people had been travelling in Germany or Switzerland.

Charlotte came up yesterday, looking very well. We went to the *Croix Rouge* to see if Comtesse d'Haussonville would like to have an ambulance at Crouy. They can offer one hundred beds with their sheets and blankets in a big old *château* with a large garden and terrace, but no staff except some volunteer nurses, and no money to run it. Mme. d'Haussonville told us at once that want of funds was the great difficulty; that they had been offered quantities of houses and beds, but without money to run the thing, they could not be accepted. The President of the *Croix Rouge*, the Marquis de Vogüé, has just issued an appeal, which is placarded everywhere, asking everyone to contribute what they can, money, clothes, blankets, anything.

We were at the *ouvroir* all the afternoon, and things are gradually getting into shape. But again we are stopped by want of funds. We don't want to work ourselves, but give work to hundreds of women who are absolutely penniless, not only soldiers' wives, but quantities of young women and girls left with no work and no money. Nearly all the big shops and business establishments are closed. I saw two nice-looking girls this morning, premieres at one of the big dressmakers of the Rue de la Paix, who told me they had just one *franc* between them. It is always the same story with that class in Paris. They spend all they earn on their backs. Three or four of them dub together and have a good room, and they live *au jour le jour,* putting nothing aside for illness or dark days. In our rooms we could easily employ sixty, perhaps more, women, give them *fr.* 1.50 a day, and one good meal. They could work all day, making clothes for the sick, the wounded, and the refugees—these last are no small item now in the Paris population.

Charlotte carried off various patterns, as she has also a work-room at Mareuil. She will surely have many refugees as we are so near the Belgian frontier. We stopped at one or two work-rooms on our way up to the rue de la Pompe, to ask about prices, meals, hours, etc., as all this sort of work is new to us, and everywhere heard the same story—the quantity of women begging for work.

Daisy Cameron came to dinner, and was most amusing with the account of her work-room for the American Ambulance. She has volunteered as nurse, and I am sure she should be an excellent nurse—she has seen so much illness and so many operations in her own family.

Saturday, August 22nd.

Charlotte lunched with the Tiffanys at their hotel. She left all her bundles, a fine collection, with me, and I went to get her to take her to the train; I could hardly get in the cab, and I don't know now how the two of us managed it; but we did. It looked strange to see that busy Gare de l'Est almost deserted, entirely under military control—soldiers on all the platforms. They were much interested in all Charlotte's bundles, asked her if she was going to the front, as she had on the Red Cross badge.

Some of the empty carriages that have come back from the frontier were rather amusing, with all sorts of rough drawings in chalk on the outside. Various heads of "Guillaume" with enormous moustaches,

31

and rather a pretty girl's head on one—"*ma gosse*" (my girl, in village *patois*). I stayed till the train started. I think the two days in town rather cheered up Charlotte. She saw a good many people, and heard more news, such as it was. It is rather an austere life at Mareuil in wartime, and she feels a certain responsibility with the children and the people of the village, who all come to her. If her mother were not with her I should have to go to Mareuil—and yet I cannot leave H. altogether. Charlotte is very brave, but misses her husband so awfully, and has so little news.

I went straight to my *ouvroir* and worked all the afternoon. Olive brought me an attractive woman, one of the *New York Times* correspondents. She interested herself at once in our work, and between us we wrote an appeal to some of the American papers, which she cabled over at once. So many Americans, perfect strangers to me, names I didn't know at all, wrote to me from the west—Kentucky, Wisconsin, Arizona, about my book on France—*Château and Country Life in France*—saying they had read it with so much interest, that I thought they might, perhaps, come to our assistance. This is what I wrote:

Appeal

So many Americans have seemed interested in what I wrote of France and my life there in happier days, that I think they may be inclined to help her in her hour of dire need. We women of France must do something for the hundreds of women who are left absolutely penniless, their sons and husbands at the war, they without any resources—as almost all the big shops and business establishments have closed—I, with some of my friends, am organizing a workroom where we give *fr.* 1.50 and one meal a day to any woman who comes. They work all day, making garments for the sick and wounded, for which we furnish the material. We have many more applicants than we can employ, and are in desperate need of funds. Can you help us?

I hope I shall get some money.

Monday, August 24th.

These are awful days. There is a terrific battle going on in Belgium. Yesterday, one was ill with apprehension; the day was warm and trying; the very air seemed heavy with presentiments. I went to the English church. The special prayers for time of war bring it home to one. As on the other day, two boy scouts were handing books and the plate. I stayed in all the afternoon. We had a great many visits—some of them most depressing, the men more than the women.

Such rumours: that we were being badly beaten; nothing would prevent the Germans from entering Paris; the scum of the population would rise in a frenzy if the fighting went on without any news; that the government would go to Bordeaux; that the German Zeppelins would drop bombs all over Paris and set fire to the city; and though my own common sense told me not to pay the slightest attention to all the rumours, one can't keep being a little impressed by them. It was a relief to have one of the Dutch secretaries, Baron de G., come to dinner quietly with us, who told us not to mind any such reports; that at his legation the report was: "Situation grave but satisfactory."

While we were talking, all the windows open, we heard cavalry passing, and rushed to the balcony, as did everyone else in the street, but it was only a detachment of the *Garde Républicaine*, which patrols Paris every night. All our nerves are on edge, and yet one must be perfectly cool and keep up the courage of the people. We didn't hear any news at the *ouvroir*, but everyone looks grave, and all throw themselves upon the special editions of the papers that came all day with nothing in them.

The communications from the front are very brief, and have become much more so, as the battle rages.

Wednesday, August 26th.

Still no news, and our days are exactly alike. I had a letter from Francis this morning from Octeville. He is very busy, but says the life is monotonous. He had seen a convoy of German prisoners arrive. They were received in perfect silence—not a word, nor a sound. The general commanding at Châtenay had given strict orders to treat them with respect. They were soldiers, doing their duty to their country, as we were to ours. Francis talked later to one or two of them; said they were famished, and not at all enthusiastic about the war.

I went to see Mme. Sallandrouze on my way home. She had come up for two days from Mareuil; looked exhausted. She had been five hours on a journey which usually takes two. The people on the train were fourteen in their compartment, and a solid mass of people with their valises and bundles, standing in the *couloir*. She would like to come to Paris. They say there will certainly be bands of Uhlans all over our part of the country, and there are wild rumours of automobiles *blindés* dashing at full speed through the villages, shooting anyone they meet. We are only three hours from the frontier, and she can't take the responsibility—would never forgive herself if anything happened to the children.

We are all under the impression of the brutalities of the Germans in Belgium, who in one of the villages shot a boy of seven years who aimed his toy gun at them.

Our boys play about the garden all day with their flags and guns, shouting "*Vive l'armée,*" and "*Vive la France.*" If they heard cavalry passing on the road, they would certainly dash out of the gates, and anything might happen. The Germans would not hesitate to shoot down two boys shouting "*Vive la France.*" I think they had better come up. I will try and go down there on Saturday.

The new ministry which is announced this morning, has been an excellent move. It is certainly the moment to sink all political feeling, and can upon the best men of all parties to come to the front. I think it will give the country great confidence, especially Millerand at the War Office. The army, which criticised his first appointment to the War Office some time ago, ended by liking him very much. Though a civilian, he understood the French soldiers, and knew how to keep up their military enthusiasm. The Radicals have done much harm with their anti-military campaign.

Thursday, August 27th.

It was cool, a lovely morning. I went to the bank with the Mygatts, to discuss our Relief Fund—as Harjes will receive any money that is sent. I rather demurred at the name: "Mme. Waddington Relief-Fund." It seemed so very personal. But the gentlemen said as I had made a direct appeal in my own name, the money must be sent to me. I shall be very grateful for anything I get, as the misery is going to be awful—not only the quantities of Frenchwomen without work, but all the Belgian refugees. One of my friends saw a lot of them the other day, all huddled together in a court of the Chemin de Fer du Nord.

He said they looked exhausted, the women carrying their babies, the men all old, well past middle-age, carrying the bundles, with all sorts of things in them—evidently put together in a hurry at the last moment—pots, boots, some clothes, bird-cages (one man had a saddle from which he absolutely declined to be parted), perfectly useless things. People were bringing food and wine to them, milk for the babies, which they accepted most gratefully. They didn't complain; seemed stunned by the appalling misfortune which had come upon them so suddenly. Some of them were perfectly prosperous farmers with large, comfortable houses, plenty of beasts of all kinds. The Germans took away the animals, burned the houses; they saw them in flames behind them when they were flying for their lives. It is too horrible to think of the misery that pretty, prosperous little country is going through.

I am getting a little nervous about the children. I am fairly brave, but can't help being impressed with all I hear. Mareuil is directly on the line from Meaux to Rheims, and a household of women would be helpless against an invasion of such barbarians.

Friday, August 28th.

Francis' birthday. We sent him a telegram. Have heard nothing from him for some days.

I dined last night with H., an *ex-conseiller général* of the Oise. He asked me to come—*"pas un dîner, une réunion de dames, en toilette d'ambulance."* Of course no one dresses in these days. I put on my red cross medal over my plain black dress, and walked over (it is only two blocks off) in the rain, under an umbrella. I found four or five men—two *conseillers d'etat*, an ex-*préfet*, one of the directors of the *Banque de France*, and a young woman, daughter of one of the *conseillers*, whose husband is at the front. The director of the bank had just come back from Rennes, where he had deposited a large amount of gold—I dare not say how many millions—in the bank. The youngest *conseiller d'etat* had also just returned from a *tournée*, a mission he had made in the north of France, with one of the generals. He said that the condition of the men, physically and morally, was excellent, and the food supply abundant and marvellously carried out. They had their two meals a day, quite hot and good.

They all spoke most warmly of the ministry; said they were doing splendid work, and also of Poincaré; say he is wonderful, very cool, knows all about everything; where each *corps d'armée* is—that of course—and every regiment, and who commands it; has no doubt as to the final result, but thinks France will lose half her army. It is awful to think of the mournings—a whole generation wiped out. . . .

Sunday, August 30th.

Still the same beautiful weather. When one thinks of what France ought to be at this time, with a splendid harvest—all the people in the country, men, women, and children working in the fields, coming in at night so pleased with their day's work, it is terrible to feel that the country is being devastated by the Germans. I was miserable all day yesterday; I had quite made up my to go down to Mareuil for twenty-four hours and bring up the children, but everybody told me I mustn't go; it would only complicate things for them, make one more person in the train; so I sent a telegram to Charlotte, telling her to come at once. Jean Sallandrouze sent one to his mother, saying the same thing. He came in just before dinner to say he had just had a telegram from Mareuil, saying they would start this morning, but would probably arrive late in the evening, as there was "*du retard dans le service.*"

I went to the American church; there were not many people. One young woman, just in front of me, was crying almost all the time. I suppose, like all the rest of us, she had some dear ones at the front. I didn't go out again until late, and then went with the Mygatts to the Bois de Boulogne, which has been transformed into a whole-sale provision camp. The two race-courses, Auteuil, Longchamp, filled with cows and oxen, sheep at the Tir aux Pigeons, and quantities of hay and food in great stacks. There were, as usual on a Sunday afternoon, many people dining *al fresco* on the grass—whole families, from grandmothers to babies, sitting on the grass and making their evening meal; but there were no games, no tennis, no football, nor any gaiety. Everyone looked grave.

I stopped at the rue d'Artois to see if there was any news of the children, but they hadn't come. The Ségurs dined with us. They had come to Paris for his *Conseil Général*, which is usually held at Melun, but in these agitated days it was judged more prudent to have it in Paris, and they met in the *Palais Bourbon* (Chamber of Deputies). They were both rather sad, having between them eighteen nephews and grand-nephews at the front, and no news of any. Ségur is always so moderate in all he says. He has no sympathy with the Republic, but thinks the government is doing splendidly.

About 10 o'clock L. de R. came in and told me that the Mareuil party had arrived well, but exhausted, having left Mareuil at 7 in the morning, and only arrived at Paris at 10 o'clock at night. It was a great relief to me.

Monday, August 31st.

It has been again a very hot day, and I am worn out tonight with heat and emotion. At 9.30, before I was dressed, Mme. Jean S. came to see me, to say that they were all starting before 12 for Orléans in autos, *en route* for Tours. I went straight over to the Rue d'Artois where

Charlotte had gone to her mother's apartment. Ours in the rue de la Pompe is shut up; it would not have been worthwhile to have opened it for one night, and Mme. Sallandrouze could take them in, and found them all exhausted, but so pleased to be out of the fighting zone.

They were told Saturday evening that they must leave at once. La Ferté-Milon, the place next to us, was being *évacué*, and there were reports of bodies of Uhlans at Laon. They all worked hard Saturday night, hiding silver, valuables, etc., and started at 7 Sunday morning. When the train drew into the station from Rheims, crowded with wounded and refugees, they didn't want to take them at once. But the *chef de gare*, who knows us well, insisted, and they got in, scattered about the train—the two boys and their nurse in a *fourgon* (baggage-wagon) with some soldiers—the others in third-class carriages—anywhere. They had long waits all along the route, being shunted all the time, to make way for military trains.

At Meaux the Red Cross ambulance was stationed at the *gare*, all the women occupying themselves with the wounded, and giving food and clothes to the refugees. They gave the children's Nanna, who is an excellent nurse, a bowl of water and a towel, and asked her to wash some of the wounded men. The boys were so tired that Charlotte, who is a Red Cross herself, asked for a cup of milk for each of them. The woman said to her: "We shouldn't give it, *Madame*; your children look strong and well. We ought to keep the milk for the babies and little ones." C. couldn't insist, but the woman was evidently sorry for the two little boys and gave one cup of milk for the two.

Charlotte thought she had better go with her mother: Mme. de R., who has a place near Tours, would take them in for a week or ten days, and she might then perhaps join Francis at Cherbourg. I quite agreed, as I should not have liked to keep them in Paris. They came here to say goodbye to H., the boys much excited at all they had seen and heard. "You will never see Mareuil again, Danny; those wicked Germans are going to burn it." Perhaps, but I don't feel as if that was before us, and was rather comforted with what Percy Tiffany said—that Mareuil, being a stone house, would be difficult and long to burn. A band of Uhlans would not stay long enough.

I went back with them to the Rue d'Artois, and saw them all start at 12 punctually, in four large autos. The chauffeurs said they would get them to Orléans at 6. They couldn't bring any baggage, and had a wonderful collection of bags and bundles. I was delighted to see them go. Poor Mme. S. looked quite white and exhausted. It had been a great responsibility for her, as Francis left his wife and children in her charge, and I couldn't leave Henrietta.

Tuesday, September 1st.

It is again very warm today, and we hear all sorts of rumours, that a great battle is going on at La Fère, at St. Quentin. The war news is so insignificant and I suppose it is right not to give details; but it is awful to think of battles going on, and not to know where anyone is.

I was all the afternoon at the *ouvroir*. We are sending off a pile of shirts and bandages to Meudon, where Mme. Marchand has the direction of an ambulance. Our Belgian friends are awfully down. No news of their children; many of their friends' *châteaux* burned, and probably their own. They always bring bad news; reduced Mme. G.'s maid to tears, saying that Sédan (her town) was burned, also Mézières. I tried to reason with her as it is not possible that something would not have filtered through the lines if two such important places had been destroyed.

Palma M. came as usual to work with us, and told us the government was leaving that evening for Bordeaux, all the Diplomatic Corps going with them. I am afraid it will frighten people. Their ambassador, Tittoni, goes. He need not, as he is not representing a *puissance belligérante*, but he prefers to go and Ruspoli remains. Palma will stay with him.

We walked, quite a band of us, the Mygatts and Olive Tiffany, down the Boulevard Haussmann, as far as Potin's, to see what was going on. Just as we got to the place we heard two or three loud explosions, then several rifle-shots. Everybody rushed out, and we saw a German aeroplane with German flags disappearing over the barracks of La Pépinière. There was great excitement in the streets, or rather curiosity, but no one seemed at all nervous. A policeman told us they had thrown their bombs on the Gare St. Lazare, but not much harm was done—one or two people hurt, no one killed. It is a curious sensation, all the same, to be walking about a quiet city in the waning evening light, with the possibility of a bomb falling on your head. I must confess it made me a little nervous. This was the first one I had really seen and heard. They have been coming for several days.

After dinner the Ambassador and Mrs. Herrick came to see us, on their way to the station to say goodbye to their colleagues who are starting at 10 o'clock for Bordeaux. The President left this afternoon by automobile Mr. Herrick says the situation is grave, but he doesn't think the Germans will get into Paris. He intends to remain and see the end of the war.

Wednesday, September 2nd.

I went to the Red Cross this morning, but could not find Outrey. I wanted to ask him what he thought about our going away. It is so difficult to know where to go. There doesn't seem to be any room anywhere. Orléans, Bordeaux, Caen crowded—the *préfet* of Calvados has put an official communication in the paper from Caen, saying that there is literally not a bed to be had at Caen. People are sleeping at the station, and in the courts of some of the public buildings. Marie suggests that we should go to Les Aulneaux, a small hamlet in the department of La Sarthe—hardly a village, though it has got a mayor—where her daughter Fernande is schoolmistress and *adjointe* to the mayor. She has a nice house with a big court and garden, and two rooms, where she could make us very comfortable—about four hours from Paris. I talked it over with H., who does not want to leave Paris.

I had a line from Charlotte, from Tours. They made their journey very easily to Orléans, arriving before 6. But their night was trying. No rooms in any of the *hôtels*, nor yet *chez l'habitant* (the peasant or workman). They finally got a small room in a hotel, where Mme. Sallandrouze, Charlotte, and Madeleine slept. The *jeune ménage* (Jean's) in a dressing-room. Maggie (the English nurse) with the two boys, and three Sallandrouze servants slept in one room, on mattresses on the floor, with ten other people—the boys, of course, enjoying it madly. Everything a delightful novelty. Frank said to Henrietta on Monday: "It's such fun to be travelling in a *fourgon* (baggage-wagon) with soldiers; you would like it." They had got to Tours, and C. was leaving at once with the children for Cherbourg, to be with Francis. If only he can stay there, but they are moving Territorials to the front.

I went with Mr. Herrick in the afternoon to the American Ambulance. They have taken the Lycée Pasteur—a fine new building at Neuilly, and can make one thousand beds, though they begin with less. All the arrangements are perfect, large, high rooms and corridors, and wide courts. I should think there was almost too much space. The work will be heavy on the nurses—all American and British, and all voluntary. We went all over the building, wards, operating-rooms, lingerie, kitchen. There were no wounded yet, and they won't have any until the fighting near Paris begins. I wanted a model of a sort of loose, sleeveless flannel jacket I saw at the *lingerie*. It looked so comfortable for men sitting up in their beds; they only had one, and would have lent it to me, but the ambassadress said she would send me one from the rectory, where they sew every afternoon.

I found the *ouvroir* very blue. The Mygatts think they must go. He has business in America, and is afraid he might not get out of Paris if he remained much longer. Every day the papers say it is the last day that automobiles can get out of Paris—but I think one could always get a pass. They don't want to leave us, but I don't think H. can undertake a long journey either in an auto or in a crowded train. Mygatt had found a man with a *camion* (a dray) of one horse, which would take him, his family, and his baggage out of Paris. They have their auto and have found a good chauffeur, very well recommended. But they must have a special permit to take the auto out of Paris. They quite saw that it would be impossible for H. to go any distance in an ordinary cart; and as we decided it was out of the question for us, they said they would propose it to the Tiffanys. He, too, has business, and wants to get out of Paris. H. and I talked it over after dinner without arriving at any conclusion. The Tiffanys came in the evening to say they were going—so our friends seem deserting us.

At 10 o'clock a line came to me from the embassy, telling Mygatt the ambassador would see him at 9 the next morning. He had written to the ambassador to ask if he could get the pass for him, so I sent it to him at once.

Thursday, September 3rd.

The news doesn't seem very good this morning. There are reports that the Germans have blown up the Pontoise bridge over the Seine, and that we have done the same at Sevres. I don't feel very happy, though in my heart I don't believe the Germans will come into Paris; but a cannonade near, with possible shells falling about promiscuously, wouldn't make Paris a very pleasant place to stay in. While I was hesitating, Henry Outrey came in with a man from the *Croix Rouge*, who had helped a good many people to get away, and who strongly advised our going—Henry, too. He would take our tickets and places in the last special train that leaves tomorrow. I consulted H., who didn't want to go at all, was not in the least nervous, and dreaded the journey; but I was uncomfortable, and we decided to start tomorrow morning. Marie had written and telegraphed to her daughter that we might perhaps come. We couldn't take any baggage—merely bags and bundles; but the man said he would send our trunks on by *Grande Vitesse*, with the Red Cross labels, which always pass first.

We were very busy all the afternoon, making our preparations. We only packed two small trunks as we did not think we would need much in the way of *toilettes* at Les Aulneaux; but there were things to be put away in the apartment. We leave no one in it, but the ambassador will have a notice put on the door, saying it is inhabited by Americans, and the *concierge* has also a paper to show. That is another of the many small things Mr. Herrick has done to help such of his compatriots as were obliged to stay in Paris. All property owned by or let to Americans has been marked. The only thing he couldn't do was to put such marks on people walking about the streets. We must all take our chance with bombs.

About 5 o'clock I walked over to the *ouvroir* in the Boulevard Haussmann, stopping a moment at the Church of St. Philippe, where there are always women kneeling at the little chapels. The poor *ouvroir* looked quite deserted, but there were piles of shirts, *caleçons*, and bandages ready to be sent off. I gave the woman in charge directions where to send them. She has some money in hand, and will go on with her work until I come back—I hope in about three weeks. Mme. Mygatt must, of course, be longer away, as she is going to America.

As I walked home the streets were full of people looking out for the German aeroplanes, but none had appeared—either the ambassador's remonstrances to the government at home, asking them to protest at Berlin against such traitorous modes of warfare, or else the sight of the French armed aeroplanes had frightened them. The crowd wasn't at all nervous, remarking cheerfully: "*Ah, l'Allemand ne vient pas ce soir; on l'aurait bien reçu pourtant!*" ("The German doesn't come this evening; he would have been well received!")

After dinner Outrey came, and we walked down to the embassy, where there were a good many people coming and going—among others, Mr. Bacon,[5] just arrived. He belongs to the Franco-American Committee, and has come over to help us in whatever way he can. The ambassador said there was no later news. He thought we had better leave Paris. We had nothing particular to keep us here. If there should be a long siege we would be weeks without hearing from Francis, and might be greatly inconvenienced by want of proper food. All the old stories of the horrors that people ate in '70 came back to me—cats, rats, and glad to have them!

---

5. Who was ambassador just before Mr. Herrick.

It was perfectly dark when we came out of the embassy, not a light anywhere, only the searchlights from the *Tour Eiffel* and the Automobile Club, throwing a weird, yellow gleam for an instant over everything. Our street absolutely black. We groped our way along.

Friday, September 4th.

We are quite ready—start at 12.30. I wonder what sort of a Paris we shall find when we get back—and I also wonder if we are right to go. There is every conceivable rumour in the air, Germans at St. Germain—Paris fortifications weak on that side. Paris population discouraged—yet in my heart I don't believe the Germans will get into Paris.

Dimanche, 6 septembre.

I leave the *mairie* paper, dear; by that you may see where we are. It all seems an awful dream. The sudden decision to leave Paris (I don't know now if we did right), and the long, tiring journey; the emotion at meeting soldiers all along the route—these going to the front, cheering and laughing, promising German bullets and sword-belts to the women who crowded around the trains; the young recruits, just twenty, of the class of this year called out, some of them looking mere children—they too, gay, with one or two exceptions—but I must begin at the beginning.

H. did not want to leave Paris—dreaded the journey, and is convinced the Germans will never get into Paris (and I think she is right), nor ever near enough to make life difficult; however, all our friends were going. Every day we saw the official order that after Friday no one could leave Paris by auto, nor perhaps by train. Henry Outrey, who is working with one of the generals in Paris, and also at the *Croix Rouge*, advised us to leave when we could; he would arrange for tickets, places, etc.

I can't say our lives had changed very much since the declaration of war. The market was just as good; we could get everything we wanted and no dearer than in ordinary times, in fact, fruit and certain vegetables cheaper, as the *maraîchers* (market-gardeners) wanted to sell at any price. We had made no extra provisions. The street was gloomy at nights; no more lights, and hardly anyone in the houses, we the only people left in ours. It was rather sad looking down from our balcony on the perfectly dark street—empty, no sounds of life. I haven't heard a laugh for weeks, and it was a relief to hear the hoofs of the horses of the cavalry patrol which passes every night in the Rue François Ier. I went on Wednesday to ask Ambassador Herrick for a pass for a friend of mine, Mr. M., who wanted to get his auto out of Paris, and he advised us to go to the Invalides, where the military governor of Paris lives, and show his card. M. came for me and it was most interesting to see the Esplanade des Invalides; at one end rows of autos drawn up which are being requisitioned for the army, quantities of officers in every direction looking very busy, but perfectly cheerful, notwithstanding the reports that we had heard in the morning that the Pontoise bridge was blown up by the Germans, and the Sevres bridge by the French.

We waited some time in spite of the ambassador's letter and my Red Cross badge, but were finally received by the officer in charge. We explained that we wished to go out of Paris that afternoon in the auto.

"In what direction, *Madame?*"

"Chartres."

"Then go as quickly as possible."

"You really think that?"

"I have no doubt of it and beg you will go at once."

Mr. M. had already made his arrangements to leave. He had chartered two drays of one horse each for himself and his family (they were four) and his luggage, from which he would not separate himself, as he was going to America and hoped to get down to the coast eventually. He wanted us to take his auto, but it had not been going very well lately. He had a new chauffeur whom he knew nothing about. I didn't dare venture, we three women alone, H. hardly walking; so, most reluctantly, they started without us. We decided to leave Friday at 2 o'clock by special train for this place, stopping the night at Conches or Laigle. We had no baggage, only what we could carry. H. was very plucky—didn't want to leave Paris—but I was nervous. I went out to our *ouvroir* late Thursday afternoon to give certain last instructions to the woman Mrs. M., whom I left in charge, telling her to send the garments which were already made to one or two ambulances where we had promised them, and left her some money to go on with the work.

After dinner I went to the embassy to say goodbye to the Herricks in case they should leave before we got back. There were a good many people there coming and going. Mr. Bacon just arrived to give us what help he can in our dark days. Mr. Warren remains too, having sent his wife and children home. The Americans have all been so sympathetic to France since the war began. It must be a most disagreeable surprise for the *Kaiser*, one of the many, I think, that are in store for him. Mr. Herrick is wonderful, quite cool, thinking of everybody, and not sparing himself in the least, working as hard and as late as any of his secretaries. Neither French nor Americans will ever forget what he has done here, and, of course, his remaining in Paris has reassured people very much.

We started Friday at 12 o'clock from the house (the train started at 2.15 from the Gare St. Lazare). Henry came to take us to the station, and I really think our bags and valises were very creditable for ladies accustomed to travel with everything they wanted. We took as little as possible, but, of course, had to provide for the possibility of never seeing our trunks again. They—two small ones—were sent by Grande Vitesse, with Red Cross labels, as all Red Cross baggage goes first. The Gare St. Lazare was a curiosity, crowded with people, quantities of children, and the most remarkable collection of bags, bundles, and household goods possible. We found already six people in our carriage and a child. Marie was obliged to take a place in a second-class carriage (she had a first-class ticket) to be near us. It is a long pull down the platform to the train. H. was very nervous, but got along pretty well, sitting down whenever she could. We hoped to get to Laigle or Conches about 7 o'clock, but telegraphed for rooms at both places. Henry recommended us warmly to the people who were already in the carriage. There were two parties—father, mother, and son going to Brittany, and a young mother, child, and two grandparents bound for Houlgate.

We started at 2.15, having been in the train since 12.30, and remained in it till 8 the next morning. It was an awful journey. We changed our direction many times, backing, turning (at one time we went back nearly to Versailles), and waiting at the stations to let pass the military trains. We met a great many—sometimes soldiers going to the front, sometimes wounded, and always refugees at all the stations, and we stopped at every one. There were crowds of people sitting on their valises, or on the floor, clamouring for seats. I was afraid we would have many more people standing (all the seats were taken) in our compartment, but we managed to keep them out. At Mantes we crossed a train of English troops, and very well and fresh and young they looked in their khakis. They fraternised instantly with the French soldiers, and ran across the track to speak to us. I asked them where they came from: from the frontier, on their way to Rouen for provisions and ammunition. There were great cheers and waving of caps and handkerchiefs when the train started.

As the evening went on it became most evident that we could not get to Conches or Laigle at any possible hour, and we all made up our minds that we must stay the night in the train. The *chefs de gare* looked anxious and overworked wherever we stopped, but were perfectly good-humoured, as was everybody, answering civilly and as well as they could to all the questions. All the *gares* were occupied by soldiers, and the line guarded. We got to Dreux about 1 in the morning, and backed and stopped and were shunted for more than an hour. Some distracted English pursued the *chef de gare* with questions.

"*Monsieur, quand arriverons-nous à Caen?*"

"*Ah, Madame, si vous pouviez me le dire!*"

They told us the town was full of people, no room anywhere, people sleeping in the *gare* and outside on the platforms. The station was as animated as if it were 1 o'clock in the afternoon. Everybody got out, even the twenty-months-old baby, who played about and was wide-awake and perfectly good. Happily it was a beautiful, warm summer night, with a full golden September moon, the harvest moon. That makes me think of one of the numerous prophecies which encourage the people in these awful days:

"*Les hommes commenceront la moisson, les femmes la finiront; les femmes commenceront les vendanges, les. hommes les finiront.*" ("The men will begin the harvest, the women will finish it; the women will begin the vintage, the men will finish it.")

They are getting in the harvest quickly. All along the route women and children are working in the fields. The weather is so beautiful, warm and dry and bright, that they can work long hours and not have too much time to think of the mournings that surely are coming to some of them.

We got through our night well. The baby was perfectly good, slept all night in its grandmother's arms. She could hardly move her arm in the morning. The poor woman was so warmly dressed she was most uncomfortable. Like all the rest of us, she too had started suddenly and could take no baggage, so she had two extra petticoats and another cloth skirt under her ordinary dress and petticoat; she said the weight was awful. Everybody shared whatever she had, water, biscuits, chocolate, but none of us were hungry. At Evreux, where we waited a long time, a train went off with soldiers to the front, all singing the *Marseillaise*, and laughing and cheering. Some of the Red Cross nurses were on the *quai*, but there were no wounded while we were there.

They told us a train of wounded had passed in the night. H. was as plucky as possible; I was worried to death about her. She is kept so carefully and watched over so at home that I didn't see how she could stand all those hours sitting bolt upright in the carriage, but she did, and is none the worse for it.

We got to Laigle at 9 Saturday morning; walked over to the hotel opposite the *gare* and got a nice clean room with hot water, where we could arrange ourselves a little. We had very good *café au lait* and *pain de ménage* on the terrace, with soldiers, refugees, and people leaving Paris. Everybody talked to everybody, but no one knew any more of the war than we did. We left H. sitting on a very hard stone bench with her knitting, and Marie and I went for a stroll. It is a pretty little town with a fine market-place, and a modern *château* standing in a wood at the top. In the eleventh century there was a fine *château*-fort built by the first Marquis de Laigle, which was destroyed by the English in 1419. This one is built on the site of the old one. The park has been cut up, but some of the old trees remain and are splendid, and we had charming glimpses of the river in the distance.

There are handsome, coloured-glass windows in the church of St. Martin. We didn't see many soldiers, though they told us they had four hundred to five hundred wounded, but we met many Belgian refugees, looking so sad and weary, with a pathetic, half-dazed expression in their blue eyes. They try to give both men and women work in the fields. While we were at the *gare* after breakfast, trying to get some information about our train, we heard the drum, the *générale*, which means something serious. In an instant the little place was black with people. All one's nerves are on edge, and we saw instantly bands of Uhlans in the distance. However, the announcement was not tragic, though significant: "*Défense de porter le pain dans la ville.*" ("Carrying bread in the city forbidden.") It tells that one is put upon war rations and everybody must go and get his bread, which, in the big cities, means standing for hours in the crowd at the baker's door.

We started at 4 for Mortague, where, in ordinary times, one arrives in two hours, but we only got there at 8. We were told we could get good accommodation there for the night. Again a great crowd at the station—whole families of women and children, and travellers sitting on their bags; military trains and long provision and forage trains passing in rapid succession, everything making way for them. It is curious to travel when the country is under martial law. Most of the employees of the railways are with the army, their places taken by soldiers who guard the stations. We had a number of young recruits on board—the class of 1914, which, properly, should only have been called to the colours this October. At all the stations we picked up others, their fathers and mothers and families generally coming to wish them goodbye and good luck, all the boys as gay and lively as if they were going off to a country fair; all manner of jokes about "Guillaume" and promises to bring back buttons and cartouches from Germany.

One young fellow came into our compartment. He looked refined and delicate (I shouldn't think he could stand much hard work), of good birth and manners, and evidently didn't care for the rough jokes of his companions. He told us he was just twenty, a Parisian, only child of his parents, had nine first cousins in the war. One saw he was accustomed to the good things of the world. He made a very good meal from a nice basket he had with him, winding up with bonbons and a large piece of cake. He helped us to take down our bags when we arrived at Mortague and looked perfectly miserable when we shook hands and hoped he would get along all right. Poor child! I am sure he cried a little when he was alone in the carriage. If we think twenty is young, what must the German mothers feel whose sons are called out at sixteen?

There were just the same scenes when we arrived at Mortague—people everywhere, not a room to be had at any hotel or any house in the town. I must confess to a moment of profound discouragement when Marie and one of the soldier-porters went off to see what they could find. H. and I remained at the station, she seated on a baggage-truck in the middle of the bags. We waited some time, nobody reappearing, and I saw the moment when I must ask the *chef de gare* to let us sleep in a first-class carriage in the station. When they finally came back, Marie and the two men, they said there was nothing to be had in the town, but the men knew a lady—*une brave dame*—who kept a small pension for the railway employees; they thought she could take us in, but it was at a little distance from the town.

Then came the difficulty of transporting H. There were no carriages of any kind; she couldn't walk. It was late, 9.30; perfectly dark; a "*petit bout de chemin*" might mean anything, from one kilometre to three. However, somebody had a brilliant idea. The men said they would get another porter who would carry our baggage, and they would wheel H. on the truck. She didn't like it much, poor dear, but they promised to go carefully, so we started, one porter in front, carrying a lantern, another alongside with all our bags, the third wheeling the truck, Marie and I on each side, so that H. couldn't fall off. It was a wonderful procession. We crossed the track, followed the road for a short time, and then began to go down a steep, rough path, the man asking both me and Marie to hold the truck back. It was such a ridiculous plight that we couldn't take it tragically, but I was thankful when we stopped.

At the end of the path we came to a garden and a nice house with open windows and lights which looked friendly. A nice-looking, gray-haired woman, attired in a black-and-white dressing-gown, opened the door and showed us into a small room where a man was supping. She said she could only give us one little room, as her best one was given to two wounded soldiers she had taken in, but she would give us two clean beds, and find something—a mattress on the floor perhaps—for the maid, and would give us something to eat. We had a good omelette, bread and butter and cider, and talked to the man, who was an inspector of telegraphs. The poor old lady was very worried at the very little she could give us, but Marie reassured her, and after hearing a great noise of moving furniture over our heads she reappeared with nice clean linen sheets, and Marie went upstairs with her to help make the beds. We consulted the porter who wheeled H. down about the way of getting to Le Mêle the next day (one train was at 4.30 in the morning, another at 9 at night, arriving Heaven knows when). He advised taking an auto; knew the patron of one very well; would go at once and ask him if he would take us direct to Les Aulneaux, and would come back with the answer. He returned before we went upstairs, saying the man would come for us the next morning at 10 o'clock.

I was so tired I was asleep, sitting up in a straight-backed chair. H. and I had a very nice clean room, a lovely garden smell coming in from the open window, and not a sound except trains moving all night. We slept perfectly well. Marie had a mattress on two chairs in the corridor just outside our room, with her dog, a wise little fox-terrier, to take care of her. I was up early and had very good *café au lait*, a fresh egg, and bread and butter, and talked a little to the man of the telegraph, who was most hopeful about the war—said wherever he went in any class, there was the same spirit of dogged resistance to the Germans; they would fight to the last man and woman.

When he had gone the old lady appeared with many apologies for the poor accommodation she had given us; she would like to present her two *blessés* to us; so as soon as H. appeared she brought them—two fine, good-looking young fellows, *fantassins* (infantry), about twenty-six and thirty; one married just six months ago. They had been wounded in the Ardennes, not very badly, each in the arm, and were dying to go back. The younger one can soon go; the other's case was more serious. They had just come from the hospital at Rheims (which is near Mareuil), as the hospital had been evacuated. We asked them if they had plenty to eat when they were fighting. They said always plenty and very good, and wherever they passed on their way back everybody was good to them, bringing them wine, cigarettes, flowers.

They told us a funny story about one of their comrades here, in one of the Algerian regiments. He appeared after the fight slightly wounded, but with a very good bicycle, explaining in his funny French: "*Moi tué quatre Prussiens, puis pris bicyclette*." He was in great request with his *bicyclette* as he got better. He had been wounded in the head; "*petite chose*," he said, but was able to go about the country and do errands. I walked about the garden while we were waiting for the auto, and when I saw by daylight the steep, stony path we had taken last night I really wondered how H. and her truck ever got down and how she ever stayed on it.

The auto with the patron himself driving came at 10 o'clock and we went first to the town to lay in some provisions. Fernande had not answered any of her mother's letters, and this is such an out-of-the-way place that it would not have been safe to arrive without certain precautions. The main street was full of soldiers; there are six hundred wounded and walking about with arms in slings and bandaged legs and heads, all most cheerful. We met the two of our house, who waved to us in the most friendly fashion. We had a charming drive, about an hour to this little place, through lovely country—all green fields, hedges, and fine trees; few villages, almost all farms and grazing country—cows, horses, and colts in the fields. We arrived about 11.30 just as the congregation was coming out of church, and you can imagine the sensation we made in the auto, crammed with bags and parcels of every description. Fernande was quite bewildered, as she had received none of her mother's letters, and three extra people in a small house is a serious thing.

Monday, September 7th.

It is an enchanting summer day. We all seem in a dream. Fernande is the daughter of H.'s Marie, who has been with her for over nineteen years. She is a schoolmistress here and is *adjointe* [6] to the *maire*, and lives in the *mairie*. It is a very nice house, with three big rooms, a courtyard, and a garden, and a high airy classroom which we used as a *salon*. All day yesterday they were arranging two rooms for us. Everybody in the village, from the *curé*, who lent a *fauteuil*, to the mayor, who lent a bed, contributing something. A farmer's wife brought a bottle of fresh milk, and everybody gave a helping hand. Fernande went to the nearest big town, Mamers, yesterday with a long list—two straw armchairs, *portemanteaux* to hang up our skirts and hats (if ever we see our trunks again and have anything to hang up), and some stuff to cover tables (boxes I standing up on one end), etc.

In all my experiences, which have been many and varied, I have never lived before in two rooms in a *mairie*, but I think we shall be perfectly comfortable and so quiet. There isn't a sound, except the *angelus*, which rings twice a day, and makes us stop for a moment in what we are doing to think and pray for all our men in the thick of the fight.

Wednesday, September 9th.

It is a most primitive little hamlet, about fourteen houses, a church, *mairie*, and schoolhouse, one shop, just off the highroad to Mamers, the big town of the neighbourhood, about ten kilometres away, almost hidden on the great stretches of fields and orchards which open out in all directions. It is a great grazing country; there are plenty of cows, horses, and long-legged colts in all the fields, and even the smallest farmer has eight or ten beasts. They sell the horses very well—one thousand five hundred or two thousand *francs*—which makes them a very good income, independent of what the farm brings. Now, of course, there are no men anywhere. The women and old men do all the work.

I went to see the *curé* this afternoon. He has a nice house with a big garden and orchard next the church. He opened the door for me and asked me to come in—into the kitchen, where a bright wood-fire was burning and a nice-looking woman sitting sewing at the window, whom he introduced as his aunt. He is tall, slight, a gentleman in manner; had on an old *soutane*, with a blue gardener's apron over it. He excused himself for receiving me in such dress, but he was working in his garden. I sat there about ten minutes telling him all I knew, which wasn't much, but my news from Paris was more recent than anything he had heard. I asked him if I might play on the harmonium; he said

6. Assistant.

as much as I liked, but he was afraid a Parisienne would not find it very good. It had been seventeen years in the church and a good deal knocked about by people who did not know how to use it. I thanked him for the *fauteuil*, and he asked me if I would like to have a sofa; he had one in his *salon*, which we went to see, but I don't think I shall indulge in such a luxury as a red velvet sofa in my room.

Another time he will show me his house and garden and orchard. The house looks large and roomy. It seems he has four very good rooms upstairs which he would let, but there is no furniture; we would have to hire it from Mamers, which wouldn't be worthwhile if we only stay to the end of the month, which I hope. Besides, we should be less free staying at the *presbytère*. Here we are perfectly comfortable with three women to look after us—Marie, Fernande, and a cousin from Belfort—an *inspectrice d'ecoles*, such a nice woman, obliged to leave Belfort, which was threatened at one time—her husband with the army.

However, I don't think the Germans will tackle Belfort this time. They know quite well how strongly it is fortified, and they need all their troops to stand the desperate resistance they will meet before Paris. We talked a little, of course, of the state of France and how this awful war had been sprung upon her, the *curé* saying she deserved it as a chastisement for the wickedness and immorality of the country. I didn't pursue that conversation, as it seems hard to visit the iniquities of the big towns which have always existed upon the thousands of brave, honest men, good husbands and fathers, leaving all they have in the world and fighting bravely and cheerfully for their country.

Friday, September 11th.

We are settling down to our life in this quiet little corner of France. If only we had more communication with Paris and the rest of France. I get a walk every morning and already know all the village. I stopped to talk to a nice-looking girl the other day who had a baby in her arms, its father, her brother, at the front. She invited me to come in and I found a nice, clean peasant's house; her father and mother very respectable, speaking quite intelligibly. Sometimes their French—not exactly a *patois*, but with a curious accent—is hard to understand. They knew all about us; had seen us arrive at the schoolhouse in the automobile, and were most curious for news from Paris. They offered me a drink—wine, milk, or cider—but I excused myself on the plea of its being early in the morning.

The country is lovely, like walking through an English park; no fences anywhere; green banks, high hedges, and splendid pasture-fields. I don't see much cultivation; I fancy horses and farm products are the principal resources. H. and I go every day about 6 o'clock to the church, which we have to ourselves, and have arranged a little service. I play and sing some hymns or bits of Beethoven. The harmonium isn't bad, only I have so little the habit of playing an organ that I forget the pedals sometimes, and then the music stops with a sort of wheeze. I always finish with the evening hymn: "Sun of my soul. Thou Saviour dear," "God save the King," and the Russian hymn. I don't dare play the "*Marseillaise*" in the church. It would upset the *curé* dreadfully, and yet it is too bad not to play sometimes for our soldiers. The next time any one goes to Mamers I will ask them to bring me back the famous *marche* of "*Sambre et Meuse*," which our troops love to march to.

We had a good mail this morning: letters a little old, and papers the second day from Paris; also a telegram from Charlotte, from Cherbourg, where she has joined Francis. She is trying to find a small house there—says the boys are highly excited seeing their father in uniform. The war news is good, the Germans retreating. For the moment they seem to have given up their march on Paris; I wonder why.

Sunday, September 13th.

Yesterday was rather a wild day, raining and blowing. However, I got out between the showers. Still nothing of our trunks, which were sent off two days after us (just a week ago). We manage pretty well. Our next-door neighbour washes our linen, and our serge dresses hold out. We each had an extra blouse in our bags, we hear all sorts of reports. In a letter today from Anne Morgan, written from her convent in England, she says:

"The great event in our quiet lives has been the passing of the *Cosaques* at our little station at Norton bridge. I am sorry I could not go and see them; all the countryside was much excited."

They are a wild lot, particularly the red *Cosaques*. They are dressed in red, have long red lances, and ride small, red bay horses. We saw them in Moscow at the coronation of Alexander III. They patrolled the streets to keep the crowd back—such a patient, long-suffering crowd. Sometimes they backed their horses vigorously into the mass of people; no one seemed to mind; the ranks thinned out a little but formed again instantly. Sometimes they charged down the street full gallop, brandishing their lances and yelling in the most awful way.

Even in times of peace it was enough to strike terror into the stoutest heart. The Russians seem to have annihilated the Austrians, who certainly have not proved themselves a very formidable foe.

I don't think they will find it so easy with the Germans, who will certainly make a desperate resistance before Berlin. For some reason we don't know, the Germans are not advancing on Paris and are retreating steadily toward the southeast—sixty kilometres—pursued by the French and English, who have taken cannon and prisoners. The fighting must have been awful, day after day, and even the very meagre official reports say there were great losses on both sides. It is heartbreaking to think of the mournings there will be in France when the lists are published. A whole generation in the flower of their strength and youth cut down on account of one man's wicked ambition.

The mayor, who comes to see us every night brought a report yesterday that two of the emperor's sons were terribly wounded and the empress gone out of her mind. If it is true, as many people say, that *she* wanted the war, and arranged it all with the crown prince while the emperor was cruising, her punishment has come quickly.

This morning I went to church, a simple country service; more men than I expected to see. The melodeon was played by a small boy with one finger, but he did sound the notes. The *chantre*, having gone to the war, was replaced by an elderly gentleman who did his best, but wasn't always at the same key as the instrument. Then the *curé* intervened and brought him back to the right note. The congregation looked respectable and well-to-do. Fernande says there are no poor in the village. All the little girls had their hair neatly braided in pigtails down their backs, tied with a blue or white ribbon. All the women wear the *coiffe* of the country, a white muslin cap with a very full crown falling low at the back of the neck, a bow of muslin on the top.

Some of the rich farmers' wives have four or five in their *trousseau*, which last all their lives and go to their daughters after them. When they are hand-embroidered they are quite expensive. A young woman came to see Marie the other day with a very pretty one which was given to her when she married, and which cost seventy-five *francs*. Marie asked her if she wouldn't like to wear a hat, but she said not at all, and that her husband wouldn't let her. "*Une fermière doit porter la coiffe du pays.*" The girls wear hats but simple ones, not so many flowers and feathers as our girls in Mareuil. Some of the farmers are very rich. One of them married his daughter some time ago and gave her a trousseau, linen sheets and table-linen, and beasts, which would have been a fortune in Paris. The wedding festivities went on for a week, all the countryside feasting at the farm. He is said to have spent five thousand *francs* on the entertainment.

Thursday, September 17th.

We are having beautiful, golden September days, but the evenings are chilly. I walk about in the mornings. All the women come to the doors of their cottages and ask me to come in. It is curious to see no men except very, very old ones, the women doing all the work. Every morning I meet a girl about twelve years old, mounted astride on a big farm-horse; a little later she appears on another; evidently takes the horses to the field, which the women plough. It is only in the country that one realises the war and the difficulty of transport and provisions. The farmers are afraid even their poor old horses will be taken away; all the best ones have already gone.

Our trunks have arrived and we are more comfortable. Until they came we didn't like to go out in the rain, as, if we got our skirts wet, we had nothing to change. We are rather short in books. I read so much to H. that we are very dependent upon books and papers. Fern-ande has put the *Bibliothèque Scolaire* at our disposition, and that may keep us on a little. I have found a history of France by Lavisse, much abridged and simplified. Still it will put the main facts back in our heads, and I shall be able to answer the boys' questions when we all of us get back to Paris again. I was very embarrassed when they were beginning their Bible history to find how little I remembered about the misfortunes of Tobit and various Kings of Judah.

There is also in the library a translation of *Uncle Tom's Cabin* and the *Last of the Mohicans*, so you see we are not very modern in this quiet little corner of France. The happy days in Mareuil seem so far off. We have had such beautiful September days there, the men shooting partridges all day, we women joining them at tea-time in the keeper's cottage, and the lovely walk home across the fields, the soft evening light making everything a picture—a peasant woman crossing the field, her baby tied in a red shawl on the back, the man plough-ing, his white oxen standing out against the sky-line, and always in the distance the purple line of the Villers-Cotterets forest.

In a letter from Tours from Madame Sallandrouze, received this morning, she spoke of the constant passage of wounded soldiers, both French and English, at the station. All the ladies take them fruit, wine, cigarettes, and above all postcards. Both Renée and Madeleine speak English well, and they say the poor men were so grateful to have post-cards sent to their families. One young fellow said most respectfully to Madeleine: "Might I kiss you, *mademoiselle?*" She instantly gave him her cheek. One regiment had been to La Ferté-Milon and Mareuil the night of the 31st (the day Charlotte and her family left) pursuing German cavalry who also passed through. As the Germans were re-treating they probably didn't have time to stop and pillage or burn our house; however, we know nothing. Francis may have some news per-haps, but his letters are very rare, postal communication is very long, and the soldiers are forbidden to give any details about anything.

Sunday, 10th September.

We get through our days as well as we can, but it is terrible to have so little news. They are fighting hard over all parts of the country—Germans perfect barbarians, burning, pillaging, shooting perfectly innocent people. There will be a fearful reckoning when the time comes. At church this morning the *curé* read us the bishop's letter announcing the election of the new Pope, Benoit XV, and ending with the prayer that he might be the means of restoring peace among nations. The service is the most primitive I have ever seen. The poor little boy who plays the harmonium with one finger got nervous this morning, lost his place completely. Everyone waited—the *curé* turn-ing round, saying, "Try the Alleluia," but no sound was forthcoming. The *curé* and the *chantre* had it all their own way—and a very curious plain-chant it was. The *chantre* also made the *quête*. He had neither plate nor bag—held out his hand and every one put the offering in the hollow of the palm.

It has been a beautiful day, a gorgeous sunset, but the evenings are decidedly chilly. I am getting a little nervous about staying much longer with H. If it begins to rain or we have a series of foggy days—already a mist rises in the fields after sunset—this little house would be very damp—besides, I seem to get more news, such as it is, in Paris. Little things always leak out, and the few diplomatists who are left keep us well informed.

Monday, 21st September.

Today Marie and I made an excursion to Mamers, the nearest big town, where there is a *Sous-Préfecture*, big hospital, and famous mar-ket. *Monsieur le Maire* drove us in his dog-cart, a most primitive little country equipage, with very high, broad wheels, and rather narrow seats. However, it was only twelve kilometres and he had a good little mare (just over two years old, too young to be requisitioned—all his good farm-horses being taken). He took us along at a fair rate. We picked up a friend, a nice-looking peasant woman, on the road; she was trudging along to market carrying a heavy basket in each hand— eggs in one, and pots of fresh yellow butter in the other. The route was charming, bordered on each side by high green banks and hedges. We ran for some time along M. d'Allières's property (the man who stood against Caillaux in the last elections), in fact through his property, as he owned the land on each side.

We went through fine oak woods, growing very thick, a clearing every now and then giving a beautiful far view over the plains. The mayor is a shrewd little man; talked a great deal; told me all he knew and I told him all I knew (with certain limitations). One of his remarks rather astonished me. We were talking, of course, about the war, and how Germany had been preparing quietly and mobilising for months, while France, apparently, was quite unprepared. *That*, he remarked, was the fault of our ambassador in Berlin, who ought to have known what was going on—that was what ambassadors were sent to foreign countries for.

Mamers is a pretty little country town, most animated today, market-day, and a most tempting market it looked, all the women busy and energetic-looking, so nice with their clean stiff white *coiffes*, standing guard over their stalls. I never saw so many eggs and tubs of fresh yellow butter before in my life. There were quantities of soldiers everywhere, one regiment of *chasseurs* passing through on their way to the Marne, and some of the wounded walking about with heads and arms bandaged. The hospital is full; if there are any English wounded I will go and see them. We made various purchases and then went on to the *gare*—quite a walk—to ask about trains and the possibility of getting back to Paris.

In the main street, just out of the market I saw an *infirmière* of the *Croix Rouge* in uniform. I went to speak to her to ask if there are any English at the hospital. She was rather an attractive-looking woman, a pretty smile and nice blue eyes. She was very civil, said there were no English at this moment, but that they were expecting a *convoi*. She would let me know if I would tell her where I was. I said it wasn't worth while; I was not at Mamers, but at a little village some distance—Les Aulneaux. She said that would make no difference, she could easily send word. I gave my name and we parted.

The mayor said to me: "*Madame sait à qui elle a parlé?*"

"*Non, pas du tout.*"

"*C'est Madame Caillaux, Madame.*"

I was rather annoyed. All that affair was so disgraceful. One felt ashamed of being a Frenchwoman. However, the conversation was of the briefest and most impersonal description. It was curious to come upon the lady the one day I was at Mamers. We walked through the Place de la République on our way to the station, a broad, handsome avenue, with fine trees, good houses with gardens at the roadside, and quite an imposing *Sous-Préfecture*, with iron gates and good entrance. The station looked deserted—no sign of traffic, but the *chef de gare* told us that the trains ran regularly twice a day to and from Paris. He advised us to go at night. We would certainly have no trouble about seats, and it would be better to arrive in Paris at 6 or 7 in the morning than at 12.30 or perhaps later at night, so I think we shall do that and leave Sunday.

We went back to the market to pick up our bundles, and found everybody reading the Paris papers, and half-mad with rage. The Germans have bombarded and reduced to ruins the Cathedral of Rheims; there were explosions of indignation everywhere. Their conduct is inexplicable, to destroy for the pleasure of destroying and putting the whole civilised world against them. One can't imagine Rheims without that splendid old cathedral, so full of beauty and mystery and the old traditions of France—her history. The mayor and one of his military friends with whom we took coffee before starting back, in a *café* filled with soldiers and small farmers, were furious, and suggested that we would do well to burn the Cologne Cathedral when our troops get into Germany. One can't quite do that, but one might destroy the Royal Palace in Berlin and a few others of the hideous buildings which adorn the city.

There was no special news from the war zone, but one serious measure—all the men up to forty-eight years old have been called out. Certainly life is made up of contrasts here. As I was jogging along very contentedly with the mayor, talking about the relative merits of oaks, which he knew about, and poplars, which I knew about, as a source of income, I asked myself if it could have been I who drove into the Kremlin in a gala carriage attired in "*a white satin gown, all finished off with a golden crown,*" as the old song says.

Tuesday, September 22nd.

Another beautiful day. One ought to be so happy merely to live in such weather, and when one thinks of all those who will never see their homes and woods and fields again, it is heartrending. We have had a very good mail today, all the papers, of course, full of the bombardment of Rheims, the English and Americans most outspoken. I shouldn't think Von Bernstorff's position in America was a very enviable one. I have a nice letter from Charlotte from Octeville, where she has found a nice little farmhouse, very clean, with four rooms, kitchen, sitting-room, and two bedrooms; orchards, big garden—*potager*—a cow, chickens, and all sorts of vegetables.

It is close to the *cantonnement*, so that Francis can come to dine and sleep every night. She is so happy, poor child, to be with Francis again. She has also found a nice, strong country girl to do the cooking and general work. Says the boys are quite well and happy, playing all day in the fields and gardens. She has friends and relations at Cherbourg— twenty minutes' walk, and curiously enough it was at Cherbourg that she made Francis's acquaintance, when her father. Admiral Sallandrouze, commanded the Atlantic squadron and was stationed at Cherbourg. She and Nanna are going to work regularly at the Cherbourg hospital.

I left off as I heard the *boulangère's corne*. She generally has news, and stops at the gate for a little talk. She hadn't any news, but gave her customers a disagreeable piece of information—she must raise her prices, and ask in the future twenty-four *sous* instead of twenty-three for the long loaf of bread which she supplies. The women protested, but she said her bags of flour had increased in price and diminished in size. She couldn't make both ends meet if she didn't ask more for her bread. She is mistress of the situation, as there is no other baker in the neighbourhood.

I suppose at the big farms they do make bread, but there would be no way of getting it; the men are all away, and the women too busy to go and get it.

Every day women come to the *mairie* to ask for news of their husbands and sons. One poor young thing with four small children is quite hopeless. Her husband was in all the fighting in Belgium; wrote or sent messages at first; since three weeks she has heard nothing. The nights are beautiful, the sky as blue almost as in the day, and myriads of stars. I wonder what horrors they look down upon.

Wednesday, September 23rd.
Today Marie and I and the *maire* have been to the other big town,

Le Mêle; just the same lovely country, but more farms and fields than toward Mamers. I should think there was more culture. We passed one big farm where there were quantities of stacks of wheat; the mayor said they had been there for a long time; there was no one to take them in; each man had as much as he could do to work his own farm. A sign of the times was the women carting. We saw certainly three or four heavy carts drawn by two old horses, filled with bags of flour or potatoes, with women walking alongside with their long whips, just like the men. Le Mêle is a pretty little town, the River Sarthe flowing through it. Just at the entrance there is a picturesque old house, now a mill, with courtyard and towers; it had been a *château*.

Usually they did a most flourishing business, the mayor told me, but today it was almost deserted—a few old men and boys staggering along with heavy bags on their shoulders. It was market-day and the town was full, but evidently a great many strangers—"*des Parisiens*," one woman told us. Le Mêle is on the highroad from Paris to Brest, and hundreds of people passed through at the time of the panic (when the Germans were near Paris), on their way to some quiet little place in Brittany. For two days, the *patronne* of our little hotel told us, two hundred autos a day filled with women, children, and baggage passed through the town. There are no soldiers, no wounded, there now. The only two doctors had gone to the front; no traces of war—a, busy little country town. When I went into a shop to ask for a pattern of *caleçon militaire*, the woman said to me, seeing my Red Cross badge, "Ah, *Madame* is come to open a hospital."

All the women in the shop were making garments for the soldiers, some of them knitting stockings as they walked along the streets. There were several autos with nice-looking people in them standing about. The market was crowded—always the same nice-looking women, so active and alert, standing at their stalls, their arms *akimbo*, smiling and eager and so intelligent in understanding what one wanted. I always say Frenchwomen of all classes are the best business women in the world. There was just the same tempting array of eggs, cheeses, chickens, and butter as at Mamers, but we get all these from the farms. We wanted some meat, which we only get once a week from the butcher. The great feature was fat little pink pigs, really quite pretty—their long hair, carefully combed, like silk.

The mayor told us they were much in demand, cost forty *francs* apiece. I shall become an expert in farms and woods. I always said I ought to have lived in the country and have managed a model farm.

It was really more my vocation than the life I have led in courts and embassies, though that had its charm too.

The poor mayor was rather worried when we got home. He found despatches advising him of the passage of a certain *black* automobile, filled with men dressed as women, flying at top-speed over the country—spies certainly—who must be arrested. Such extraordinary rumours get about. He was going to communicate with the *gendarmes*, as he alone—he is a little man—could do nothing. Usually nothing passes—some children, a few carts and wagons, and a great many geese, who are as good as watch-dogs. It seems they hate strangers, fly at the children sometimes, and always cackle and flap their wings when any one passes. They are enormous in this country, as big as swans.

It really is a lovely view I have out of my window when I open the shutters wide early in the morning and look straight across the narrow country road to a high green bank and hedge, behind it pear and apple trees loaded with fruit; just around the corner a little white house with a red roof, with a small garden in front, where a red-cheeked, white-haired old woman sits all day in the sun, and invites one in to pick some of her flowers. They make their cider here much more with pears than apples, and very good it is, though very strong; I add a great deal of water.

Friday, September 25th.

Still beautiful, bright days. We sit out all day; take our meals (except dinner) in the garden. Yesterday I went with Marie to one of the famous farms near here. The *fermière* came for us in her little trap—a dean, energetic little woman, dressed like all the peasants in a short black skirt, and wide, blue-and-white check apron, which hid her dress entirely, but no *coiffe*, her hair very neatly done. She has eight children—seven boys, three at the war, and one girl, and now they do all the farm work themselves, as they can't get any labourers. The court looked very clean and sunny, all the buildings in good order. We saw everything conscientiously. It was amusing when the boys drove in the brood-mares (which have just begun to work a little). They let out the colts, who all galloped madly to their mothers.

The farm is very well known. They got the second prize for the best-kept farm, and would have had the first, if there hadn't been a bottle of *cornichons* in the dairy, which the judges said was not in its proper place. She gave us milk, cider, everything she had, and we carried home a pot of thick yellow cream.

This afternoon's mail has brought us bad news from Mareuil. I was sure it would come, but it has distressed me very much. One of our friends, M. Pernolet, was *en tournée* in our part of the country and stopped at Mareuil to give us news. This is what he writes:

"The 1st of September the English arrived and did a little harm, but they only passed through. Then came the Germans, who stayed eight days. They have entirely demolished the inside of the house, stolen linen, dresses, all the *batterie de cuisine*, twenty-nine lamps, the silver broken, and spoilt all the furniture. In the cabinet stolen medals, arms, ransacked and thrown about all the papers; all the bedding spoilt; one new automobile taken; an old one left; the outside is intact."

I don't think we could have prevented it. I could not leave Charlotte there alone with her boys to face these savages, and even if I could have left H., I don't think I could have prevented anything, a woman alone, but it is awful to think of our house ruined and so much of value taken. All my husband's papers were there, locked and padlocked in a case, but that, of course, was easily smashed. I must get back to Paris and then down to Mareuil. I have written to our woman down there who went away with all the rest when they were told to *évacuer*, and also to the *curé*, but I must get there. It would have been a miracle if we had escaped, as our place is directly on the highroad from Meaux to Rheims. We had also a letter from Comtesse Gyldenstolpe (née Norah Plunkett), wife of the Swedish minister, from Bordeaux. She says:

> I shall never forget our hurried departure from Paris that night, that endless train, crowded with people of all nationalities, from a small Chinese baby up to the most important ambassador, everybody divided up by countries. I never knew we had so many colleagues before. As we travelled through the night we passed one train *militaire* after the other, crowds both of soldiers and evident refugees all along the line, so many wounded too. I shall never forget it; everybody so anxious and preoccupied, and at the same time each one asking for his baggage and wondering how he could caser himself when one got there. The heat too; there are no words to describe what it was; no words either to describe the crowd, soldiers, political people, diplomats, stray foreigners, who really had nothing to do here, and anxious relatives, who wished to be at headquarters to obtain news. . . .

I think the crowd has diminished a little now, but, of course, as long as the government is at Bordeaux it will always be the great centre. We have been up to the church for the last time, and I went to say good-bye to *M. le Curé*. He received me in his *salon* this time—really quite a nice room, with a red-velvet sofa and armchairs, a bookcase, and a big window opening on a pretty garden. I told him if I had been more familiar with the chants of his church I would have offered to play for him. He said he hadn't dared ask me. He was much interested in all I told him about Mareuil and how our house had been *saccagé*. It was a beautiful evening, soft, pink sunset clouds; the yellow moon just rising over the trees; not a sound in the quiet little place until the evening *angelus*. I shall miss the bells; they seem to speak of peace and hope.

Paris, Monday, September 28th.

We arrived this morning after a long night in the train, the carriage full. However, we had no adventures. We left Les Aulneaux looking quite charming in the sunshine about 3 o'clock yesterday afternoon. I had sent for a carriage from Mamers for H., as I was afraid she would appreciate neither the mayor's conveyance nor his conversation, but his trap followed with our luggage and the two women. The drive was charming; our old horse went quite fast enough. The harness was a little casual; the driver got down once or twice to arrange something, finally asked Marie if she had a pair of scissors and a piece of string. She produced both, and he mended whatever was wrong, and we got to Mamers without any adventure.

The town was full of soldiers—many wounded, a group of *Turcos* sitting in the sun. Two of them looked badly, stretched out on *couvertures*; they couldn't speak—just smiled when we talked to them. These fierce fighters that caused such havoc with the Germans, and are such a wild, formidable enemy, had good simple faces, almost childlike. We stopped at the Hôtel du Cygne on the Place de la République, and sat on the terrace till nearly 9 o'clock, much interested in all that was going on. There was evidently a general or superior officer staying in the house, as orderlies were going and coming all the time with despatches. I asked a nice-looking old colonel if there was any news.

"*Cela va bien, Madame; nous n'avons qu'attendre; nous attendrons.*" ("All is going well; we have only to wait. We will wait.") The dinner was good, served by women; was entirely military—one long room filled with *sous-officiers*, the other reserved for the officers and the few passing travellers. There was a great jingle of spurs and sabres when they all trooped in—and a very good-looking lot of officers they were—and then a flow of conversation; all were most cheerful. We had a little table at one end of the room; too far to hear any of the talk, which I was sorry for. Some of them were evidently just from the front, some very smart *chasseurs* with their light-blue tunics and red trousers, which showed distinct signs of wear. I caught every now and then the names of familiar places in my part of the country: La Ferté-Milon—Villers-Cotterets. They might perhaps have given me news of Mareuil, but I didn't like to ask.

Our carriage came a little before 8 to take us to the station, where there was again a great crowd—as many people apparently wanting to get into Paris now as there were who wanted to get out three weeks ago. We took a little country train to Connerets and there got the *rapide de Brest* for Paris. Any illusion we had had of a carriage to ourselves—or even a comfortable seat—was quickly dispelled. The train stopped for a very short time; we were hurried into the first-class carriage (there were only two on the train) and found one seat (we were four) for H. I began my night sitting on my valise in the *couloir*, but after a little while the people in the carriage where H. was made room for me, and I got through the night fairly comfortably, though it is years since I have sat up straight all night in a crowded carriage. I was thankful when we arrived at 7.30 at the Gare Montparnasse, and I hope I won't have to take another railway journey while the country is under martial law.

October to December 1914

I have been ill for two or three days. The visit[1] to Mareuil upset me entirely. However, I have got my nerve back. Things might have been worse, and after the war, if all goes well with us, it will be interesting to reconstruct our house and our lives. Nothing can ever be the same again.

After breakfast, I walked down to the embassy to thank the ambassador for having given us an auto and an officer to go down to Mareuil. I found there the new Spanish ambassador, Marquis de V., a fine soldierly-looking old man. He remains in Paris, having stopped a few days in Bordeaux to present his credentials.

They were both much interested in all I told them of the state in which I found my house and the village; and they rather comforted me, saying that any troops would have taken blankets, coverlids, and saucepans out of an uninhabited house. I couldn't have refused them, naturally, to our own soldiers; but *they* wouldn't have taken pictures and silver and souvenirs of all kinds.

It is beautiful weather. I enjoy the walk over to the *ouvroir*, should enjoy it more if there were not occasional Tauben flying about. No one seems to mind them. Everyone runs out into the middle of the street when they hear one coming, though people have been warned to stay indoors. One hears them from a long distance.

Mrs. D. came in late to the *ouvroir*, rather afraid she may be *évacuée* a second time, as the Germans are unpleasantly near the ambulance. She carried off a large parcel of sheets and pillowcases we had made for her. I went to dine with her at the Hôtel Crillon. There was no one but ourselves in the dining-room, but the *gérant* told us there were several people in the house.

---

1. This visit is described later in this chapter.

64

They had an Englishman with them whose name I didn't catch, a tall man, dressed in khaki, with the Red Cross brassard on his arm. He had been to the front in his motor to look for his son, reported missing, whom he didn't find. He said people were very kind, trying to help him, but that it was impossible to get anywhere near the front: all sorts of vehicles, provision-wagons, munition, cannon, and autos—squads of cavalry crowding on the roads, which are getting very bad and cut up with so much passing; a few heavy motors struggling helplessly on the side of the road—and in the fields.

I came away early as I didn't like driving about in the dark. The Champs Elysées are scarcely lighted. It is now a long, black avenue, the trees on each side making a high dark wall.

Thursday, October 8th.

I was at the *ouvroir* all the afternoon. We want now to make packages to send to the front. We have many more applicants for work than we can employ, and it is hard to send the women away. They look so utterly miserable; but we can't increase our expenses. I stopped at the Automobile Club who send off autos filled with warm clothes once or twice a week. All the packages were piled up in the courtyard, and each one was weighed, as they must not exceed a certain number of pounds. There were all kinds: An old woman came in with such a small packet, wanting to send it to her son, and the soldier in charge, a smart-looking young *réserviste*, was so nice with her, looking to see if the name, company, and raiment were distinctly marked. I asked her what it was. "Only a flannel band, *Madame*; I have nothing to send and he asks for nothing, but he always liked his flannel belt." They are very useful; we make dozens of them, some in flannel, some knit or crochet.

I am going to ask the women in our street, the *épicière* and the *patronne* of a little *café* at the corner where the *Croix Rouge employès* and boy scouts breakfast, if they won't knit me *cache-nez* and stockings, if I supply wool and needles.

I dined out tonight—a rare occurrence in these times—with Sir Henry —— to meet Lord and Lady R. C. He is over here with the British Red Cross Society. There was also an English banker who is banker for all the British officers. The talk was interesting. I really think the British hate the Germans more than we do. We spoke of old times, and Hatfield, of course, when all were young men, unmarried and at home, and a very cheerful, united family party they were; and all so clever. Lord R. told me his brother Edward had lost his only son. The mother came over to see if she could find his body. He was reported missing after the Battle of the Marne. She went down to Rheims, made all sorts of inquiries—heard of many good-looking young Englishmen killed—even had some of the graves opened (the clothes and belongings of each dead man are put in a bundle at his head), but could find no trace of her boy. She is one of a million mothers who will never hear anything more of their sons.

The drive home is always disagreeable; so dark and the streets so deserted; I think our street is the darkest of all. It doesn't seem like Paris when one crosses the Avenue du Trocadéro, usually so light and so many carriages dashing about, and the trams a long line of light which are seen at a great distance. Now it is quite black. Suddenly a figure emerges out of the darkness, quite close to you. A little further on one just gets the glint of the bayonet of the sentry at the foot of the hill. I don't believe a creature has come back. There is no sign of life; no lights anywhere. As long as the Germans are still near Pairs and the Tauben flying overhead, people won't come back.

Saturday, 10th October.

It is beautiful summer weather and the days slip by. We were quite numerous at the *ouvroir* this afternoon. Madame de Sinçay, who is *infirmière* at the British Red Cross hospital installed at the Hôtel Astoria, asked me for some "Nightingales." I didn't know what they were, but the boys' English nurse told me: a loose, sleeveless jacket which the men like on their shoulders when they can sit up in bed to read or write. They were invented by the famous English nurse, Florence Nightingale, in the Crimea, and called after her. We sent at once for some flannel, and will have some made as quickly as possible, all the ladies working hard.

At 7 o'clock C. came for me and we went to dine at La Rue's, one of the popular *cafés* in the Rue Royale, to see the aspect of the boulevards at night. There were a good many people dining—a very good dinner. One long table filled with British officers, who attracted much attention from some of the pretty young women, *dames seules,* who were dining quietly in the corner—almost all with the badge or brassard of the *Croix Rouge.* Women of all classes have formed that society, and some of the best nurses are young actresses and dancers from the Paris theatres.

D. dined with us. He goes every day to the Jockey Club and hears their view of the way things are being done, and how now, after the first burst of patriotism, politics are beginning to play a part.

I think the government is doing very well; and if there are individual cases of treachery (it seems an awful word to use in connection with any French soldier or minister) it will have no effect on the public.

War always brings out the best qualities of people of all classes— except the Germans, who have developed such barbarity and cruelty that we ask ourselves how they were ever considered a Christian, civilised power. They imposed upon all the world with their *Familienleben* and their sentimental music and poetry.

A little after 9, the waiters began to bring the hats and coats of the diners, and gradually to put out the lights. At 9.30 two policemen appeared at the door, and in ten minutes the *café* was empty.

We walked about a little, but the boulevards were depressing; very dark, and one needs as much outside light as possible in these sad days.

Wednesday, October 14th.

The days are so alike that one hardly realises that the autumn is slipping away. The weather is beautiful still. I went up to the Rue de la Pompe. Maggie is there, and we went to the hospital installed in the Lycée Janson, just opposite our apartment, to see an English soldier, a nice-looking young fellow, not wounded, but almost dead with rheumatism and pneumonia. He had been four days and nights on his gun (was an artilleryman), sometimes in a pouring rain. He said everybody was good to him at the hospital, some ladies even bringing him tea and buns every day. We promised him some warm clothes as he was to go back to the front in a day or two. He was dying to get on his gun again and have another shot at the Germans. Told us horrors he had seen; but said the Germans were drunk (he was near Rheims); their officers had no control of them.

Friday, October 16th.

Maggie came in after lunch with the gunner who was to leave for the front the next day. He looked better but delicate still; was dressed in the clothes we gave him, and had had a good "English" lunch at one of the restaurants. The *médecin-chef* had allowed Maggie to take him out until 5 o'clock. The Mygatts were here, and we were all much interested in all he told us. He never had his clothes off from the 20th August until the 15th September. His boots had to be cut off, they were so hard and stiff. When they wanted to give him another pair at the hospital, he refused absolutely; said he would never put on boots again—went for days in felt slippers.

Saturday, October 17th.

Our beautiful sun has gone in. Today it is grey and damp. Mrs. Mygatt and I went to see the mayor of our arrondissement to speak about some poor women who wanted work. He was not there, but we saw a lady, very important, who was in charge of the *ouvrières sans travail*. She recommended two women, soldiers' wives, one a *culottière* (woman who makes trousers), and the other a *piqueuse de machine à coudre*. They would be very pleased to come every afternoon from 2 to 6 for *fr.* 1.50. Poor things, it is nothing for clever Paris workwomen. One gained 10 *francs* a day, with two meals, at one of the good tailors; the other about the same. We don't say we will give any meals, but we will give tea and thick slices of bread and butter, and later a bowl of soup.

Mme. del Marmol, our Belgian friend, came in quite happy, poor thing, as she had had news of her children in the country in Belgium, for the first time since the siege of Liège. She is just starting an *ouvroir* for the Belgian women; says their misery is appalling; some of the children have no shirts or underclothes of any description, only a dress or a coat over their skin. One woman came to the *ouvroir* with her baby, a month old. They put it in a basket near the fire, and the little thing was quite happy and slept peacefully, all the other women crowding around it. She says they don't complain; seem half stunned by the awful catastrophe that has fallen upon them.

Poor, pretty, smiling little Belgium, with gardens and farms and thriving, busy, happy population! It is sickening to think of black burned plains, and whole villages smoking ruins!

Mme. de Sinçay came in about 6 o'clock to beg for garments for a military hospital at Villers-Cotterets, where they were in need of everything. Someone down there asked her if she knew me; said Mr. Waddington had represented so long that part of the country that they were sure I would help them. She carried off a fine bundle of flannel sheets, warm *caleçons*, red flannel *ceintures*, and rolls of bandages of all sizes.

I found M. sitting with H. when I came home. Her husband is an *infirmier* at the American Ambulance, works there every day from 8 in the morning until 7 at night. She says he is tired out, stoops like an old man; has his dinner as soon as he comes in, and goes at once to bed. She had just seen her eldest boy (22), who is in a French *cuirassier* regiment. He is a Russian subject, was in Canada when the war broke out, and couldn't get back in time to enlist in a Russian regiment, so joined the French Army, as did the son of Istolsky, Russian ambassador in France, who was also too late to get to Russia.

Sunday, October 18th.

There was an innovation in the American church this morning— almost all the boys and young men of the choir have been called away either as soldiers or scouts, and they are replaced by girls dressed in black with white surplices, and little white caps on their heads, only a few older men remaining.

We had a few visits in the afternoon. Mrs. Watson, the rector's wife, came late. She was most interesting, telling curious stories of Americans of all classes stranded here at the beginning of the war. The Ambassador and Mrs. Herrick, Sir H. L., and Pauline de B. dined. Lt. G., the young officer who took me down to Mareuil, came in after dinner. Lt. G. had just come back from the front, where he had picked up wounded and brought them back to the hospital. He said shells were flying about in a pretty lively manner.

The Harjes have done a most generous thing: fitted out and equipped entirely—nurses, doctors, and ambulance—a field-hospital in a *château* close to the firing-line. Everything is arranged so that the *whole* hospital can move on to another place in two hours, if there came a serious attack.

I thought the ambassador looked tired; he does so much and sees so many people—not only his own colony, but many of his colleagues, who go to him for advice.

He is reading the life of Washburne, who was United States Minister here in 1870, and remained in Paris all through the siege and the Commune. He said it was most interesting to read it just now, when he was doing the same thing, but under such different circumstances.

Tuesday, October 20th.

A. H. came to breakfast this morning, and we went after breakfast to see Mrs. W. at the rectory. She had promised to show us her *ouvroir*. I had never been inside of the house. It is pretty and original, very comfortable for two people. No clergyman with a family could get into it. She showed us some of the upstairs rooms over the church, which had been most useful at the time of the American invasion, as they had put beds and mattresses everywhere, in the library, in the corridor, and even in the cloisters. The weather was so warm and beautiful all those first days of the war.

The *ouvroir* was very well arranged, a large light room—cupboards all around the walls; about twenty women, all French, working at a long table, some by hand, some with sewing-machines. There were two women in charge—a *surveillante* who gave out and examined the work, and another who had the *caisse*, received any money that came, and paid the women. It was most orderly. In some of the cupboards were all sorts of clothes, both men's and women's, sent in trunks to Mrs. W. by people who were going back to America and were willing to leave their contents for less fortunate compatriots who couldn't get away with the first rush, and who had no clothes except what they had on their backs.

Most of the useful things had been given away, but there were still some evening cloaks, one or two pretty dresses with *fichus* and sashes, fancy shoes and blouses, and petticoats with lace and embroidery. Mrs. W. told me that one woman carried off a pair of white satin slippers. She rather protested, thought it foolish, but the woman persisted. She returned three or four days afterward with a pair of nice black shoes on. She had covered the white satin slippers with some black stuff, and had a very neat pair of shoes.

We carried off some patterns, a plastron, and some loose stockings to go over swollen or bandaged feet. Nothing is lost in the *ouvroir*. They use the selvage as it is cut off the flannel. It makes strong twine to tie up packages.

Wednesday, October 21st

There is very little war news. I wonder if it is right to keep the public in such ignorance. The Germans have not succeeded in getting either Calais or Dunkirk, but we haven't dislodged them from their trenches near Soissons, and as long as they are in France one can't breathe freely.

I went with the M.'s this afternoon to visit a hospital of the *Petites Soeurs des Pauvres* in the rue Lafayette, near the Gare du Nord. We passed a house which had been destroyed by bombs dropped from a German Taube. Roof, windows, *façade* gone, a crowd in front of it. The hospital looked very peaceful and well ordered in a convent on one side of a big courtyard. The church at the bottom. The *supérieure*, a good, kind, helpful woman, took us into the wards. They only have twenty beds—as they have very little room and no surgical cases, for they have no surgeons or doctors in permanent attendance. They are very poor; depend entirely upon what people will give them. When the first wounded came they had nothing—gave up their own beds, and made first bandages out of their own chemises.

We saw one young officer with his right arm amputated—twenty-eight years old—with a wife and child, another one on the way. He had been moved there as soon as possible after his operation. I stopped to talk to him a little when the party moved on. I am very shy about talking to the men. I think they must hate a party of sightseers, who come to inspect the hospital and say a few banal words to each man. He looked so sad, I said to him:

"It is melancholy to see you like this at your age."

"I don't complain, *Madame*, it might be worse. I am glad to have been able to serve my country; but I am a cripple for life."

The *mère supérieure* told me his wife didn't know yet that his arm had been cut off. They were going to tell her the next morning. I said: "Don't tell her yet, poor thing, in the state she is in; wait until her baby is born."

But the good nun answered, putting her hand on my arm: "Oh, yes, *Madame*, she must be told; she must bear her cross like so many women in France today. She must be thankful to have him back even a cripple; many women will never see their husbands again."

I was haunted all night by the poor fellow's eyes, so big in his white, drawn face.

Saturday, October 24th.

Our work is going on well. The mayor sends us women every day, but we can't employ all, and it is hard to send them away. Some of the women who asked at first to work at home have now asked to come to the workroom, where they have fire, lights, and company. Usually nine or ten French girls working together chatter all the time; but now one scarcely hears a word except something to do with the work. They all look sad, and what is worse, they all look hungry. I suppose a good bowl of *café au lait* and a slice of bread helps a little, but it isn't a meal for working, growing girls.

We have had no Taube for several days, but French aeroplanes are always hovering over Paris—which of course the Germans know, as they know everything. They are bombarding Lille and Arras. Soon northern and eastern France will be as completely devastated as Belgium.

Sunday, October 25th.

I didn't go out at all today, though the sun was shining brightly. We had visitors all the afternoon, and Mrs. B. and Lord W. dined with us. Lord W. had brought our despatches and had been to the front; said everybody seemed quite satisfied, but all the same the fighting in the north is terrible, and the wounds ghastly. Some of the German prisoners tell stories of hunger and of being forced to fight, and show no enthusiasm for the war or the *Kaiser*. But the officers as a rule are reserved and arrogant. There is always a note of gaiety even in these tragic days, when one talks of the *Kaiser* and his intimate relations with God. An Englishman who happened to be at Potsdam on Good Friday, was surprised to see the Imperial flag on the palace at half-mast—hadn't seen in the papers that any member of the Royal Family was dead. He asked the driver (of the *fiacre* he was in) what it meant; who was dead? The man grinned, and pointing to the flag, remarked: "*Familientrauer*" (family mourning).

Monday, October 26th.

The weather is beautiful, and there are a few more people about in the daytime, but the streets are melancholy at night, quite dark and deserted. When we come back late—7 o'clock—from the *ouvroir*, we generally come *en bande*, walking; but if it rains, we take a taxi between us, which takes each one home. Everybody walks; no one has a carriage. There are only Red Cross and military autos.

Mme. Marchand came to tea with us, and we promised to send her a packet for the front where her husband has a command. He has many *Turcos* in his brigade, and says they are shivering. Poor fellows! how will they ever stand the real cold weather when the winter begins?

Very nice-looking women came to ask for wood this afternoon, one with such good manners, looking and speaking like a lady, implored us to not send her away. We gave her some work. She told the *caissière* she hadn't 50 *centimes* in her purse.

Thursday, October 29th

B. and M. came in this morning. They are installing an ambulance in their *château*, which means putting in *chauffage central*—extra bathrooms and various other changes so that for the moment the house is not habitable—as B. says there are holes in the walls everywhere—they are in Paris for a few days.

She read me a charming letter from J. (my godson) who is corporal in a regiment of *cuirassiers* somewhere in Belgium. She didn't know where, as the soldiers are not allowed to put any address on their letters, but "at the front." When he wrote, he was acting as interpreter for the British. He says they are wonderfully equipped, have plenty of warm clothes and excellent food. He had tea with them sometimes in the trenches, and they gave him some jam. Half of his regiment is now *à pied* in the trenches, as they have no more horses. There is nothing for the cavalry to do now. Their turn will come when the Germans retreat, and we drive them out of France. Those who are dressed for it manage pretty well, but he is still in his *cuirassier's* uniform, high boots, spurs, cloak and *casque*, and doesn't find that very convenient for crouching in the trenches. As he is very tall—over six feet—the trenches are not much of a shelter for him.

He says, as they all do, that the British fight like lions; but they are most independent; can't stay in the trenches. When they hear the noise of any explosion, they start up and get killed at once.

I went to the embassy for a few minutes after breakfast; found people there, of course. They keep open house always; have people lunching and dining. Dr. H. was there, who was American ambassador in Berlin some years ago. I asked him if he wasn't surprised at the brutality of the Germans. He said he couldn't understand them, above all the *Kaiser*. He had often talked to him about all sorts of things; found him intelligent, well-informed, with a strong sense of his position and responsibilities. He had raised his country to such a height of prosperity; everything—army, navy, commerce, colonies, so firmly established—that it seemed incredible he should have sacrificed it all for his own insane ambition.

Mrs. Herrick had a charming letter from Queen Mary, thanking her for all she had done for British people. It was a pretty, womanly letter. Both she and the ambassador will have many more before the war ends. Their staying here through all the darkest days will never be forgotten. The big gates and doors of the Embassy were always wide open, and there was a continuous stream of people pouring in, asking for advice and help.

Saturday, October 31st.

Always the same meagre war news, but one feels that things are going well with us. I have again letters from the *curé* of Mareuil and Mme. Gaillard, my concierge, begging me to come down. Mme. G.

says she has soldiers quartered always at the house, and that they are very exacting, must have fires of course (*"Madame sait comme le bois est cher"*), and would like blankets—but as the Germans took all mine, I can't give them any. I must take some down when I go. This is the list of the necessary things I must bring down, Mme. G. says: Coal, petroleum, lamps, candles, tablecloths, napkins, towels, blankets, china, knives, forks, spoons, sugar and salt, pillows—*batterie de cuisine*. She hasn't got a kettle or a saucepan in the kitchen. Also, will I bring down some warm clothes for the women and children? People have been very kind in sending me clothes. Mrs. Watson sent me a good package from her *ouvroir*, and I will take some men's shirts from mine.

They also write from La Ferté-Milon for hospital shirts, warm clothes, and bandages. The sisters have wounded men at the Hôtel-Dieu, and very few resources. La Ferté was occupied by the Germans, and the town had to pay a heavy indemnity to prevent them from bombarding and destroying their beautiful churches.

Monday, November 2nd
(*Jour des Moris*).

We have had two beautiful days, and I have been so homesick for Mareuil. The *Toussaint* is such an important day in our little village. Early in the morning the children come to get flowers to decorate the church and the tombs. I seemed to hear the clatter of *sabots* and the shrill voices of the children as they trooped into the courtyard, and to smell the chrysanthemums which they carried off in quantities. Then came the *sacristain* with two choir-boys, carrying with much pomp the *pain bénit* we always gave on that day—an erection of *brioches*, going up in a pyramid, with a wreath of flowers at the base. The church was always full the next day (*Les Morts*). I never went. The black draperies and funeral service, and the names of all who died in the year read out, made such an impression upon me the only time I went, that it left a haunting memory that lasted for weeks every time I went to the church. But I always went to the cemetery, after the service, and stood with the village people who were praying for their dead. It never seems quite the same day in the city.

Wednesday, November 4th.

We are going to Mareuil tomorrow. Maggie will go down with me. We were busy making our packets all the morning, and went in the afternoon to get my *sauf-conduit*. They always make a difficulty about it. My *pièces d'identité* are not sufficient. They want my *certificat de mariage*, which is at Mareuil—and are most unwilling to give any *sauf-conduit* for a village in the war zone. I wanted to get a permanent pass from the governor of Paris, but he won't give me that, as I am not connected with a hospital or ambulance at the front.

Mareuil, Thursday, November 5th, 1914.

I am writing in my own room, in one corner of our house which has been disinfected and thoroughly cleaned. The servants have made it as comfortable as they could with the chairs and tables the Bodies have left me. I have an excellent lamp which I brought down with me, and a bright, crackling wood-fire, with pieces of wood about as big as matches which come from the saw-mill opposite. The little girl brings them in her apron. It is the first time I have fully realised what the German occupation meant, and how much can be taken *out* of a house, and how much dirt left *in* in eight days.

Mareuil is a peaceful, sleepy little village of about five hundred inhabitants, in the heart of the great farming country of France. It is directly on the highroad between Meaux and Soissons, about twenty miles from each. It is surrounded by big farms and woods. The fields stretch away to the horizon, on one side; on the other to the great forest of Villers-Cotterets. There are no local industries, no factories; the men work in the fields and woods. The women do nothing but look after their houses and children.

Of course all the men, except the old ones, left in the first days of the mobilisation. My daughter-in-law with her two boys, aged eight and nine, had remained in the house.

The farmer next door and the miller promised to look after the women of the family, and the month passed quietly enough. Toward the end, there were rumours of the Germans having broken through the "wall of steel," and small parties of Uhlans were said to be hovering about Rheims and Laon, also armed autos were reported dashing through the villages, firing at every one they met.

Suddenly on Saturday night, the 29th of August, Charlotte was told she must leave the next day as early as possible. The village was to be *évacué* by *ordre militaire*—everyone to leave, mayor, *conseil municipal, curé*, women. They spent Saturday night hiding all the valuables they could—papers, medals, etc., and left at 7 o'clock Sunday morning, with the greatest difficulty. The train was crowded with refugees and wounded soldiers. They could not have got seats even in one of the *fourgons* (baggage-wagons) if our *chef de gare* had not insisted.

They had an awful journey, taking fourteen hours to travel a distance which usually takes two. They were shunted at almost all the stations, to make way for military trains going to the front, filled with soldiers cheering and singing. The passengers got out, and the wounded were attended to, sometimes on the roadside, sometimes at the stations. At Meaux there was an ambulance of the *Croix Rouge*, the nurses dressing the wounds, giving food to the soldiers and refugees, children frightened and crying.

The whole party were exhausted when they got to Paris, but a night's sleep restored them, and they started the next morning for Tours by automobiles.

I was glad to see them out of Paris, which was no place for children with the great heat, and Tauben going about. I wanted to come straight down here. I had a feeling of shirking responsibility, and leaving the village to its fate, which was very disagreeable to me; but all my friends protested vigorously; besides, I could not get a pass to go directly into the fighting zone. I was very uncomfortable, but there was nothing to be done. I heard nothing for weeks, but gathered from the *communiqués*, and the few people one saw who knew anything, that fierce fighting was going on in that part of the country—*châteaux*, houses, and villages sacked and burnt. It wasn't possible we should escape with our house standing so invitingly on the highroad.

About the end of September, we heard through a friend who had been there, that our house was completely sacked, the four walls standing, but everything taken out of it.

We had gone to the country, to a quiet little village in the Sarthe for three weeks, but as soon as I got back to Paris I determined to come down here. It wasn't easy—impossible by rail, as the bridges were blown up and no private conveyances were allowed on the road. I applied to Ambassador Herrick, who, as usual, did all he could to help me, and gave me one of his automobiles with a young American officer as escort, Lt. G. I asked the Tiffanys to come too, as they had stayed so recently at Mareuil, and Olive and Charlotte had moved all the furniture and pictures and rearranged the rooms.

We started about 9.30, couldn't get a *sauf-conduit* all the way to Mareuil, only to the next village, but Lt. G. said he would certainly bring us here, and he did. The journey from Paris to Meaux was almost normal, except for the absolute lack of traffic or movement of any kind. There were the same long stretches of straight white roads, bordered with rows of poplars which always mark the highroads in

France. Nothing passing but military autos, long trains of munition and provision wagons, and ambulances with wounded soldiers. The villages were empty, a few very old men, women, and children standing in the doorways or at the well, the resort of all the women in the country when they want to gossip a little. No one in the fields, no sign of life, and above all, no *sounds* of life. No loud talking, nor singing, nor whistling.

Meaux looked just the same, the beautiful old cathedral untouched, and the old mills on the river intact. I was afraid they had gone. They are so picturesque, built on a bridge. Everyone goes to see them; they are quite a feature of Meaux. The other bridges were destroyed.

About half-way between Meaux and Mareuil we began to see signs of fighting; all the big trees down, their branches blown off, lying on the road—roofless houses, holes and gaps in stone walls, fields cut up and trampled over, barricades across the roads, trenches and mounds in the fields, a few dead horses. Soldiers everywhere, the whole road guarded.

We were stopped once or twice, but the officer's pass and the embassy carriage were all-powerful, and we came straight to our gates. From the outside one saw nothing changed. The four walls were intact, the iron gates standing, but inside . . .

We had not been able to send word to the *concierge*, neither telegraph nor telephone worked (don't yet for civilians), and the post was most irregular. She heard the auto and came to the gates, not knowing who it was. The poor woman looked twenty years older. She and her son, a boy of eighteen, had gone away with all the village. Sometimes a farmer's wife would give her a lift, but mostly she walked, for miles, weary and footsore, sleeping in the fields, under the hedges, occasionally in a barn; no clothes but what they had on their backs, and hardly anything to eat, frightened to death, seeing a Uhlan in every creature that passed, and tormenting herself as to what was going on at home. She was so agitated at first that I could do nothing with her—assuring me that she had not deserted the place, that she only left when all the village did. I comforted her as well as I could. After all I had not come down myself to set the example, and could not expect others to do what *I* didn't do.

We began our *tournée d'inspection* at once. In the garage Jean Sallandrouze's auto had been taken, our's left, but smashed. It seemed they could not make it go at once, so they broke it. They had also left a light trotting wagon.

The inside of the house was a desolation. It had been cleaned—four women working hard. Mme. G. said the dirt and smells were something awful. The bedding was in a filthy state. For twenty-four hours after they had begun to clean, they couldn't eat anything. "*Si Madame avait vu la saleté, jamais plus Madame n'aurait mis pied à la maison!*"

Perhaps it is just as well that *Madame* didn't see all, as the actual state was bad enough.

She had sent me by a messenger a first statement of what was missing. Everything in the kitchen (except the range, which they couldn't move), twenty-nine lamps, china, silver, forks, spoons, and a tea-pot that were forgotten in the hurry of moving, glass, sheets, and blankets, cover-lids, pillows, rugs, pictures, old English engravings, family miniatures, linen—all my son's and daughter's clothes; and what they did not take they spoilt. A satin dress and lace dress of C.'s on the floor with great cuts in them.

They evidently were of a practical turn of mind—took all the useful, solid things, cloth dresses, cloaks, two excellent Burberry waterproofs, canes. They took the billiard-balls, broke most of the cues, but did not break the table—neither the piano, an Erard grand. I rather expected to see it standing out in the fields, as some of my friends found theirs.

In the drawing-room chairs and tables were broken, drawers pulled out, their contents scattered over the floor, quantities of papers and letters torn. I hadn't time that day to verify—put them all in a box upstairs.

Mme. G. had left two rooms, C.'s *boudoir* and Francis' dressing-room just as she found them when she came back after her ten days' wandering. The floors were covered up to our ankles with papers and books. In some of the books pages were torn out in the middle—such useless, wanton destruction.

I had no time to look into everything, but of course I went all over the house. Some of the hiding-places had not been discovered. We found the silver and some old china just where C. had hidden it. It seems the officers slept in the house, the men on straw in the garage. The names Schneider, Reisnach, etc., were written on the doors of the bedrooms, and on the shutters of the drawing-room, in German writing, "*Geschäftszimme*"—with the names and number of the regiment. In another part, "*zwanzig Männer.*" I told Mme. G. to leave the writing so that when Francis comes back—if he comes back—he can see in what state the Germans left his house.

After we had been through the house, Mme. G. weeping alongside of me, and telling me all she had gone through, we went into the garden, which was too awful. They had kept their horses there. Lawns and flower-beds all trampled over and destroyed, a few climbing roses left on the walls.

It was a beautiful day, a clear blue sky, yet all the time we heard the rumbling of thunder. I said to the young officer:

"How extraordinary to hear thunder with that cloudless summer sky!"

"Don't you know what it is, *Madame?*—cannon—about twenty miles away."

I had visits from the *curé*, the mayor, and one of the *conseillers municipaux*—all full of their exodus and the weary days and nights of tramping along the road.

No other house in the village seems to have been treated like mine—except the poor peasants', where they stole and broke everything. When a French peasant marries, his first investment is a large wooden bedstead and *armoire*, which is the pride of his heart. These the Boches couldn't carry away, but they broke them up for firewood, and carried off every poor little pot and pan they possessed.

The women are sleeping on straw. I made a turn in the village, went into the two shops. Nothing left—empty shelves, the floors still covered with the remnants of broken pots of cereals, *pâtés*, dried fruit, grains of all kinds, the entire stock of a country shop. The women were standing about helplessly, not knowing what to do.

I saw a pile of berets and jerseys in one corner; was surprised they had left anything so useful; when I touched them they all fell apart, had been cut and slashed in every direction—again such useless destruction.

No harm was done to the church, a fine old twelfth-century specimen, and no houses burned nor shelled. The outside intact everywhere, but everything gone inside.

The mayor was very blue, and I don't know how we shall get through the winter with all these women and children, with no work nor money, and no clothes.

We started back about 5 o'clock, so as not to be too late on the road, and the impression was melancholy; such intense stillness, as if the war-cloud was hanging low over us. We met three or four farm-wagons between Mareuil and Meaux, with women and children, and odd bits of furniture—poor people going back sadly to their homes.

It was tragic to see some of the villages we passed through—Vareddes, May, etc—the black, roofless cottages told their own tale, as well as the mounds in the fields where many soldiers are buried. Little is left of the peaceful, happy little hamlets we know so well; no more women standing smiling at the doors of their cottages, nor men ploughing the fields with their fine teams of big white oxen—utter desolation everywhere!

I promised to come down again as soon as possible, but I could not manage it until today. I could not come alone; was obliged to wait until I could find someone willing to go into the "war zone," and was not sure if the railway would accept the quantity of luggage I would have. Everything had to be brought from Paris. I couldn't come by our usual line, the Est, as the bridges are not yet mended, and the journey was much longer by the Nord. I went to the Gare du Nord, and had some difficulty in getting the necessary information. I found a capable, intelligent woman, however (there are, of course, numbers of women employed at all the *gares*, as the men have all gone). She was much interested in my journey down to a village which had been devastated by the Germans, and we found that I could take as much luggage as I wanted, *if* I could get a *sauf-conduit*, which she seemed to think doubtful.

I did have some trouble with the *commissaire de police*, who didn't at all want to give me a *sauf-conduit*, and was not satisfied with my *pièces d'identité*. I hadn't got my *certificat de marriage*, which is at Mareuil. When he finally made up his mind that I was Mme. Waddington, he still hesitated to give me the *sauf-conduit*.

"*Mais, Madame, pourquoi aller àMareuil*; it is absolutely in the zone *militaire*; it is no place for women—it is not really reasonable to go there." And when I insisted again on going: "But why do you want to go just now?"

"Because, *Monsieur*, I live there; my house has been completely sacked, so has the entire village. I must go down and take clothes and provisions to the poor people."

That mollified him a little, and he made out the paper grumbling to himself all the time, saying when he finally handed it to me: "I really ought not to give it to you. It is no time for women to travel about in that part of the country at *your age*."

We started this morning. Maggie, the boys, English nurse, who is now nursing at the American Ambulance, and an Englishman, one of our humble friends, out of place for the moment, and very glad to do any odd job. He speaks French well, having lived many years in Paris. We had two cabs—Barling in one, with piles of bundles and cases around him, as we had to take down everything—among others, a large case of Quaker oats, which Dr. Watson sent me, a basket of china, another of groceries, two big bundles of blankets and linen; a trunk of clothes which friends had sent me, also one from my *ouvroir*. Maggie and I in another with a bundle of clothes Mrs. Watson had sent me from her *ouvroir*, cartons with lamps and shades, a basket of vegetables, another of saucepans and kitchen things, a valise of knives and forks and spoons, and a holdall full of things sent at the last moment—bandages, woollen socks, etc.

There was a great crowd at the station. The Belgian refugees are still there in one of the covered courts, where *couchettes*, a sort of bed made of planks, and covered with rugs and blankets, had been arranged, and big marmites to cook their food. People flock to see them, bringing them clothes and food.

There was a great deal of confusion as there was not half the usual number of porters—soldiers everywhere. Everyone made way for Nanna in her nurse's dress, and the porters were much interested in the ladies who were taking down food and clothes to one of the mined villages.

It has been a beautiful day, clear and warm, and the route through the Villers-Cotterets forest was lovely. We went very slowly, stopping at every station, a long crowded train. We had a long wait, two hours at Ormoy, in the heart of the forest. From there to Mareuil there were traces of war everywhere—almost all the little forest stations completely wrecked, roofs off, no doors nor windows, nothing but the four walls half tumbling down.

They are repairing now as much as they can, but it is difficult to get workmen; the soldiers give a helping hand when they can. I should have thought some of the Belgians would have been glad of the work, but there are few able-bodied men among the refugees; they are all old, old men.

Mareuil is *occupé militairement*—soldiers at the *gare*, and a *poste* on the highroad, just at the entrance of the village. They stopped me and wanted to know where I was going, and who I was, but the *brigadier de gendarmerie*, who was lodged at our house, and had seen me at the station, hurried up and explained.

Mme. G. had not received my letter, and was much flustered at the

arrival of three people. However, it was quite early in the afternoon.—
2.30. She had plenty of time to make fires (it was not at all cold—a
bright, beautiful sun), and beds, and prepare our dinner.

I walked about the garden while they were unpacking. The lawns
are entirely cut up; horses were tethered there. The flower-boxes quite
spoilt; but there was one bed of chrysanthemums left—some of the
big yellow ones, which gave quite a touch of colour and life to the
wasted garden.

The dining-room and *fumoir* were fairly comfortable though very
bare; still there were chairs and tables. I dined alone and am finishing
my evening in my own room. The stillness and darkness are oppressive.
There is not a light in the village or station—no trains passing—not
a sound on the road. I am haunted by the thought of those brutes in
our house.

Friday, November 6th.

It has been a beautiful bright, mild day—extraordinarily clear,
hardly any mist on the hills and woods. One sees a great distance. I
have had a procession of visitors—first the *curé* with a list of the most
miserable people, and all day the women and children. It is a pitiable
sight. They have no clothes but what they stand in, as they went away
at very short notice, and could only take a very few things tied up
in bundles (which some threw away *en route*, as they could not carry
them).

There is nothing left of their cottages but the four walls. The village houses are all stone, not easy to burn. But the Germans took all
they could carry off, and destroyed what they couldn't take—broke
furniture, chairs, tables, all the beds. The women sleep on straw and
club together to make their soup in a marmite, like the soldiers. They
have no clothes. When the woman washes her chemise, she lies in bed
(on the straw) until it dries. One of them said to me: "Would *Madame*
please give her a *casserole*" (saucepan)? *"Vous êtes bonne, ma fille. Les Allemands m'ont pris tous les miens; je suis arrivée avec deux ou trois dans ma
poche pour faire ma cuisine ici!"*

Some of the boys—strong, handsome boys of ten and twelve—
had nothing on but the linen jacket they went away in (it was warm,
beautiful summer weather when they left) and no shirt nor tricot, the
jacket over their bare skin. Thanks to my friends and my *ouvroir*, I can
supply the first necessities, but to clothe a whole village requires time
and money.

All the afternoon we spent going over the house and seeing what was left. They seem to have made a clean sweep of all the small things that accumulate in a house—pens, pencils, scissors, frames, pincushions, fancy boxes and bags. Some of the trunks in the garret are untouched. They were locked, but of course could easily have been forced open. All the silver things that had not been hidden have gone, inkstands, frames, vases.

The *concierge* has lost everything, even her wedding-wreath carefully preserved under a glass.

I went into the billiard-room and *salon*, opening the windows wide to let in the last rays of the sun. In the *salon* drawers pulled out and broken—books taken—great gaps in the rows—music torn and scattered over the floor, but the piano not hurt. I tried to play a little in the twilight, but it makes me so homesick for the children; I seemed to hear their little voices singing their Christmas carols; and always saw that awful German writing on the shutters, "*Geschäftszimmer*"—but I must leave it for Francis to see.

We still hear the cannon, but more faintly. I don't feel now as if ever I could be gay or happy again in the place, but perhaps that feeling will pass when the war is over, and "the troops are marching home again with gay and gallant tread"—but when?

Saturday, November 7th, '14.

It was foggy but not cold this morning. I walked about the village a little after breakfast; always the same story of pillage and misery. Most of the women and children have no clothes left, and no money to buy any. Everybody was very sad, as a funeral service was going on for one of the village boys, twenty years old, a little shepherd, *tué à l'ennemi*. Of course we all think of our own at the front, and hardly dare to pray that they may come back.

The *curé* has made me a first list of a hundred children, ranging from one year old to twelve, boys and girls, all wanting warm clothes. I found some flannel in the village which will make shirts and petticoats; that will give the women something to do; they will be glad to earn a little money; and it will be easier for me than buying the things in Paris, particularly as they don't send anything yet by rail.

We had sent for a carriage from Thomas at La Ferté, but at 3 o'clock nothing had come, and after 6 no equipages are allowed to circulate. We tried to find one in the village, but there are scarcely any horses left. Finally the farmer next door lent us his little country dog-cart, and we started off with our *sauf-conduit*. Nanna and I sat behind, and Barling in front with a package of hospital sheets and bandages.

The road was absolutely deserted except for military automobiles, and there were soldiers everywhere. It was really dark when we got to La Ferté at 4 o'clock, and I was rather worrying over our return, as we had no lights. La Ferté is quite changed. I should never have recognised the dull little provincial town, with no movement of any kind except on market-day, when a few carts were drawn up on the mall, and the neighbouring farmers jogged along on their funny old-fashioned cabriolets. Now it is full of soldiers; cannon and munition-wagons on the mall; the bridge over the canal, blown up and replaced by a temporary rickety wooden structure. The shops were open and lighted, I should think doing good business.

I had some difficulty in getting some petroleum. I was received with enthusiasm; everybody wanted to talk, to tell me their experiences and to hear mine. The town had suffered very little during the German occupation, thanks to the *curé*, the Abbé Detigne, who remained all the time, and certainly saved the town by his courage and coolness.

I went to the *presbytère* to see him. He was out, but his sister told me she would find him in the town and send him to the Hôtel-Dieu. I went there to see the sisters and leave my parcels, stopping on the way at the butcher's to buy a *gigot*, as I had asked our *curé* to dinner. I had a nice talk with the sisters, who asked me if I would give them some wool as they have taught the girls to knit socks, but can't get any wool in the country. They had only a few wounded Germans. "*Madame voudrait les voir?*" No, *Madame* didn't feel as if she could see a German, coming directly from Mareuil where they worked such havoc. The old *mère supérieure* did not insist; merely remarked: "*Ce sont des soldats, Madame, qui font leur devoir commie les nôtres.*" It is quite true—all the same I didn't want to see them.

The *abbé* came in just as we were starting. He was very preoccupied about our return in the dark, along the lonely road, with a child driving, and wanted us to stay the night at the *presbytère*—couldn't imagine that it was possible to stay at Mareuil; at any rate we had better dine with him. He evidently thought I had no shelter nor food, and nothing to cook it in if I had any. However, I reassured him; told him we had our dinner in the cart, and the *curé de* Mareuil was coming to dine with me. All I wanted was a lantern. The sisters procured me one, and wanted to give me hot wine and biscuits to eat on the way—but that was really not necessary, as it is not more than eight kilometres and the road was fairly good—not too much cut up.

It was a mild evening, a little damp, but we had warm cloaks, and Barling held the lantern up high, swung on a cane. It was pitch-dark, nothing on the road, except military automobiles, which dashed by at full speed, their great lanterns lighting up the road for a few seconds. No one molested us, nor asked for our papers, though we didn't get home until 7 o'clock.

Mme. G., rather anxious, was at the gate. The *curé* came to dinner, and he sat afterward for about an hour in the *fumoir*, and he told me of their hurried flight from Mareuil, and the fatigues of the journey, the whole party sleeping in the fields, under haystacks, with very little to eat or drink, hardly daring to stop at night for five or six hours to rest, for fear of being caught by the Germans. In some of the villages the Germans forced the fugitives they met on the road, to go back to work for them. One poor old man in our village was not quick enough, nor strong enough to carry some wood. They pricked him with the bayonet, telling him he wouldn't die yet; he would live long enough to become a German. The village was away for thirteen days, wandering along the roads, delighted when they could get a bundle of straw in a barn to sleep on.

Sunday, November 8th.

I didn't go to church as the service was early, 8 o'clock, but I walked about the village and found more flannel and cotton which I can leave here. The women can make chemises and petticoats for themselves. The poor people look dreadfully depressed without work or money. It is very difficult to know how to help them. However, I promised to come down about Christmas and bring some warm clothes. I would like to start a knitting class, but the *curé* tells me so few people knit.

We leave at 2.30. I have made an exhaustive tour in the garden with the boy and a gardener who works for us occasionally. It must all be dug up; lawns, flower-beds—and in the spring, if the Germans are out of France, we will see what can be done. As long as they are so near us there is no use doing anything, as they will certainly burn and ruin all they can as they leave.

I couldn't find out anything about the people in the neighbour-hood in the different *châteaux*. It is a curious feature in this war, no one knows anything about anyone. Unless you are in the country and pass a house or farm that was burned or knocked to pieces, no one knows.

The cannon was loud and incessant this morning. I ask myself all the time: Am I really at Mareuil, our quiet little village, or is it all a bad dream? Ah, what a wicked war!

Paris, Thursday, November 12th.

We got back Sunday, to dinner. A tiring journey, and I must have caught cold as I have been stiff and rather miserable ever since. Didn't go to the *ouvroir* until today. Mr. Mygatt has brought over excellent stuffs and wool from London, better and cheaper than anything he can get here. The big room looked very business-like with its piles of cloth and flannel. Mme. del Marmol brought us a doctor (soldier) who was starting a field-hospital near Châlons, just behind the last line of trenches. He came to ask for help for his hospital.

"What do you want?" we asked him,

"Everything," was his prompt reply; and we made him two enormous bundles with everything we had in stock, from sleeping-bags to socks. Unfortunately we had no hospital stores, but he thought he could get them from the *Croix Rouge*. He helped make the trunks, kneeling down on the floor, and carried them off in a cab.

The fighting is terrible on the Yser, the Germans attacking furiously, but making no progress; but the loss of life on both sides is awful. They say the Yser runs red with blood in some parts. The lines of the Scottish poet, Thomas Campbell, which I learned as a child, come back to me all the time:

On Linden, when the sun was low,
All bloodless lay the untrodden snow.
And dark as winter was the flow
Of Iser, rolling rapidly.

Tuesday, November 17th.

It has been a bright, beautiful day, just enough crispness in the air to remind one that autunm was coming to an end. It was really a pleasure to be out. I always walk over to the *ouvroir*. It takes one about twenty minutes. Little by little, the shops are opening, quite a number in the rue de la Béotie. Almost all, except the grocers and bakers, have soldiers' things: waistcoats, jerseys, *passe-montagnes* of every description. We are always looking for models of the simplest kind, with as few buttons, strings, and pockets as possible.

The equipment of our *poilus* is much simpler than that of the Tommies. Some of the older, old-fashioned officers are astounded at the baggage which follows the British Army.

About 3 o'clock I went with the Mygatts to one of the hospitals of the *Petites Sours des Pauvres*, in the rue Lafayette. Cardinal Amette, the Archbishop of Paris, was coming to see the wounded. We took over ten of our *paquets militaires* and bundles of *pansements*, as the hospital is very poor. The sisters have given up their beds. They had so few extra ones.

The *paquets* are very good, shirt, drawers, jerseys, socks, and *passe-montagne*, a sort of helmet which goes over the *képi*, and protects the back of the neck; everything in wool. We prefer to give fewer things but in good quality. It is useless to send cotton to men in the trenches.

There was quite a stir in the street when we arrived at our destination. The church at the end of a long narrow court, with its big doors open, the altar brilliantly lighted; the body of the church dark, outlines of kneeling figures just visible; quite a number of people waiting at the door of the convent.

The cardinal came very punctually. (It was a pleasure to see the red cap and robes.) He is a good-looking man, tall, rather the military type—spoke charmingly to the *mère supérieure,* who was waiting at the door—and went with her into all the wards, speaking to each man. A Sénégalais convalescent, black as ink, standing in the row of white beds, was a curious sight. I don't think he understood anything the cardinal said, but he smiled and showed all his dazzling white teeth.

The cardinal said he would come and *bénir notre ouvroir.*

Mrs. Herrick came in late and was charming, always so ready to help and doing it all so simply. She thinks they will go soon, but I can't think the government could make such a mistake.

Thursday, November 19th.

I had a line from Mrs. Herrick last night saying they were leaving on the 28th. It doesn't seem possible. I went to the embassy after breakfast; there were several people there, all much disturbed by the ambassador's sudden departure. He was quite smiling and composed. I think he is deeply sorry to go while things are in such a serious state. He has been so interested in France and all she has been going through in those tragic months that it will be a wrench to leave it all just now. Of course, once the break is made and he has got back to America, he will find so much to do that France and the war will gradually recede into the past.

I think Mrs. Herrick is glad to go back to her children and grand-children, though she enjoyed the life in France. They have made quantities of friends over here.

Sunday, November 22nd.

Another enchanting day. I walked about a little after church and sat on a bench in the Avenue de l'Alma, and talked to three wounded soldiers who were sitting there in the sun. They all had crutches, but told me they were getting better, and none had lost arms or legs. They had all been wounded at the Battle of the Marne; were not in the least discouraged, and were pining to get back and have another shot at the Boches. One of them, with quite an educated voice and language, said: "They thought they were going to get Paris, *Madame!* They will never have it, our beautiful Paris. They would have to walk over bodies, not only of soldiers, but of women and children, before they could get in!"

One or two passers-by stopped and joined in the conversation, and we ended by discussing the Battle of the Marne: "A miracle," someone said.

It is astonishing the camaraderie this war has brought about; everybody talks to everybody; and everybody helps.

Monday, November 23rd.

I lunched at the U. S. Embassy this morning, and went afterward with the ambassadress to the American Ambulance, where I had given *rendezvous* to two French ladies, Duchesse de T. and Princesse d'A., who wanted very much to see it. They made a most thorough inspection, and were delighted with the order and beautiful cleanliness of everything. The big ward looked most cheerful, brightly lighted. The rows of beds spotlessly clean and tidy. All the nurses in white, many ladies we know; some professionals, and quite a number of young men of society who were unable for some reason or other to join the army, but were anxious to do something to help. They, too, were in white, the regular *infirmier's* dress, and the wounded seemed quite at ease with them, evidently liked to have them about.

I talked a little to two young Irishmen, each of whom had lost a leg. They were quite smiling and ready to talk. Sometimes it is not easy to make conversation; the men are shy or tired. The doctor asked me if I would go into one of the small rooms where there were some *grands blessés*—four in one room. I didn't want to, very much, as I am very impressionable, and could do nothing to help them—but I didn't like to refuse. Two of the men buried their faces in their pillows, evidently didn't want to be talked to, and the others tried with such a pitiful smile to answer and be grateful for our sympathy; but what can one say to them?

We went down afterward to the tea-room. Every afternoon, three or four ladies provide tea and cakes for the nurses and various functionaries of the Ambulance. We found the tea-room quite full of white aproned nurses and *infirmiers*, and big, burly chauffeurs of automobiles, and three or four boy scouts. The ladies behind the long table were kept very busy, and teapots and plates of buns and good heavy substantial plum cakes were being constantly replenished.

My French friends were much interested in the hospital. Such abundance of everything, so much given, and so wonderfully light and clean. No detail escaped them, not even a corner of a corridor, where some women were washing and preparing green vegetables.

Thursday, Thanksgiving Day.

I went to church, as I feel I have much to be thankful for, in this awful year which has brought mourning to so many homes. We had a quiet dinner—very unlike our Thanksgiving dinners at Mareuil, where we had always that day a regular American menu: Turkey, cranberry sauce and pumpkin pie for those who liked it. No French of any category ever tasted the pie. They are just as conservative about their food as they are in everything else, and only eat what they are accustomed to.

I wander what next Thanksgiving will bring us. France has held her own wonderfully, so far, and has shown such quiet, steady determination, besides her splendid fighting qualities.

There must be so many changes all over the world after the war, and surely a change of mentality. The men who have fought such an awful fight, and the women who have lived through the suspense and trials of these terrible days, can never shake off those memories and take up the old, easy life again.

Friday, November 27th.

I had a long afternoon at the *ouvroir*. We had a great many soldiers and some of the older men looked sad! It is terrible for the men of the *pays évacués*. They have been for months without news of their families.

I went later to say goodbye to the Herricks, who leave tomorrow. Their *salon* was full of people, all deploring their departure. I waited until nearly 8 o'clock to see the ambassador, but he didn't come in. I walked home in the dark, thinking regretfully that I should never cross their hospitable threshold again. . . .

December 1st, Tuesday.

Quiet day at the *ouvroir*. We are getting through a great deal of work, and have at last arranged to get our wool and stuffs from England. Here everything is *hors prix*, and besides taken by the government. One of my friends went to buy some wool the other day, and would have taken a large amount, but while the woman was getting it together, two men with military brassards on their arms, came in and forbade the woman to give it. They took all she had for the army. My friend remonstrated, saying she too wanted hers for the soldiers, but they wouldn't let her have any. It is comfortable in one way being under martial law. One feels so absolutely protected, but there is no appeal possible if they tell you a thing can't be.

I found a telegram from Charlotte when I came home this evening. Francis' regiment is ordered to the front. She and the boys come to Paris on Thursday.

Thursday, 3rd December,
Rue de la Pompe.

It seems strange to be here again in my apartment, but I can't leave Charlotte quite alone. I have divided my time between here and the Rue de la Trémoille. C. and the boys arrived at 7 o'clock. I went to the Gare St. Lazare to meet them. They all look perfectly well; boys splendid. We sent the luggage straight up here, and dined at la Trémoille with Henrietta. The boys have grown so much older, with so much to tell. They had seen the regiment start, and "Papa *armé* with his rifle and revolver!" Poor little things! they have seen so much sadness since the beginning of the war. The regiment is at Aulnay, near Paris, for a few days only, *en route* for the front. Where, they don't know—Belgium, I suppose.

I think we shall be comfortable here. We shan't use the *salon* and my room, but live all together in Francis' part, where we each have a bedroom, with dining-room and *fumoir*.

Friday, December 4th,
Rue la Trémcoille.

We all lunched here and went afterward to the *ouvroir*, where we had the visit of Cardinal Amette, Archbishop of Paris. We had asked several ladies who knew him to come: Duchesse de Trévise, Comtesse de B., Comtesse de B—nes, etc. He was quite charming. Two or three priests came with him, and he looked at our stuff, and was so simple and interested in everything; said, as everyone does, that the soldiers needed warm things. He spoke very nicely to the women, all soldiers' wives and refugees, who were working in one of the rooms. It was nice of him to come as he has so much to do. I was so glad to see the red robes again. They always recall Rome and the happy days there— so long ago—when I think that we all saw Pio Nono.

Monday, December 7th.
Rue de la Pompe

The boys began school this morning. Charlotte went with Mrs. Mygatt to see about some stuffs for the *ouvroir*. She had a telegram from Francis asking her to come and see him at Aulnay. She went off about 3.30. It is close to Paris—would take about half an hour by train in ordinary times, but the service is very irregular—so many employ-ees are at the front, and the passenger-trains are constantly stopped to let troops pass.

I came up here after the *ouvroir* and dined with the boys. C. came in about 9.30; said Francis was very well, had a very nice room, and wanted us to go and see him tomorrow. We can only go late as women are not supposed to go out there, but after dark no one pays much at-tention, and the officers shut their eyes. It is so near Paris, only an hour by train, that they would certainly have not only the soldiers' wives, but women of a certain class, which would not be desirable.

Thursday, December 8th.

We had two hours with Francis today. C. and I took the 4 o'clock train, stopping at a *pâtissier's* on the way to buy two large tarts for the mess of the *sous-officiers*. Soldiers are such children. They always want *bonbons* and cakes, cigarettes, or picture papers. We were in a very long train, had German prisoners on board, the first I have seen. They got off at Le Bourget. Quite a crowd assembled on the platform to see them pass as they walked down guarded by a few French *fantassins*.

The men looked young—tired, but their uniforms were clean— didn't look as if they had been fighting lately. Nobody said anything or made a hostile demonstration of any kind. There was absolute si-lence.

Francis met us at the station as it was dark. It was the first time I had seen him in uniform. He looked very well, very sombre; wears no longer the red *culotte*. All the men at the front wear dark blue, even the buttons of his coat were dark. He took us to his room in the only hotel near the station, where he had made himself very comfortable, and was on the best of terms with his *patronne*. He gave us tea and chocolate. The *patronne* made us very good toast, and smiled all over when he complimented her on her tea. We had a nice white *nappe*. There were only two chairs in the room, so he sat on the bed. He was very cheerful, said there was no chance of his getting to Paris. We hoped he might have come for Christmas. He didn't think they would stay long at Aulnay. Had no idea where they would go. He is so pleased to get to the front and see something of the fighting. It was nice to see him again. He looked well, but older and graver.

We left about 7. The streets of the little place were full of soldiers and their wives, who apparently had managed to get out to the regiment.

Thursday, December 10th.

I was at the *ouvroir* all the afternoon. C. took the boys out to Aulnay. While we were at dinner she came in, looking rather white and upset. Raiment ordered to the front, somewhere between Rheims and Soissons; starts tomorrow morning, 4 o'clock.

Francis and Charlotte went shopping at Aulnay. He had to buy himself flannel shirts and drawers as his things were at the wash. Poor little Willy was quite nervous and tearful as his father told him he was going to the front; might never come back, and that he must be very good and take care of his mother and little brother and D. How many soldier-fathers all over France have said the same thing to their boys!

Monday, December 14th.

We have decided to go down to Mareuil, Charlotte, the boys, and I, on the 18th. I have written to Mme. Gaillard to have the house well warmed. We shall take down a provision of warm clothes. Thanks to our friends, we have been able to get a lot of things.

Wednesday, December 16th.

We are very busy at the *ouvroir* fitting out the children of Mareuil. We have very long lists from the *curé* and the schoolmistress. When I went over just now, I found Charlotte established in one of the small rooms, and surrounded by piles of coats, costumes, dresses, petticoats, shirts, drawers, socks of all sizes, from a baby of eight weeks to an old woman of ninety-five. Mlle. Jeanne was sorting the things and pinning tickets with the names on the garments. Our bundles will be huge, but Mr. M. has lent us his auto-*camion*, which will take the things from door to door.

Thursday, December 17th.

We filled the *camion* this afternoon, as the man wants to start early tomorrow morning. The boys wildly excited, helping put in the packages, and suggesting that they should go, too, in the *camion*.

Mareuil, Friday, December 18th, 1914.

I am writing at night. Although it is only 10 o'clock, the whole household is wrapped in slumber, as we have had a tiring day. We left Paris, Charlotte, her boys, the maid, and I, at 9.30, still with a fair amount of packages, provisions mostly, as Mme. Gaillard wrote us we could not get anything at Mareuil but bread, butter, and apples. She thought the butcher from La Ferté would come when he knew we were there, but wasn't sure.

We had a tiring journey, a long, cold wait at Ormoy; and the boys were much impressed over the various traces of the war. In one field we saw three graves with a little French flag to mark the spot. A little farther on, quite a row with a cross made of sticks at one end. They looked so lonely in the middle of the bare field.

From Ormoy to Mareuil, at almost all the stations, roofs were off, the houses—doors and windows gone—bare walls. We got to Mareuil about 2 o'clock. Of course Mme. G. hadn't received either letter or telegram, but the *camion* had arrived and prepared them for our coming. Our friend, Mr. Mygatt, lent us his auto-*camion* to bring down all our things. It was so much more convenient to load it directly at the *ouvroir*. We had no troubles about trunks, or tickets, or weighing. Bundles of all kinds and sizes were crammed into the car; some blankets and thick coats just tied up with a string, as the auto went from door to door. We loaded it yesterday afternoon late at the *ouvroir*, and I was quite astonished when all the packages got in.

The chauffeur, the faithful Marius, had already unloaded boxes and trunks, which had been carried into the house. He started straight back, as he wanted to get into Paris before dark. It was a bright, lovely afternoon, and the boys dashed at once into the garden to see if the Boches had spoiled their garden and gymnasium. The poor garden looked awful, all dug up, only two or three pots of chrysanthemums were left in the tool-house.

The *curé* came to tea, and we plunged instantly into lists: warm clothes, blankets, etc. He had two hundred and odd children on his list. (He had been to every cottage in the village to make sure that no

93

child was left out.) Also about sixteen or eighteen young mothers, with babies in their arms, girls and boys up to eighteen—all the old people. It seemed rather an undertaking to clothe so many people, but our bundles and trunks held a great deal.

We decided to make our distribution on Sunday, as we really needed all day Saturday to sort out the things; besides I had promised to go to La Ferté in the afternoon to see the Abbé Detigne, and take some wool to the sisters. The house was cold though there were fires everywhere—but such fires! still no coal, only little blocks and ends of wood we got from the sawmill, and it has naturally an empty, uncomfortable look.

We put all the rugs and blankets we possessed on the beds. There weren't many, as the Germans had carried everything off.

Saturday, December 19th, '14.

It has been again a lovely day, the sun shining in at all the windows, showing us more distinctly even than yesterday all that has been taken. Still we are comfortable enough in our corner, and I suppose ought to be thankful that we have anything left.

We had people all the morning asking for warm clothes and looking, I must say, utterly wretched, half-starved, and frozen. Our village was not so perfectly miserable, but some of the refugees from the environs of Soissons and Rheims were in a pitiable condition, weary and cold and terror stricken. They had been chased out of their villages, their cottages burned, all the old people, grandfathers and grandmothers, left to die probably on the roadside. Even in our village some people have never come back. No one knows what has become of them. The children had a frightened look in their eyes, which was heartrending to see. The mothers didn't complain; were very grateful for anything we gave them, but they all had a hopeless expression on their faces, a quiet, half-dazed acceptance of the ruin which had come upon them.

We breakfasted early and started for La Ferté before 10 o'clock (we had to have *sauf-conduits* from the mayor) in the *tapissière* of Bourgeois, the grocer—a most primitive vehicle, a cart with a canvas cover, no springs, and very hard, narrow seats. The cover was so low that Charlotte had to take off her hat and hang it on a nail on one side of the curtain. The road looked exactly the same as when I was here the last time—nothing passing but military autos, a few officers riding. At Bourneville there is a sentry-box just outside the gate; a *service de ravitaillement* is stationed there.

There was a good deal of movement at La Ferté, soldiers, cannon, and munition-wagons everywhere. We went first to the *presbytère* to see the *abbé*. He wasn't at home, but we saw his sister, and asked her to tell him we hoped he would come and lunch with us on Monday. Then we went to the Hôtel-Dieu and left a good package of clothes and wool with the sisters. The old *mère supérieure*, who has been there for forty years, was so pleased to see us—told the boys she remembered their father when he was a baby in long clothes. She gave them a German knapsack which they were delighted to have, as they are making a collection of all the German war material they can find to make a *musée de guerre*.

It was lovely coming home; except for the unnatural quiet—not a sound, no children playing on the road. The *curé* came to dinner with a supplementary list, and we worked hard all the evening. It was not easy to sort and mark all the garments. The boys helped at first, sitting on the floor among the heaps of blankets, rolling them and pinning on tickets until they were dropping with sleep!

We have only two bedrooms. I have one, my own room, and Charlotte and the boys are next to me. We moved two beds into the room, and they are quite comfortable.

Sunday, December 20th.

We have made our distribution, and I think have not only given pleasure, but encouraged the people. We went to church this morning and the *curé* announced from the pulpit that there would be a distribution of warm clothes at the *château*—to which every child in Mareuil was bidden, also the girls and young men still in the village. He hoped they would all assemble quietly and punctually in the courtyard, at a quarter to 3, directly after vespers.

We had cleared the dining-room, taken everything, carpet, chairs, and tables, out of it, then opened the folding-doors into the *fumoir*, and put a table across. Charlotte stood in the *fumoir* behind the table. On one side there was a pile of clothes which Mme. G. passed to her, telling her the names. On the *other*, two large baskets filled with cakes and chocolates which our maid and the little *lingère* from the village distributed. We couldn't undertake a *goûter* with hot chocolate and brioches. We hadn't any cups and saucers except the few we had brought down with us, and we couldn't have found a hundred in the whole village.

By 3.30 the courtyard was filled with children and their mothers. In fact the whole village—but we only allowed the children inside.

First came the schoolboys, marshalled by the *curé*. (The schoolmaster is mobilised, but a youth of nineteen comes every day from a village near and takes the class.) The boys were rather shy and awkward; didn't say much, but I think they were pleased. Everyone got a pair of trousers or warm cape with a hood, like what they all wear here. The little ones got a suit, and all got two cakes and a big piece of chocolate. Then came the schoolgirls led by the schoolmistress and her *adjointe*— about a hundred. They, too, got each one a dress, cloak, or warm petticoat. Then they trooped out, and another hundred arrived—boys and girls mixed—mostly little waifs and strays—not schoolchildren; and at the same time young mothers with babies in their arms. Then there was a fine pandemonium. The women talked, the babies cried; various children whose names were on the list didn't appear, and there were several quite unknown children, refugees, or from the neighbouring hamlets, who had heard of the distribution. They were in rags, sorely needed clothes, and all got something.

Then came boys and girls from twelve to seventeen. Some of the boys looked like men, so tall and broad. C. said she felt quite shy offering them chocolate and cakes, but they all took them.

It was after 5 when the distribution was over. C. was very tired, having stood ever since breakfast. She did it very prettily and graciously. She knew all the children, having had them in the garden all the month of August. She had organised a *garderie*, where the children could come every day while their mothers were working in the fields, getting in the harvest. They had games for the little ones, and the older girls worked at socks or shirts for soldiers.

The *curé* announced that the blankets for the old women would only be distributed the next day, also the wool for the *tricoteuses*, who were told to come at 10 o'clock Monday morning.

The children had all remained in the courtyard, and there was a fine noise of clattering sabots and shrill little voices. The air in the dining-room with the smell of muddy boots and damp clothes, was something awful. We opened all the windows wide, and dined in the *fumoir*.

We heard the cannon all the afternoon.

Monday, December 21st

Charlotte had her *tricoteuses* this morning early—about twenty.

Of course we supplied the needles and wool, which was carefully weighed, each woman receiving the same quantity. Some of the older ones knew how to knit socks, but the younger ones were a little unwilling—could make *cache-nez*, but that we absolutely refused. Charlotte was very severe with them; told them she didn't know either how to knit stockings until the war, but she had learned, and now made all her husband's socks. One of the ladies of the village said any woman who wanted a lesson could come to her any day between 1 and 2, and she would help her—and Charlotte left a sock as a model.

The Abbé Detigne, *curé* de La Ferté, came to breakfast, and was most interesting. He is a very clever, cultivated man, a good earnest priest, devoted to his church, but very large-minded, understanding beliefs he doesn't share, and never intolerant. He behaved splendidly all through the German occupation. They had Germans for ten days at La Ferté. Almost all the official people—*conseil municipal, percepteur*—went away. The mayor was arrested at once, kept in prison, and the *curé* and one *conseiller municipal* had all the responsibility. He said on the whole they behaved well; but their revolvers were always pointed at one if there was the slightest discussion or delay.

They began by asking a ransom of *frs.* 20,000—which the little town couldn't possibly pay. The *curé* asked for a little patience, said he would do what he could, and, escorted by four German soldiers with fixed bayonets, made the round of the town, knocking at every door. He got *frs.* 7,000— with which they were satisfied. He had soldiers at the *presbytère* and in his churches (there are two fine old churches at La Ferté), which he asked them to respect, and they did; remained at the bottom of the church, didn't go up to the high altar. He thought once or twice his last hour had come when some of the officers either didn't understand all he said (though he said most of them spoke French well), or were not satisfied. Instantly the revolver was pointed at him, and a curt order given to the men. He waited calmly and bravely, merely thinking that, if he was to be shot, he would ask to be shot on the *Calvaire*, the cross near the woods—which we all know well—have often sat and rested on the steps after a walk in the woods—until he heard the welcome words: "*Vous êtes libre, Monsieur le Curé.*"

The last day, while the soldiers were getting ready to start, a young officer came in whom he hadn't seen before. He saw at once that he was a personage. The men seemed petrified. He gave a few instructions, then turned to the *cure*, drew up an armchair and sat down, saying: "*Causons un peu. Monsieur le Curé*" ("Let us talk a little"), and instantly plunged into a discussion on the war.

"What do you think of the war, *M. le Curé?*"

"*Monsieur*, what do you expect a priest to say? A war is a wicked thing."

"Yes, but war is *war*, and you would have it. We didn't want the war." Then turning to his men: "That is true, isn't it, my men? We Germans didn't want the war; it was forced upon us." There was a growl of assent from the men. He then continued: "War always brings horrors, and misery. Have you any complaints to make of my men?"

"None whatever; they respected my church, didn't molest the women and children."

"I am glad to hear you say that, *M. le Curé.*"

Then he got up and put out his hand, saying, "*Au revoir,*" but that was too much for the *abbé.*

"That, *Madame*, I could not do—give my hand to a German. I stood up, looked him full in the face, and made the *salut militaire.* He stepped back, hesitated a moment, and then gave the military salute, very stiffly, saying, '*Je vous comprends. Monsieur l'Abbé,*' turned on his heel, and left the room.

He heard afterward that it was Prince Eitel Fritz, whom he had never seen—the first time in his life, probably, that anyone had refused his hand.

The boys, of course, sat speechless, their eyes fixed on the *abbé.* He told us hundreds of details too long to write; but said there were no atrocities nor violence of any kind at La Ferté, though in some of the farms and villages near awful things had been done—but he personally had not seen any acts of cruelty. He has certainly made a fine record. When the war is over, all his friends will try to have some public recognition of what he has done for La Ferté.

After he had gone Charlotte and the boys went to the *poste des gendarmes*, and gave them what we had left in the way of socks. Just as we were starting for the train we had the visit of an officer *du train de ravitaillement*, to thank us for what we had sent his men. He told us he was the first person to come into our house after the Germans had left, and that no words could describe the filth. His men put a little order, and picked up and put in drawers some of the papers that were lying about.

Among other things that the Germans took was all the writing-paper stamped "Mareuil-sur-Ourcq, Oise." I had just got over a lot from England. One wouldn't think that would be very useful in Germany!

The *curé* came in after dinner, and we made an our arrangements for the women's work, sewing and knitting. He says the village is very pleased with our coming down—not only the material help, but the encouragement. One old woman, the widow of a carpenter, who had done much work for us, came to say that she would cut out the shirts. Her father had been a *chemisier* in the Rue de la Paix, and she knew all about it; would also look over the women's work and see that it was well done. She wanted no pay (at our Paris *ouvroir* we give a tailor 5 *sous* for cutting out a shirt), was very happy to do that for the soldiers. We leave tomorrow, early.

Paris, Thursday, December 24th.

Charlotte and I went out this morning to do a little, very little shopping. She won't have a Christmas tree, which the boys quite understand. "War times" explains everything. But they have their *crèche* as usual, as all the animals and *rois mages* are there; and hung up their stockings—one for father, and we will send him a Christmas *paquet*, with a plum-pudding.

Christmas Day.

I went to the American church this morning. I felt I must hear "Hark the herald angels sing." There was quite a large congregation; several soldiers in uniform. Our dinner was as cheerful as it could be under the circumstances. We had the Sallandrouzes, Madame and Madeleine, Jean and his wife, the W.'s, and C. and the boys. We had a small tree in the middle of the table, just to mark the day. We tried not to miss Francis too awfully; choked a little when we drank to our men at the front. I wonder what next Christmas will bring us, and how many places will be empty at the Christmas dinner. But we mustn't look forward, only be thankful that after five months of war none dl our men are touched.

Sunday, December 27.

It was odd and bright this morning. I went to the English church in the Rue Auguste Vacquerie. I like Mr. Cardew so much—always stay for his sermons; they are so simple, suited to everybody, and yet so scholarly and thought out.

Tuesday, December 29th.

The days are so exactly alike. Time slips by without our realising how fast it goes. The English papers are amusing this morning: All the Tommies so pleased with their plum-puddings and Christmas gift from the queen and Princess Mary.

I am writing late, just to see the old year out. The street is perfectly quiet and dark. No balls, no *réveillons*. This tragic year finishes in darkness and silence. Certainly if Paris had become too frivolous and pleasure-loving, she is expiating it now. The people themselves are so changed. They are not sad; that isn't the word, but serious, engrossed with the men in the ranks and the women and children left behind them.

Paris is caring well for all her children. There are *ouvroirs* and free meals (very good) everywhere.

January to June 1915

Saturday, January and, '15.
It was bright and cold this morning. I had an interesting visit from a Quaker lady, Miss Fellowes, whom Austin Lee sent me. She has come over with friends to do what good they can to the civil population of the north of France, and is now working in the department of the Aisne, which has been frightfully devastated. Their religion forbids them to have anything to do with soldiers, or the fighters of the world. They will find much suffering and distress in all the country where the Germans have passed.

Friday, January 8th.
Today is Willy's tenth birthday. We couldn't let the day pass without some little rejoicing. They didn't want a party or any little friends, but he had his cake and candles, and whatever money he got was put away for "Papa's soldiers." Francis begs us to send clothes and blankets for his regiment whenever we can.

Sunday, January 10th.
Still no war news. The *communiqués* are very meagre. I suppose it is right not to give too many details, but one longs for something from the front.

Two days ago the Germans bombarded Soissons furiously, and tried to advance to our trenches, but were beaten back.

I went to tea this afternoon with the Duchesse de T. Only about eight people. Mmes. de B. and d'A. were there. Neither of them have had a line from their *châteaux* or villages since sometime in September. Comte de B. remained in his *château*—is practically a prisoner there— as he has a German general with his staff in his house. He would not leave; sent his wife away, but said it was his duty to stay in his place and keep his village from being burned, and the women and children

101

shot. It has been reported once or twice that he was shot; but the news has filtered out that he is alive. The Germans told him he might write to his family if he would use a German stamp, and date his letter: "Folambray [the name of his village], Deutschland," but that he refused absolutely to do.

In all the countries occupied by the Germans, they have established their own post-office, and use German stamps.

The Comtesse d'A.'s *château* is also occupied by Germans. None of her family are living there. She is a widow, her two sons in the army.

Saturday, January 16th, '15.

We had a nice letter from Francis this morning. He is getting used to the shells; doesn't mind them so much. The first two or three times that he carried despatches at night over impossible roads, deafened by the cannon—quite dark; the only light the shells bursting all around him—he didn't like it much, particularly being alone. When there are two of them it doesn't seem so awful.

Monday, January 18th.

The *curé* came to breakfast, giving us all the Mareuil news. He brought up forty pairs of socks our *tricoteuses* had made, and wanted more wool, which we will give him tomorrow, when he goes back. He says the village is trying to readjust itself and take up its normal life again. If only we would come down and settle in the country; but that is not possible.

I dined quietly with the Ségurs. I don't much like going out at night; the streets are so dark and empty, but they promised to send me home in their auto. They have still no news of Claude Perier. They have had a letter from one of his men who saw him fall at the head of his company, but he thinks he was not killed, only wounded and a prisoner.

We sat in S.'s library (no one opens their big rooms) and we two women knitted, and he read the paper to us. It would have been a peaceful, happy evening if we hadn't been so oppressed with the thought of what might still come to us.

Saturday, January 23rd.

It was beautiful this morning. I walked over to Mme. de J.'s for lunch. She had Mmes. S. and M. We all talked war and *ouvroir* hard. The ladies asked me why Francis was not with the British army as interpreter, knowing French and English as well as he does. It seems that some of the Frenchmen who have gone as interpreters speak such extraordinary English that the British officers can't understand their orders.

M. d'H. came in after breakfast. He is frightfully changed since the war. His *château* has been entirely destroyed—bombarded, burnt, pillaged. He and his wife and daughters had just time to get away. Mme. d'H. arrived in England without a hat. The poor man is almost crazy, but puts all the fault on this infect *gouvernement*—but one can't discuss with him. He is quite unbalanced for the moment.

We had a procession of soldiers at the *ouvroir*, starting for the front and wanting warm clothes. There were eight gunners, *conducteurs d'automobiles blindés*, fine, strong young fellows. All had been wounded, but were quite well and crazy to go back. After them, some *réservistes*. That was rather pitiful, as all had wives and families; some of them looking as if they could not stand much hard work. However, the spirit was just the same as in the younger men. All quite ready to go, and confident that their wives and would be looked after.

It seems some of the *réservistes* have developed into capital soldiers after four or five months of training.

Francis' captain is a *pâtissier* de Montmartre; didn't look very military at first, but has become a smart, well set-up officer. I think they are all anxious to do well, and prove to their country that she can count upon all her sons in her hour of need.

Francis' own position is amusing, as he is only a simple *soldat*; no rank at all. He can't live with the officers; but when off duty the officers and men all call him *Monsieur* Waddington, and the colonel invites him to breakfast.

Friday, January 29th, 1915.

We didn't have many people at the *ouvroir*. Mmes. Seillière *et* Siméon—the last always most interesting. Francis couldn't get her any news of her house at Rheims. They haven't been allowed to go there lately, as the Germans shell the town furiously every now and then.

Our stuffs are giving out, and our poor women increasing in number. Some of them look too awful, half starved and half clothed. I didn't like to ask one poor thing who came with two children, both practically babies, four weeks and one year old, if she had any clothes on under her dress—I don't think she had. She knew nothing of her husband; had had no news since the beginning of December.

We must start a Women and Children's Department—and have ordered from London a thousand yards of flannel and a thousand of cotton. We get it quickly enough. It is sent over through the British Red Cross direct to us at the *ouvroir*.

The Tiffanys and Charlotte dined. C. had an interesting letter from Francis. He is getting accustomed to the shells, learns how to dodge them, but says the heavy cannonading is terrific—seems to take his head off.

Tiffany is always interesting, as he sees so many business men, both British and Americans; says there is no doubt of the American sympathy for the Allies, though they are struggling to remain neutral. . . .

Sunday, January 31st

The Quakers came to see me at the *ouvroir* to-day; they couldn't say enough of the Abbé Detigne, our *curé* of La Ferté-Milon, and all he had done for them. They were obliged to give up the farmhouse they had taken between St. Quentin and Soissons (it was too near the firing-line), and had established themselves at La Ferté. They have spent a great deal of money, and have distributed many clothes and blankets to the miserable people of the *pays envahis*. They don't do any hospital work, care exclusively for the civil population. They don't wear the Quaker dress, and don't use the "thou" and "thee" that I remember as a child in some parts of America. But the women have earnest, gentle faces. They left us quite a large order. Of course we are delighted to sell a little. We have sent off so many *paquets militaires* that our funds are getting low.

Tuesday, February 2nd, '15,
Rue de la Pompe.

Charlotte and I took our *paquet* for Francis to the Invalides this morning, which was accepted at once. The last one was refused. We heard the explanation later. We took over two enormous *paquets* one day, much over the regulation size, but as we said they were clothes and blankets for the soldiers, they took them. It is much the best way to send packages, as they go through in one day by the military autos. All we send by rail, goes first to Caen, the *dépôt* of the regiment, and from there to Francis, near Rheims, which makes an enormous loss of time. When there are any eatables (he clamours for green vegetables and fruit) the *trajet* is long.

It seems that the two big packages, instead of being delivered to Francis at his regimental *bureau*, were sent to the Division Headquarters, and dumped in the general's anteroom. He went into a rage at seeing these packages for "Soldat Waddington" in his anteroom; and an *aide-de-camp*, a friend of Francis, motored over in hot haste to Francis to see what it meant. Francis was much disgusted, and explained that the *ballots* contained clothes and blankets for the regiment, sent by his mother from her *ouvroir*. The *aide-de-camp* said he would make that all right, and started off for headquarters. He reappeared with the *ballots* and a message of thanks from the general, and the hope that Mme. Waddington would send some more warm clothes for the men. But in the meantime, the young officer at the Invalides had been hauled over the coals probably. All's well that ends well, however; and now they take our packages.

Thursday, February 4th.

I didn't stay long at the *ouvroir*, as I was going to dine with the W.'s at their *hôtel*. Two nice people came to their *salon* after dinner—a M. Perritet and his mother. He is from New Orleans, speaks French well, and goes often to the front, to a hospital organised by Mme. de P., *née* MacMahon (the marshal's daughter). He is going again soon, and expects to take a great many things.

He says the American Clearing-House is wonderfully filled with every imaginable thing, from bedsteads to boxes of Quaker oats.

It was a bright, cold moonlight night. W. walked home with me. The streets are perfectly dark and deserted. A footfall on one of the narrow streets quite startles one. I think ours is the darkest of all. Hardly anyone has come back. There are no lights in the houses, and only one lamp at the bottom of the street.

Saturday, February 6th.

I was rather tired at the *ouvroir* today. There were so many women, and they all talked so much, and knew so much; apparently everyone had constant and confidential communications from General Joffre.

I met Henry Outrey at the door and told him he must take me somewhere for a cup of tea. I was tired with so much female conversation. Outrey is working at the *Croix Rouge*; goes three or four times a week to the station at Aubervilliers, near Paris, where the trains of wounded soldiers arrive. They stop there to have their wounds dressed. There is a hospital on the quay. The Red Cross nurses always there. He stays all night (so do the women), and says the sights are awful; some of the men too badly hurt to go on are taken out of the train and laid on mattresses or piles of straw, on the quay, until they can be attended to. They never complain; try to smile and thank when anyone brings them a bowl of soup or a cup of hot coffee.

Henry says they are *terrible* objects, their uniforms filled with dust and blood, which stiffens on the thick cloth of their *capotes*, unwashed, unshaven. I suppose one must go on to the bitter end; but I ask myself sometimes, if it is worth the frightful sacrifice of life. I often stop at the church of St. Philippe du Roule on my way home. Already there are so many women in deep mourning—what will it be later?

Tuesday, February 9th.

Mme. Thénard (*de la Comédie-Française*) gave a conference on Déroulède this afternoon at the *ouvroir*. She is always interesting, and though she has lost her wonderful voice, she uses such beautiful language and speaks with so much emotion that the audience, quite numerous, was moved to tears. She recited the *Clairon*, and wound up with an appeal to the women of France to lead more earnest, simple lives. Men are what women make them, and the mothers and wives have a terrible responsibility in these awful days. There was a wounded officer in the audience, just from the Yser, with his arm in a sling, and a Belgian boy scout sixteen years old, who had been nineteen times through the enemy's lines, and had been decorated by the King of the Belgians, who pinned his medal himself on his coat. He was, of course, surrounded and questioned after the conference, but looked very shy and uncomfortable, finding himself the object of general attention. However, I don't think anyone kissed him, which sometimes happens in these emotional days.

Thursday, February 11th.

There is startling news this morning. Gerard, U. S. Ambassador, insulted at a Berlin theatre—most angry, hostile demonstration. Of course we have it only in the papers. It may be exaggerated. I can't think that Germany wants to quarrel with America. It would be about the last blunder she could make.

I don't know Mr. Gerard, but I hear that he is a cool, clever lawyer, who would resent the least slight to America.

Friday, February 12th.

We were busy all the afternoon at the *ouvroir*, making *pacquets militaires*. We sent off a good one to Mme. Machery, the "Mayor of Soissons." My husband knew Soissons well in earlier years when he was senator for the Aisne. Mme. M. has shown wonderful courage ever since the war broke out, and for the last two or three days there have been appeals in the papers for the refugees, who are leaving it *en masse*. Half the town is in ashes. Such a typical old French cathedral town, with its broad, quiet streets, with old-fashioned houses behind high walls—the beautiful ruins of the St. Jean des Vignes—and on market-days the main street and hotel (the "Cheval Blanc") crowded with farmers and country people. What all that country will look like when the Germans finally retreat one can't imagine; they will certainly burn and destroy all they can. It will take years to restore any kind of trade or prosperity.

Mareuil, Saturday, February 13th, 1915.

We got down yesterday at 2.30. The boys had a holiday for *Mardi Gras*, and of course wanted to come to Mareuil. It was a cold, boring journey. We had the same long wait at Ormoy. but we did not mind it so much this time as the station was crowded with soldiers. Two military trains with dragoons and *cuirassiers* arrived just after us; all of them, officers, men, and horses, looked very well and cheerful. They had come from Amiens; hadn't had much fighting yet, and were on their way to the front. They didn't know where. The little station was in an uproar at once. The officers asked for papers. There were none at the station, nor at the *café* just across the road, so we told the boys to give ours, which they accepted gladly.

The fatigue-dress of some of the officers was most remarkable— brown corduroy breeches, a khaki coat—and one big, rather red-faced man had a knitted polo-cap, green and yellow, on his head.

The country looked still very desolate, and the work of repairing goes very slowly; but there was a little more movement—some women in the fields, one with a plough and a donkey, trying to turn up the ground a little. Soldiers, of course, everywhere. Even the little country line from Ormoy to Mareuil is strictly guarded, particularly at all bridges and tunnels. I think they must be afraid of spies still, for no troops pass on that line.

We found the house fairly comfortable. Mme. Gaillard had received our letters, and she and Lucie had worked hard to make the rooms habitable, collecting all the *whole* chairs and tables from all over the house. It was not oppressively hot, though there were fires in our rooms and the big stove in the hall was lighted—but as we cannot get any coal, of course we can have no great heat with the very small pieces of wood they send from the *usine*.

We found quite a pile of shirts, drawers, and socks in the lingerie— really very well made; the socks much better than we expected. There were two or three pairs that were a little eccentric as to shape—heels a little wide—but I fancy our poor soldiers in their trenches, half full of water, won't be very particular as to shapes, so long as they have something warm to put on.

We have very few Belgians in the village, though we are so near the frontier, and they are all very quiet and grateful for whatever is done for them. In Paris, we heard complaints. At one big Belgian *ouvroir* the refugees declined the clothes that were given to them, wanted to go to the *vestiaire* and choose for themselves.

Sunday, February 14th, '15.

It was lovely today—a bright sun. It was so cold in the church we had to change our seats, and even then could hardly stay. A large pane of glass is out in the window just over our pew, and there is no glass in the country, and no workman to put it in if there was any.

We took a long walk after breakfast through the big quarries on the La Ferté road, coming out on the Montigny hill. We had the fields to ourselves. Not a soul to be seen. The quarries are enormous, stretching far into the woods, and one can understand perfectly how strongly the Germans are intrenched in the Soissons quarries, which we stupidly and thoughtlessly put at the disposal of a delightful German *en civil* (some people say it was General von Kluck), who settled some time in Soissons. He took a house there, made himself charming to all the inhabitants, rode all over the country, and finally obtained permission to grow mushrooms in the quarries. Of course, as one looks back now, our *naïveté* seems colossal, to use the German's pet word.

They have carried off many French women and children, who live with them in the quarries, cook for them, and go into Soissons to buy food, the Germans threatening them with terrible reprisals if they don't come back, keeping their children as hostages. One of the difficult questions after the war will be what to do with the German babies born in the trenches. One Belgian priest said from the pulpit that they ought to be killed at once, or not allowed to be born; but I suppose one can't resort to such drastic measures. They will be allowed to live probably, but sent to the "*Assistance Publique*," and then to the colonies.

It was warm walking, and the sunset lovely. The *curé* came to dinner and told us more details of their wanderings, which seem already ancient history—events have gone so quickly since. He told us that for nights after their return to Mareuil, he couldn't sleep; all night he heard the trample of cattle and the roll of heavy cart wagons on the hard roads. He said the women were wonderful. Many of the farmers' wives led their caravan of women, children, and beasts. The village travelled for days alongside of one large, well-known farm.

The *fermière* led the procession in a *cabriolet* with an old horse the Germans didn't think worth taking; beside her an equally old *contremaître* (overseer); oxen, cows, sheep, and geese directly behind. Then a train of farm-wagons filled with women and children. When they came to a *carrefour* (a square place where several roads meet), she made signs to her *troupeau* (flock) with a red parasol over the top of her cabriolet. They halted at night—all drawn up on one side of the road, and she and her *contremaître* went off to see if they could find food or shelter in a hamlet or farm—happy if they could be taken in, in a barn or a wood-shed. My poor women slept two nights in a field under the haystacks.

Monday, February 15th.

It was an awful morning, hail and frozen snow and an icy wind. We all shivered even with our coats on, and an expedition to La Ferté seemed impossible; but it cleared up bright and mild at 12 o'clock, and we started directly after breakfast—always in Bourgeois's *tapissière*—the only available vehicle. Charlotte, remembering her last experience, when she had to hang her hat on a nail on the side, had put on a soft felt with only a ribbon around the crown, and we all managed to get in and jolted along very uncomfortably. We met nothing on the road until we got to Marolles. There we fell in with an army of auto-buses and big lorries, taking up the whole road and making it very difficult for us to pass. It was the *service de ravitaillement*. Their headquarters are at the Château de Bourneville and La Ferté. There were three hundred lorries at La Ferté. They radiate from there in all directions. The town was crowded with soldiers and officers.

We didn't see the Abbé Detigne. He wasn't at home, and his sister didn't know where to look for him. We went to see one of our friends, Mr. C, and rang a loud peal at the door-bell, not observing—as the door was wide open—that a notice was posted up: "*Etat-Major.*"

There were one or two soldiers in the courtyard, and two officers came running up to ask what we wanted. We explained that we wanted to pay a visit to Mr. C. They said he was not there, and that the staff were occupying his house—but wouldn't we come in and pay them a visit, and what could they do for us? That we declined, but talked to them a little while, and asked them if there was any news. We met them again as we were talking to some of the lorry-drivers, who told us the lorries were all American, marvellously light and easily managed; turned so well in the narrow streets. They were evidently very curious to know who we were, suddenly appearing in La Ferté, where certainly no *femmes du monde* were to be seen in these days. One of them made friends with Frank, and carried him off to his rooms over the barber's, to get some chocolate. They brought out a box of Marquis chocolates and distributed it freely to us all, filling the boys' pockets.

We had *goûter* at the Sauvage—very good chocolate, *café au lait*, bread and butter and jam, but none of the cakes for which the house was famous in the old days. The son of the house, who is an excellent pastry-cook, is at the front. Mme. Thomas was so pleased to see us, telling the boys she remembered their father quite well when he was much smaller than they. She wouldn't let us pay anything, brought in the *goûter* herself, and sat at the table with us and talked. She just remembered '70, and seeing the Germans in La Ferté. However, she said they behaved well this time, paid for what they took, and did not molest the women and children.

We went into all the shops, buying what we could, and hearing each one's experience during the German occupation. They really didn't suffer very much. They had time to hide money and valuables of every kind, as the British passed through twenty-four hours before the Germans, and told them they were coming. It was more the dread of what might happen. Some of the people left, and their houses were sacked, but nothing was done to those who remained.

One of our friends left her cook in her house. The woman preferred staying. When the Germans arrived, the officer in command sent for her, ordered all doors opened, and asked her where her mistress was; knew all about her, that she was a widow living alone with her servants. When the cook answered that she had gone away, he said she was wrong. "We don't hurt women and children."

The cook replied indignantly: "Perhaps you don't hurt them, you kill them!" Upon which she was told to hold her tongue and leave the room.

We left about 4.30. It was curious to hear such a racket of military life in the quiet little town—a continual rumbling of heavy munition and provision autos, small detachments of cavalry, every now and then a military auto filled with officers dashing full speed through the narrow street; men carrying large marmites of soup and baskets of bread, and girls standing at the doors, laughing and talking with the soldiers. I rather tremble for the morals of La Ferté with so many good-looking young soldiers about, but it is difficult to do anything: "*On ne peut rien refuser au soldat!*" is the phrase on everybody's lips.

We were decidedly exhausted when we got home, cramped and stiff from sitting so long on the hard, narrow seats of the *tapissière*. The village was perfectly dark—only a light flashed for a moment on the bayonet of the guard at the bridge, who stopped us to see if we had our pass.

Mardi Gras, February 16th.

It has been a bright, beautiful day. One could hardly believe it after the cold rain and hail of yesterday. We walked about the garden in the morning—if garden it can be called. All the lawns and flower-beds have been dug up. The house stands in the middle of ploughed fields. We are debating what we shall plant—potatoes and beans, I think, so that we can have our vegetables in winter, as well as improve the earth. They say potatoes purify the soil, and perhaps next year, if the war is over, we can have new lawns, but we shan't do anything to the house and garden until the Germans are out of France—when?

After breakfast, we walked up the Montigny hill. The boys wanted to see what was left of a German aeroplane which had caught fire and burned on the hillside. The sun was really too hot on our backs. We had to take our coats off. As we were passing a field where a very old man, with a very old horse, was ploughing, he called out to us. We couldn't hear what he said, thought he wanted something, and told the boys to run across the field to see. They raced off as fast as they could, talked to him for a few moments, then dashed up the hill across the ploughed field. We saw them poking at something with their sticks; then they came galloping back with red cheeks and eyes shining with excitement, calling out to us: "Mother, Danny, come and see; there is a dead Boche up there; they have just turned him up with the plough."

We were silent for a moment, declining their proposal to go and see; and then Charlotte said: "Ah, think, boys, perhaps somewhere in Germany, far away, a mother and her two boys are walking along the road, just like this today, talking of the father whom they may never see again."

The boys were not in the least moved—rather surprised. "Why, mother, it is only a Boche"—as if it were a rat. I suppose all the ugly sights they have seen, bridges and houses blown up, and the quantities of miserable, half-starved, half-clothed children, have hardened their childish hearts. I wonder if all this will have an effect upon the mentality of the young generation. Will they grow up hard and cruel?

There are many Germans buried in the fields around us, quite close to the surface. Sometimes one sees a rustic cross made of sticks, sometimes a stick standing straight up, just to mark the spot. There will be thousands of those lonely soldier graves all over France.

We found the wreck of the aeroplane on the top of the hill. There wasn't much left—some linen and bits of steel which the boys carried away as a souvenir.

Souvenir makes me think of the British troops. They carried off a good many things, but I suppose all soldiers do. Their reasoning was simple, logical: "*Nous prenons souvenir; si prenons pas, Allemands prennentt!*" The Germans were about twenty-four hours behind them.

It was lovely sitting on the hillside; the sun through the trees making little patterns of light on the white roads, and the beautiful valley of the Ourcq stretching away into the blue distance; it should have been a peaceful, happy scene, but the country is quite deserted; no passing, no workers in the fields, nor children playing about while their mothers worked. A cloud of sadness hovers over everything, and we always hear the dull, steady growl of the cannon, which means mourning and anguish for so many of us.

It seems centuries since I galloped over those hills with W., listening to his recollections of '70, and the first time he saw a *pickelhaube* (German helmet) appearing in the twilight at the window of his library at Bourneville—a disagreeable moment.

We were rather tired after our scramble up the hill, and didn't have a very long evening. The *fumoir* is perfectly comfortable, heats easily, even with the modest wood-fires, but it looks bare and strange; no sign of habitation, nothing but the newspapers and our work.

We always have socks and jerseys on hand.

Ash Wednesday, February 17th.

We have had a cold, raw day, which we didn't expect after the beautiful summer yesterday. The night, too, was beautiful, bright starlight. I love a starlight night in the country; the stars always seem so much nearer than in town.

It didn't rain, so we turned the boys loose in the garden, and made a depressing and exhausting tour of the upstairs rooms, missing something at every turn. The wardrobe where we keep our reserve of poor clothes, had been opened, and everything taken. We both of us feel so strongly that our house has been soiled, can never be the same to us again. I hope the feeling will pass. We have been so fond of our quiet country home —have had so many happy hours there. Perhaps when the war is over and Francis comes home, it will be different.

We decided to move the best furniture and trunks, boxes, etc., into two of the rooms and lock them. I don't think we shall have any more Germans. We are not on their way home; but perhaps British and French. One must be prepared for any surprises.

The Abbé Detigne came to breakfast. It seemed almost the old times to see his little cart coming to the gate. He was, as usual, most interesting. He was amusing over a "*belle dame de la Croix Rouge,*" who came down to La Ferté to take charge of an ambulance established in the *Ecole Maternelle*. She looked very nice in her *infirmière* dress, and gave a great many orders, and didn't find any of the arrangements satisfactory; but she wouldn't touch a wounded soldier, neither wash him nor dress his wounds, nor take off his rags—for clothes they could hardly be called—when the poor fellows were just out of the trenches, or had been lying for days on straw in a shed, waiting to be taken to a hospital. Whenever there was a badly wounded man or a fever patient, she wanted him sent to the Hôtel-Dieu, where the poor sisters had more than they could attend to; when the *abbé* and the mayor remonstrated the lady's husband appeared on the scene, saying:

"*Ma femme n'est pas habituée à retirer les chaussettes des pieds sales d'un soldat, ni de leur laver les pieds!*"

Then their patience gave out. They had the sick and wounded men wrapped up in blankets and carried them off to the Hôtel-Dieu, where the sisters gave up their *réfectoire* and lingerie—and then the authorities closed the hospital.

We gave him some warm shirts and drawers, and said we would go and see them the next time he came down.

The *Croix Rouge* has done, and is doing such splendid work that one is sorry such disagreeable incidents occur; but of course in all large societies there must be all kinds, and alongside of some of the volunteer nurses who have given their time and their strength, and sometimes their *lives*, there are women who only want the notoriety and right to wear the nurse's dress, which is becoming. The poor *abbé* was quite put out.

While we were at breakfast they brought us the news that Mr.

Profit, a young farmer of the village, was wounded; they said, "*grièvement blessé.*" It will be a great loss if he is killed, as he is one of the best men in Mareuil, has had a very good education, and has travelled a little.

I was quite surprised when he dined with us one night when the Bishop of Beauvais was staying with us, to hear how easily and intelligently he talked. They are a family of perfectly respectable, well-to-do farmers, who have big farms in this part of the country. I have often heard it said that the Profits could walk from Mareuil to Paris without going off of their own ground.

We went to see Mme. Profit after the *abbé* went. She was very agitated, but brave and helpful, was going off at once. We went afterward to see the miller's wife, also one of our friends. They had had Germans in their house, but they hadn't done much harm; drank up all the wine they could find (they had hidden their best), and carried off blankets and coverlids.

Our *curé* came to dinner, as we are leaving tomorrow morning early, and we spent all our evening making lists and prices of the work to be done. We had brought down several pieces of stuff which we left with Mme. Gaillard to be cut out and given to the women, also weighed the wool so that each woman might have the same amount for her stockings.

We leave tomorrow morning at 9 o'clock, and by the Est, this time taking the military road, which will be very interesting as it was made to suit the convenience of the army, and passes recklessly, they tell us, through gardens, farmyards, and orchards.

Paris, Thursday, February 18th.

We got back this morning from Mareuil, taking the military line as far as Tréport; it was made apparently with an absolute disregard of people's property, running through farmyards, orchards, gardens, sometimes close down to the river, sometimes close under the windows of a small *manoir*. Soldiers still working on it, and keeping the rickety little wooden bridges in order. We went naturally very slowly—a light train. They say all military roads go straight from one point to another, and this one is certainly no exception to the rule. I found H. rather anxious as people had told her we could not get back for several days, for there was a great movement of troops and cannon on the Chemin de Per de l'Est. We couldn't telegraph her (the telegraph only works for the military authorities), and our letters arrived *after* us.

Saturday, February 20th, '15.

There is news this morning. Yesterday the allied fleets, French and British, appeared suddenly in the Dardanelles and began shelling the Turkish forts. It was a great surprise to the general public. The move was so quietly made. I am afraid they have a difficult task before them; still, in the end, Constantinople must fall, and there will be one of the many difficult problems to solve when the war is over.

This is always a busy day at the *ouvroir*. The women bring back their work and ask for more. We had, too, a good many soldiers.

We like it much better when the men come for their *paquets*. Then we are sure that they get them. So many people complain that the packages they send never arrive at their destination.

It is amusing to see Mrs. M., who is a tall, handsome woman, measuring the men across the chest, to see if the shirt and jerseys are broad enough.

I went for a few minutes to the American rectory to see Mrs. Watson. I found her in her Belgian room at the *ouvroir*. It was piled high with cases and packages of every description. She is doing an immense amount of good, helping so many people.

Tuesday, February 23rd.

The days are all alike, but somehow or other the time passes. There is a lull in the fighting. Everyone predicts fierce struggles with the advance of spring and the mild weather. Until the Germans get out of France I can't feel quite happy. I don't see how they are ever to get them out of the trenches near Soissons. Report says the trenches will be blown up by the British. The French can't, as there are many of their women and children in them.

Someone read aloud at the *ouvroir* today some letters filled with German atrocities. I suppose some things are true, but they can't have committed some of the horrors laid to their charge.

I dined quietly with the Ségurs, with our old friends the Savoyes. No one dresses; the men wear smoking or redingote, with black ties, the women, high dresses. Ségur had seen some one at the club—a diplomat—who had just come back from Berlin. He said the city was absolutely normal. Shops and theatres open; streets well lighted; plenty of people walking, almost cheerful. He had a very good dinner at one of the good restaurants. There were several German officers in uniform dining. He thought they were attached to the War Office in Berlin. He didn't see any black bread, nor any want of white. Said the soldiers and people certainly had black bread, but that didn't mean anything, as the German peasant always eats black bread.

Sunday, March 7th.

It was cold and rainy this afternoon, a day to stay at home by the fire. We dined early, 7.30, so that Willy could come down and dine with his mother. Ever since his father said goodbye to him at Aulnay, when he was starting for the front, and told him he must be a big boy and take care of his mother, he has felt a great responsibility. He misses his father awfully, like all of us; but we try to be brave, though the sight of the young men walking about with legs and arms amputated takes all my courage away. Yesterday I met Mme. de G., an aunt of Charlotte's, in the rue La Béotie; so changed I almost passed her. Last year she was fresh, animated, interested in everything. She has grown thin and pale, with a wistful look in her eyes that rather haunts one.

Her eldest son, an officer, is at the front; her baby—just twenty years old, a simple soldier, is a prisoner in Germany. He has sent her three or four postcards saying he is fairly well treated. But so many people say they don't dare tell the truth on open postcards that she is not quite happy. While we were talking, a soldier, young—not more than twenty-two or twenty-three, with his leg amputated just above the knee—the empty trouser hanging loose—looking thin and pale—came along on his crutches—a woman with him. Everybody spoke to him: "*Bon jour, mon ami!*" A little girl detached herself from a group of children, ran across the street to shake hands with him, and gave him a bunch of violets, saying: "*Bon jour. Monsieur.*" He looked so pleased. It was a pretty sight. For a few moments there was nothing but the wounded soldier in the street.

Monday, March 8th, '15,
Rue de la Pompe

A horrid day, snow falling at intervals. I came up early to dinner. C. had a nice letter from Francis. He had been for the first time in the trenches, found officers' quarters very comfortable, seats, tables, fire, books and papers. The soldiers, not quite so good, but very fairly comfortable. He started back in the dark; said it was rather melancholy passing graves of some of the men of his own regiment. He met some officers in autos, who told him to be very careful crossing the bridge over the canal, as the Germans were watching it very closely, and sent shells at anything they saw crossing. He waited until one shell had fallen, then dashed over as hard as he could—a shell falling just behind him. It was a serious performance, but he seems to have grown accustomed to shells.

He says the colonel and all the officers beg for his books. We send him every week some illustrated papers for his men. Hanotaux's pictorial history of the war (*Histoire de la Guerre*), the *Revue de Paris*, which has very good war and foreign articles, and the *Times*. Walter W., who is quartered about ten miles further back, asks him for books—Walter being his cousin, Walter Waddington, who is lieutenant-colonel of a regiment of *cuirassiers*.

Sunday, March 21st.

We had an agitated night—our first experience of Zeppelins. For some days the police have been very strict about lights, not only in the streets, but in the houses. If the slightest gleam escapes through barred shutters and closely drawn curtains, they come up at once and protest vigorously.

I was sleeping quietly, didn't hear the *avertissement* (*pompiers*, rattling through the street, not ours but the Rue François Ier at the corner, sounding the alarm, "*garde à vous*," which we all know too well now), and was astonished when the maids appeared in my room much excited. The little one who sleeps *au sixième*, had been waked up by the *appel* and the noise in the street—our *concierge* ordering all lights out. She saw the Zeppelins quite distinctly from her window, passing over the *barrière de l'Etoile*, and heard the cannon and *mitrailleuses* from the Eiffel Tower. However, by the time she got downstairs the danger was over. The street and house were quiet, and she returned to the sixth floor. I put on a warm cloak and stood on the balcony a little while, but saw nothing; the street was perfectly quiet and dark, except when the searchlight threw a long yellow ray.

About an hour later there was another alarm, but it was not serious, though the *pompiers* with their "*garde à vous*" rattled under *our* windows this time.

It was too much for the poor little maid; she rushed downstairs quite unnerved and frightened, and slept in the *lingerie* all night. Almost all the *locataires* of the 5ième spent the night in the *concierge's* lodge.

Before 9 o'clock this morning Charlotte arrived, quite white and trembling. They had been waked out of a sound sleep by the noise: First the bombs—one fell in the avenue Malakoff, near the Rue de la Pompe—and then the firing from the Tour Eiffel, and the few French aeroplanes that were flying. The children and maids were terrified, so they all went down to the concierge's lodge, getting quickly into whatever clothes they could find, groping about in the dark, and spent the rest of the night there. Various other *locataires* did the same, the concierge making occasional excursions into the street, which was black as ink, to see if anything more was happening.

Evidently there was much more disturbance in their part of the town. They are so close to the Tour Eiffel. Charlotte felt rather better when she had had a glass of Marsala, and talked it all over with us; and she went back to the house to bring the boys here to breakfast. They looked a little pale when they arrived, but were much excited, having been waked out of their sound sleep by the noise and the autos, and then being hurried into their clothes and passing the night sitting up in the lodge. Poor little things, they have had various experiences since their hurried flight from Mareuil at the beginning of the war. They will never forget "wartimes." All they do and all they don't do is subservient to the one absorbing idea: "War."

We had quite a number of visits at tea-time, all of course full of the alarm. The T.'s sleeping peacefully in their rooms on the court of their hotel, heard nothing, and read the news in the papers this morning. In almost all the hotels people were waked up and told to come downstairs. They say the assemblage at the Ritz was wonderful, though most of the women had made themselves presentable with long cloaks and *fichus* tied over their heads, but some had been too frightened; had only one idea, to get downstairs, and nature stood revealed most unbecomingly.

March 22nd, '15,
Rue de la Pompe.

We had a second Zeppelin alarm last night about 9 o'clock. We had just finished dinner, all lights were ordered out, and the *pompiers* dashed through the street sounding their *"garde à vous."*

The shrill, strident notes set every nerve on edge. There wasn't a sound to be heard; no cannon nor noise of falling bombs. We sat by the window, making occasional excursions to the balcony, but there was nothing to be seen. No one in the street; a few men standing at the doors of the houses; one just saw them like shadows when the searchlights played around.

A little before 12 the *pompiers* passed again more slowly, playing "danger over," and calling out: "Danger over; you can light." They were cheered all along the streets.

Willy called from the window: "*Sont-ils partis, les sales Boches?*"
"*Oui, mon petit, oui. Vous pouvez vous coucher.*"

There was another alarm after we had got to bed, about 12 o'clock, but it didn't amount to anything. Still these are agitated nights.

Wednesday, March 24th.

I was at the *ouvroir* all the afternoon. Mme. M. had seen the Zeppelin quite distinctly. It passed over the house; she said it looked extraordinary, all lighted, brilliant shells bursting around it in all directions from the *mitrailleuses* and French aeroplanes.

Tuesday, March 30th.

The Duchesse de Bassano and Lady Lee came in late this afternoon. They were just back from Versailles, where they had been to the British Red Cross Hospital at the Hôtel du Trianon. They say it is wonderfully installed, so clean and spacious, and under strict military discipline. The *duchesse* took flowers and tobacco and picture papers to the soldiers, and said they were very pleased—just like children— particularly with the flowers.

Lady Lee occupies herself very much with the hospitals, not nursing, but seeing that they have all they want, and writing letters for the soldiers.

Versailles is quite changed with so many British about—officers in khaki, sometimes with their wives and children; British Red Cross nurses and automobiles. The two little tea-shops are doing a thriving business. We went into one the other day and might have thought ourselves in London: British at every table, all having tea and muffins. Our boys are always taken for English, as they are fair and speak English with their English nurse, which makes them most indignant. "We are French boys; father is a French soldier!"

Good Friday, April and, '15.

The churches were crowded yesterday and today; a great many women in mourning, a great many wounded soldiers. At one of the churches, in a little chapel where the Christ was exposed with an abundance of flowers and candles, a young soldier, not more than twenty-two years old, with one leg off, looking very white and weak, came in, but couldn't get a seat. He stood for a few minutes leaning on his crutches. A child got up, ran over to him, saying: "*Viens, mon ami, mets-toi là à côté de Maman.*" He demurred, but the lady made a sign to him to come. He took the seat, and the little girl knelt alongside of him on the stone pavement.

Easter Sunday, April 4th.

I went to the American church. C. and the boys came to breakfast. We had coloured eggs for them, and they had already had a fine collection at their own house—useful gifts from *Bonne Maman* and Danny: carnets, pencils, gloves, etc, and a big chocolate bell from Lady Plunkett. She is here with Nellie, staying with Norah G., and nursing at the British Red Cross Hospital at the Hôtel Astoria. I fancy she is an excellent nurse. She has had capital training at Lausanne, at one of the great hospitals there; and besides, has a real vocation, is thoroughly interested in all medical work.

Friday, April 9th.

The week has been very quiet, everybody following the action of the fleets in the Dardanelles. Things have not gone as quickly and easily as one expected. Before Easter, Mr. de P. told us they were betting at the dubs that Constantinople would fall for Easter. He wasn't quite so sanguine, thought it might perhaps fall by the Sunday after, but thinks he will lose his bet.

It is astonishing how the time slips away when one does the same thing every day. The *communiqués* don't tell us much about the war, nor private letters either. Francis writes fairly often, but except when he has a night in the trenches or a reconnaissance with the general, or some of officer friends, there is not much to tell.

Walter Waddington is about ten kilometres from Fancis' *cantonnement*. He and his officers are very comfortably lodged in a small *château*, and Francis goes over to lunch and dine with him sometimes. The other day he took over one of the sergeants of his regiment—a singer from the Opéra-Comique, who has a charming voice, and sings very well.

There was quite a good piano at the *château*, and they made music all the evening, Francis accompanying his friend. Then Francis played the national airs and our famous march of " *Sambre et Meuse*," winding it up with "It's a long, long way to Tipperary," all the officers joining in the chorus.

When Francis and his friend were starting back the cannon was going again, hard, and shells were whistling through the air. The men told Francis to be very careful at a certain bridge, which the enemy always aims at. They don't seem to mind the shells more than tennis-balls, yet men are killed around them every day.

I am going out to Mrs. Depew's tomorrow.

April 10th, '15,
Château d'Annel.

We had a lovely afternoon yesterday; leaving the Hôtel Crillon at 4 and getting here about 6.30. The road, as usual, was deserted. We met no private conveyances of any kind, merely military autos, which go an awful pace, particularly the British ones—and occasional convoys of munition-wagons or food—the fields empty, no ploughing nor work of any kind going on, women and children standing at the doors of their cottages.

We passed through Senlis, which is tragic. In the one long street, all the houses in ruins—roofs off, windows out, walls fallen, heaps of stones and charred beams everywhere. It quite reminded me of Pompeii; and over all this black ruin, the beautiful blue summer sky, and the great stillness of the country. We were stopped several times, but only for a moment, as the car with its English chauffeur dressed in khaki, is well known on the road. Then we got to the bridge of Compiègne, where we were stopped again. There were a great many people much excited, pointing to the sky, where I saw nothing, but the others did. It was a French aeroplane being fired upon by German shells. Mrs. D. saw the aeroplane quite distinctly, as well as the little puffs of smoke looking like white clouds, made by the German shells. The officer at the bridge told us we could go on; there was no danger, as the aeroplane was some distance ahead, and we were behind the firing-line.

It is curious how in wartimes everything seems natural, even to taking an afternoons turn in the country with shells flying over your head.

In one of the small villages we passed through, close to Annel, a regiment of *spahis* was quartered. They looked most picturesque with their bright red cloaks and white turbans; were tall, dark, handsome men. I suppose they are not allowed to fight in that costume; they would make a fine target for the enemy, even for the old gentlemen of the *Landsturm*, who don't seem very efficient with a rifle.

Our evening was pleasant. The hospital staff—about eight men, doctors, gentlemen chauffeurs, etc., dined with us. All were in khaki. We heard the cannon quite distinctly until 9.30, and went out on the terrace to see if we could distinguish any rockets, but all was quite dark.

As soon as the lights are lit in the *château*, heavy black curtains are lowered over all the windows, which give a ghastly impression in the house, as not a gleam of light must be visible. They are too near the front, only ten miles from the German trenches.

It all seems very comfortably arranged. The family lives in one wing, quite apart from the hospital. Mrs. Depew will take me over the wards tomorrow.

It is lovely this morning; I shall go for a stroll in the park, and at 11 o'clock there is mass in the small convalescent ward.

11 o'clock.

We have had a most interesting day. I had a nice walk with Mr. D., who showed me the graveyard in the park, at some little distance from the *château*, where the soldiers who have died in the hospital are buried, until the end of the war, when their families can come and claim their bodies. It is very well arranged. There are about thirty graves, a simple wooden cross at the head of each, flowers on the graves, and a little hedge of box around the enclosure.

We went in at 11 to the mass. It was held in the old music-room, now turned into a convalescent ward. There were eight beds; most of the men propped up on pillows, and several nurses and doctors in their white uniform. Mrs. D., in her nurse's dress, played the organ. Francis the violoncello. It was an impressive scene; and at the end the *aumônier*, with his *vêtement* over his uniform, finished with the prayer that we hear in all the churches now: "*Prions pour nos soldats au front, pour nos blessés ici, pour tous nos morts dans toute la France; et que Dieu donne aux mères et aux femmes le courage d'accepter avec résignation les sacrifices que le pays leur demande.*" And all to the sound of the cannon, which had been growling again since 10 o'clock.

After lunch I went into the big ward with Mrs. Depew. The men looked most comfortable and well cared for. The room is large and bright (the old ballroom), on the ground floor, doors and windows opening on the fine old courtyard, and a flood of sunlight streaming in.

Then we went for a turn in the motor to a village some little distance off, nearer the front. We went up to the top story of the doctor's house, from where we had a fine view of the plain and our trenches and barbed-wire entanglements. We saw very far beyond the line of our trenches, a long stretch of plain; then a wood, and behind that, the German trenches.

When we got back to the *château*, all the patients were out in the courtyard, in the sun, their beds wheeled out. Various French officers came in to tea, and it was a real pleasure to see the *pantalon rouge* and light-blue tunic of the *chasseurs*, after all the khaki, which is, of course, more serviceable in campaign than the bright colours, but it doesn't look military. Everybody wears it: chauffeurs, orderlies at hospitals, etc.

They are giving all our men other uniforms, a sort of blue-grey, for the front, but the men hate it; they love their red trousers.

I saw for the first time that afternoon, painted horses. All the horses of the *Chasseurs d'Afrique* are small grey horses, which, of course, made them a fine mark for the enemy. One orderly, who came with his officer, was riding a pink horse, which, they said, with time and exposure in all weathers would turn a *bai rouge*. Another had a bright *yellow* one, which would become *alezan* (chestnut) by the same process. They looked funny in the present stage, with the men's red trousers.

We had a pleasant dinner; made a little music in the evening, singing "Tipperary," which is a good marching tune, and another regular silly, catchy English song: "Susie's sewing socks for soldiers." I am leaving tomorrow morning.

Paris, Wednesday, April 14th.
The days pass quietly. We don't hear much news. All interest now is centred in the Dardanelles. Everyone seems to think that Russia will be most exacting when settling-day comes, and she will, of course, want Constantinople; but I don't think Great Britain would mind that now with the Suez Canal and the firm footing she has in Egypt.

Saturday, April 24th.
We had a procession of soldiers at the *ouvroir* today, coming out of the hospital with four or five days' leave before joining their regiments. Most of them were men from the *pays occupés*, with no friends in Paris and no money—the *fr.* 1. 25 they got from the government being quite insufficient to give them food and lodging. There must be houses or shelter of some kind for them, but we don't know where. One poor fellow had had no word from wife or children since September. He was a small farmer from near Laon; had had no time for preparations of any kind. He was on the first roll-call. The order for mobilisation came on Saturday afternoon, August 1st, at 4 o'clock. He was at the market in a little town not far from his farm; had just time to get back, kiss his wife and children, and take the first train at 9 o'clock that evening. Had heard nothing of any of his belongings. There are hundreds in the same plight, yet they don't complain.

Tuesday, April 27th.

Antoinette, Charlotte, and A. H. lunched with us today. Antoinette was interesting, telling all the work she had done at Dinard. She is quite miserable about her German companion, Fräulein Pauline, whom we all know, and who had been with her for years (twenty, I think). The poor thing had never been back to Germany, had no relations there—a sister married here to a Frenchman, and two nephews in the French Army. Antoinette kept her as long as she could, but it wasn't possible to go on any longer. The people in the village even the servants in the place, who had known her for years—she had nursed them when they were ill, and taken care of their children—got excited. After all, she was a German, probably a spy. At last the mayor and *curé* told Antoinette she must go; they couldn't protect her if some sudden fury seized the people—a piece of bad news, a reverse of the French; some new German atrocity might happen at any moment, and they couldn't hold the people. So most tearfully and reluctantly the poor woman started for Germany.

We talked a little of old days in Rome, so long ago. Will Italy move? I doubt it.

Friday, April 30th.

We had a nice letter from Francis this morning. He had made an interesting expedition with his general to the trenches to choose where a new line was to be made. They went in motors to the entrance of a long tunnel leading into the trench, stayed there a little, talking to the soldiers, who, he said, looked most comfortable—had made themselves chairs and tables out of old boxes and planks—had lamps.

Then their party—about eight or ten men, left their shelter and came out on the plain. They were told to throw away their cigars, not stay too close together, also to talk as little and as low as possible.

He said it was a curious situation; the night quite dark, very still, except for the shells which came screaming through the air, and every now and then a great roar from the big guns. They walked about for an hour, choosing the ground for the new line of trenches and dodging the shells which generally flew over their heads and fell at some little distance off. They heard the Germans distinctly, talking in their trenches; spoke very little and very low themselves.

He fretted so at O. all summer, seeing nothing of the fighting and never hearing the cannon. He hears it enough now.

Tuesday, May 4th, '15.

We had a little concert today, at the Swedish church for the benefit of the hospital and *ouvroir* which Comtesse G., wife of the Swedish Minister to France, organised as soon as she got back from Bordeaux. The church was very prettily decorated with plants and flowers, and very full. All the Swedish colony of course, which is quite large. Mme. Delcassé, wife of the Minister of Foreign Affairs, Mme. M., wife of the Minister of War, and a good many of Comtesse G.'s personal friends. All the soldiers who were well enough were seated on benches close to the chancel. Some of them looked very young, mere boys. The music was very good. Two Swedish singers with that high, dear northern voice—so unlike the rich, full Spanish and Italian voices—sang very well.

After the concert was over we went into the hospital, which is very well arranged, in a large high room on the ground floor, very light and airy. The beds were partitioned off with screens, making nice little rooms. The men looked very smiling and comfortable; they were all convalescents, no *grands blessés*. All the ladies had brought picture papers, tobacco, and chocolate.

Wednesday, May 5th.

I lunched today with a country neighbour, *Conseiller Général* of the Oise. He has a charming *château*, just touching the Villers-Cotterets forest. It has been occupied ever since the month of September, 1914; first Germans, now French; and the French I think have done and are doing more harm than the Germans!—horses and heavy camions all over his park; walls knocked down, the men finding the big gates too narrow to allow six or eight horses to pass abreast—and the inside in an awful condition. He was most unfortunate in the regiments that fell to his share.

In some of the *châteaux* the French soldiers mended the furniture and took care of the gardens.

Among other people we had at breakfast Mr. P., Chef de Cabinet of the Minister of War, at this moment I should think the most overworked man in France. I was quite ashamed to ask him for anything, but I did. Francis wants to go as interpreter on the staff of one of the British generals. He says he feels he could be very useful, as he knows English, of course, as well as French, and is accustomed to English ways and life. Some of the interpreters on both sides have been utter failures. They say the Englishman who knows a little French gets on better than the Frenchman who knows a little English. The French-man is accustomed to hearing his native tongue badly spoken, and understands more quickly; the Englishman on the contrary is slow to understand; must have very precise orders.

The breakfast was quite a war breakfast, served by a parlour-maid and a soldier in uniform, with his arm in a sling. He was our host's *valet de chambre*, had been wounded, and was finishing his period of convalescence in his master's service.

The general talk at table was interesting; very little criticism on what either government or army was doing, and an absolute certainty of ultimate victory—"*qui nous coûtera cher; toute notre jeunesse y restera!*" That is the tragic side of this awful war.

When we see a regiment starting for the front, all the young faces so flushed and smiling and eager for the fray, we think of the hundreds who will never come back, and of whom their families will never know anything—merely "missing," in the long lists of casualties.

Thursday, May 6th.

Mrs. W. came to breakfast, and we went afterward to the Japanese hospital, installed at the Hôtel Astoria. It looked perfectly well ordered and beautifully clean. We asked for the *directrice*, Mme. de L., whom we know, and she took us over the hospital. The *pharmacie* was quite won-derful—so neat and orderly; all the bottles and packages wrapped up in soft white paper, and the curious Japanese signs or letters that one sees on all their packages of tea. Mme. L. introduced the head of the *pharmacie* to us. He knew very little French, but English well; would be so pleased if we would talk to him. Accordingly we had one of those halting, one-sided, impossible conversations one has sometimes with people who know a little (very little in this case) of a language. I understood very little of what he said to me, and, judging from his answers, he absolutely nothing of what I said to him.

We saw several of the nurses all in white, with a curious high square cap. They are a funny collection of little yellow women, very polite and smiling and curtseying. I can't imagine that our soldiers like to be nursed by such ugly little yellow creatures, even though they dress the wounds most skilfully. They say their touch is very light, and they work much more quickly than our nurses. All the same I should think the men would prefer a nice *white payse*, even if she was a little rough.

I didn't go into the operating-rooms, but Mrs. M. did. She said they were splendid, at the top of the house, large and airy, with every modern scientific invention. There were several ladies, nurses, in the wards and corridors—French and Americans. I don't know exactly what they do, as the Japanese nurses do all the dressings—don't allow any foreigners to touch the patients.

Saturday, May 8th.

There is awful news this morning: the S.S. *Lusitania* torpedoed and sunk by the Germans off the Irish coast. I didn't think even they would have dared to do such an awful thing. The first account says only six hundred people saved; the boat went down in twelve minutes. I should think this would rouse England and America. Still, the Americans were warned; they came at their own risk; a certain number of passages were cancelled.

Friday, May 14, '15.

Nobody talks of anything but the *Lusitania*, and wonders what America will do. There was an animated discussion at the *ouvroir* this afternoon between Col. B.—a wounded French officer still on his crutches—and Mr. H. W., a clever Englishman with French relations, married to a Frenchwoman. I think in his heart, though he wouldn't own it, the Englishman thought the Frenchman was right: "that Britain should have protected her ship, not braved the Germans." Of course she never thought, nor did anyone else, that Germany, even Germany, would do such a cowardly act. However, she has set the whole civilised world against her now. Many of the Americans here, particularly the women, hope that America will fight. I hope she won't.

Sunday, May 16th.

I went to the English church. The rector didn't officiate, and the clergyman who took his place asked the prayers of the congregation for the rector and his family. Their eldest son, a soldier, is reported "missing" since Tuesday. I went to the rectory directly after the service, and the servant told me it was true—a boy only eighteen, as she said. "He was a child last year, *Madame*, when he came home for his holidays and asked me for cakes." I remember all the boys perfectly; didn't think any were old enough to be soldiers.

We had a good many people at tea-time, among others, Professor Hall of Harvard with his wife and daughter—clever, sympathetic people, all much interested in France and the terrible struggle she is going through. He sent me a generous contribution to my *ouvroir*. I so rarely see American men of that type that it was a great pleasure to me to hear an impartial opinion from the outside world.

Saturday, May 22nd, '15.

I dined this evening with the Ségurs. Quite like old times, with all the nieces and nephews, M.'s and H.'s. Young Mérode is at the *Ministère de la Guerre* (was in uniform, the new colour, "*bleu horizon*," which they say is very good, blends perfectly with sky and trees). He knows German well, translates the letters found on prisoners or dead. M. says they are not very interesting, the wives in Germany finding the war very long, the cost of living very high; not much enthusiasm.

Sunday, May 23rd.

We had a few people at tea-time; Bessie much excited over Italy's moving. She will have three grandsons and two nephews in the war: five *Ruspolis!* The Duchesse de Bassano, Stuers (Dutch Minister), and the Gyldenstopes dined. We all talked war, of course. They were hard on Bülow and his fiasco in Rome—but it really was an ungrateful mission. He was beaten even before he began to negotiate. There was a splendid patriotic demonstration in the Roman Chamber yesterday.

Monday, 24th May.

Italy has declared war upon Austria only (not on Germany). People are afraid for Venice; think Austrian aeroplanes will throw bombs on St. Mark. It would be too awful.

We had rather a disagreeable communication from Mareuil this morning, saying our house had been requisitioned by the military authorities, and the officer in command of the group of *automobilistes* had asked for seven rooms and the use of the kitchen and dining-room. It is a great bore as we want to go down ourselves for a week or ten days; but we can't refuse in war times, with the whole country under martial law. We talked it over with C, who had come in from Versailles for Comtesse Foy's funeral—and gave Mme. G. her instructions. She could give six rooms in the *new house*, and the use of the kitchen. I reserved the dining-room and old house until we were able to come down and see what arrangements we could make.

Thursday, May 27th.

Went out to the American Ambulance this afternoon. There were a great many people there, as it was visiting-day. All the doors and windows were open, the convalescents sitting out on the terrace and *perrons*; almost all had friends and presents—flowers, cigarettes, illustrated papers.

Thérèse de Ségur is at the head of one of the great Paris hospitals; was delighted, thought everything from wards to kitchen was so splendidly clean and airy.

We stopped at Charlotte's *ouvroir* on our way down, and she was much interested in all the garments the ladies were making. There are two sewing-machines, a cutting-out table, and they really get through a great deal of work. It is quite different from our *ouvroir*, where we don't work ourselves, merely give work to women, and see the soldiers who come and ask for clothes—always shirts; and a great many, even in this warm weather, still prefer woollen socks to cotton ones.

Friday, May 28th.

I went up to Rue de la Pompe to see the contents of a box just received from the Clearing-House. All good things. We had a quiet afternoon at the *ouvroir*, but one or two blind soldiers, so sad—one quite young man, a tall, broad-shouldered, good-looking fellow, led in by a comrade. I talked to him a little, asking him what he wanted. He said to me: "Je *ne puis pas vous voir, Madame. Etes-vous jeune, ou mère de famille?*"

"*Non, mon ami, je ne suis pas jeune; je suis mère de famille—même grand'mère, et j'ai un fils au front, comme vous.*"

"*Que Dieu vous le garde, Madame; je ne verrai jamais plus les miens.*"

But not a word of complaint. I couldn't make any phrases to him of losing his sight in a glorious cause—a young, strong man, not thirty years old, in total darkness for the rest of his life! I put my hand on his sleeve, saying: "*Mon pauvre ami!*"—and then the poor fellow broke down and cried, and I beat a hasty retreat, feeling a choke in my throat. Of course the government will look after them, and they will all be taught trades, but it is pitiful to see them.

It seems there was a group of wounded and one blind man on the terrace of one of the hospitals one day, all rejoicing in the bright sunlight that gave a touch of warm light to everything; the Seine, the hills in the distance, and pointing out to each other the fortifications and trenches of the *camp retrenché*. The blind man stood apart, looking sad and lonely. A young nurse went up to him, took his arm and led him into a corner where he could fed the sun, and holding his fingers, pointed out the various points the men were talking about. By degrees, all the other men joined them, explaining and talking to the blind soldier, who was quite excited, as the nurse moved his hand backward and forward, and almost seemed to see the various points;

forgot for a while his misfortune and fought his battle over again with his comrades.

It seems that some of them were so miserable when they realised their sight was gone that they did not tell them at once, waited until they were strong enough to bear the blow; let them think it was a temporary deprivation of sight.

Mareuil, Thursday, June 3rd.

We came down yesterday. For the last week we have been getting letters from the *curé*, from Mme.. Gaillard, telling us the house was always full of French soldiers, who behaved very badly; the officer, ordering all the rooms opened, established himself in my bedroom, and wished to put his orderly in one of the good *chambres d'ami* next to him. They wanted extra blankets and lamps, and Mme. G. to do their cooking. At last the poor woman came up to Paris, saying she couldn't take such a responsibility and face the situation alone. Her son has just been mobilise. She is alone with one young maid in the house. That morning's mail had brought me a letter from an officer, saying my servants were very impolite, etc., so we thought we had better go down.

I wrote to the officer and the mayor, saying what rooms I would give and, above all, what rooms I *wouldn't*; and agreed to go down as soon as I could. I also gave Mme. G. a letter that she could show to the officer, telling her what rooms to give, and that we were coming down as soon as I could get away from my work in Paris—and here we are.

We took the 5.30 train in the afternoon and got down a little before 8. Though we are no longer in the military zone, we still had soldiers at the station, and had to show our *sauf-conduits*. Our first surprise was seeing Mme G. at the station with a rather smart-looking *ordonnance* and her wheelbarrow—the well-known wheelbarrow which we always use for carrying the small parcels backward and forward.

The courtyard of the station was full of big American lorries and autobuses. It seems the *Corps de Ravitaillement* is stationed here, and our *militaires* are the gentlemen chauffeurs of the autos. We walked to the house, rather wondering what we should find, and were met just inside the gate by a young officer in uniform, who introduced himself as Lieutenant D. (the gentleman with whom I had corresponded). He asked me if he could do anything for us. He had wanted to send his automobile to the station, but Mme. G. told him we always walked, but that his *ordonnance* had gone. He thanked us for our hospitality; said he and his comrades would give us as little trouble as possible, and retired by the garden entrance. It was too dark to see his face, but he had a gentleman's voice and manner. All the same, it seemed funny to be welcomed in our own courtyard by a perfect stranger, and to see the garage and kitchen lighted, and silhouettes of soldiers everywhere.

We went into the house to see what arrangements we could make. The table was laid for us in the dining-room, and Mme. G. told us the gentlemen hoped we would allow them to send us some *filet de boeuf* and *asperges* for our dinner, also a bottle of good wine. I wanted some soap and went into the office to see if my bag was there—a very good-looking young soldier, tall, fair, rather like an Englishman, was standing there, lighting a lamp. He came forward, introducing himself; had a very good, easy manner. What could he do for me? Would I allow him to send me some soap? I said I had plenty, was looking for my bag. He went to see if it was in the hall, and through the half-open door I saw several soldiers in the kitchen, and there seemed to be about seven or eight dining in the small courtyard, just outside the office.

We made the best arrangements we could for the night, and when we went down to dinner found the boys in a wild state of delight. They had made acquaintance with all the seven soldiers who were dining. My eldest grandson, aged ten, said: "They were all very polite, Danny, got up when we came into the court, and Mme. Gaillard told them we were '*les jeunes maîtres de maison*,' and the lieutenant introduced all of them to us."

After dinner Charlotte and I went out to speak to them. They are a nice-looking set of young fellows. We asked them all to dine with us tomorrow. We are comfortable in the old house. I sleep in the nursery, which is my old room, and is still full of the boys' toys and books. The Germans didn't take anything from there, except one charming little statue of the Virgin which Charlotte had had all her life. It is certainly many years since I have slept with a hoop over my head, but it seems solidly hung. I hope it won't come down in the night. The boys will sleep to-night on their mattress on the floor, in Charlotte's *boudoir*. She is in her own room. Tomorrow we will settle ourselves better.

The house is very still; we don't hear a sound; would never imagine it was full of men.

★★★★★★

It has been a lovely warm day. It was delicious to be waked up in the morning by the smell of roses climbing into the windows. The roses are lovely—quantities of them, and all the trees and bushes grown enormously—but the lawns, planted with potatoes, beans, and peas, look too awful; but there was nothing else to do. They had been so cut up and trampled upon with horses picketed on them, that the only hope of ever having decent lawns again was to dig them all up and plant potatoes.

By 7 o'clock the boys were in the garden, playing about with some of the young men. They sent us their chauffeur to help move some of our heavy furniture. We shall settle ourselves for the present in the old house, as we shall always be liable to have French troops or British, so long as the war lasts.

We have put up a curtain at the end of the corridor, in the wing, so we are quite shut off, and none of the men ever come up the big staircase or into our part. The lieutenant uses Francis' *fumoir* as his *bureau*, and they take all their meals outside on the children's lawn or playground, the only one which has not been cut up, under the big pear-tree.

It is beautiful weather. If it rained, of course they would have to come inside. I suppose one office could be arranged as a dining-room for them. They certainly don't deprive themselves of anything in the way of food, seem to have the best of everything, and are constantly asking what they can send us. It is always a *filet de boeuf*, as the army lives on beef.

The chauffeur has also mended our motor which pumps the water upstairs. We sat in the garden all day, being quite lazy and quiet. The boys played about with the soldiers. They have quite taken possession of the premises; have a pig—"Anatole," and chickens. There was wild excitement at one moment when Anatole escaped from his house and trotted about among the young potato-plants. I sent for one of the men and explained that I couldn't have the pig running about the garden; he must be shut up.

We invited all the gentlemen to dine tonight. We had brought down chickens and ham, vegetables and fruit from Paris, and they accepted with pleasure, sending us word by Mme. G. that they had a *filet de boeuf*, which they begged we would accept. We asked them, all seven, and the two little maids were rather nervous as to how they could serve so many people. We would be eleven, and we were rather nervous too, as to knives and forks and spoons, as we have not replaced what the Germans had taken—bringing down merely what we wanted ourselves, But about 4 o'clock the lieutenant sent us word there would only be four of them, the others were *de service*. (The maids told

132

us they were too shy to come.)

The dinner went very well. The chauffeur helped in the office. The lieutenant was the only regular officer. He had been wounded at Charleroi, left rather delicate and a little deaf, and had been given this place for a rest. The other men were sons of rich *industriels*, two from Lille, which is now occupied by the Germans. They have had no news of their families for months—one, a nice young fellow—Pinto d'Arringo, son of a Brazilian naturalised Frenchman, with an English grandmother. They had all seen a little service. One broad-shouldered, nice young man had been in the fighting all around us at Vareddes-Barcy. They were a little shy at first, but the boys helped us. They asked so many questions, and were so intensely interested in everything the young men said, that it put them at their ease.

We went into the big salon after dinner, which looked ghastly; no table-covers, nor cushions anywhere, and bare spaces on the walls where the Germans had taken pictures. We had a wonderful collection of lamps, some old ones that Mme. G. had found in the garden, one borrowed from the grocer, and one or two small ones belonging to the soldiers; but in war-times it didn't matter. The piano was not too bad, and we made music. One man played the violin well, and Pinto sang quite prettily. We sang various choruses, ending with the national airs and "Tipperary" and the famous march of "*Sambre et Meuse*."

Friday, June 4th.

It has been very hot all day. Charlotte and I were busy upstairs putting away all sorts of things, as we shall lock up two rooms. The present lot of soldiers are perfectly civil and reasonable, but one never knows what the next may be.

After tea we walked up to the church to see the statue of the Virgin and Child the *curé* has had put up in gratitude for the saving of his church. When the Germans were approaching Mareuil, and the village was *évacuée par ordre militaire*, he went to the church before leaving, to take a last look. He had hidden all the vessels and archives. Kneeling at the altar, praying that his church would not be bombarded nor desecrated, he made a vow that if it was untouched (it is a fine old church of the twelfth century) he would put up a statue to the Virgin. Nothing was touched, and as soon as the village settled down a little after fourteen days of exile, he began his work.

The statue stands very well at the back of the church, on the hill overlooking the canal. It is very well done, very simple, and can be seen at a fair distance from below, and from the canal.

We walked home by the canal, stopping to talk to all the women—and seeing soldiers everywhere. I don't know what will happen with all those good-looking warriors about, quite changing the usual aspect of Mareuil. The war will be answerable for all sorts of incidents. I think the *curé* is very anxious.

Saturday, June 5th.

We had a most strenuous and interesting day yesterday. With much difficulty we got *sauf-conduits* to go to Villers-Cotterets, about fourteen miles from us. We heroically decided to take again the grocer's *tapissière*—that most uncomfortable, narrow, springless four-wheeled cart, but he had a good horse, and we thought we were quite safe with our *sauf-conduits*—but the grocer hadn't any! We hadn't thought of him. We consulted our lieutenant, suggesting that he might, perhaps take us in *his* auto. But he was overwhelmed at the mere idea. He couldn't take any *civilian* in his car, and above all, no woman—not even his own wife if she were there, or a Red Cross nurse. However, he did what he could; said he was going into Villers-Cotterets on duty Saturday morning, and would come back as soon as he could; but not before 10.30. So we gave him rendezvous at the bottom of the Bourneville hill, where the *poste des gendarmes* is stationed, and started at 10 in our most ramshackle vehicle.

It was rather amusing waiting at the *poste*. The *gendarmes* knew us well. Two of them had been quartered for some weeks at our house, and I presented them each with blankets when they went away. They brought us chairs, and we sat on the bank, under the trees, and saw all the people (not many, only military) who passed; the *consigne* was very strict; every auto, even with officers in it was stopped. There was a barricade across the road with a narrow opening, just wide enough to let one carriage pass. As soon as the *gendarmes* saw a carriage coming down the hill, one of them stepped forward, holding up his gun horizontally, to bar the way. One unfortunate young woman was most indignant. She had bicycled all the way from Meaux, twenty-five miles, in the boiling heat, and thought her papers were all right; but the captain of *gendarmes* was very stern, and wouldn't let her pass. They are still afraid of spies, and unfortunately some of the worst are women.

Our lieutenant appeared very punctually at 10.30 with the grocer's *sauf-conduit*, and we started. It was very hot creeping up the long hill, just out of La Ferté; but once in the forest it was delightful. The big trees made a perfect thick shade. It was very still, not a sign of life or culture. We met nothing but military autos and trains of lorries and autobuses, which made long trails of dust, and filled the air with the smell of petroleum. We were certainly the only *civils* on the road. At the entrance of the town, just before we crossed the railroad, two *mitrailleuses*, most sinister-looking objects, were stationed. Villers was bristling with soldiers, as it is the headquarters of the 6me *armée*.

We went first to the Hôtel du Dauphin, where we always used to breakfast in the old days, when we hunted in the Villers-Cotterets forest, but it does not exist any longer as a hotel—is turned into a military administration of some kind. An officer who was at the door advised us to go to the Hôtel de la Chasse, some little distance off, and quite unknown to me. It looked rather nice, with a large courtyard and flowers in the garden, which was filled with officers breakfasting, who were all much interested in the sudden appearance of two ladies and two children so near the front.

They listened hard while we explained to the *patronne* that we had come from Mareuil, and were very hungry. She gave us a very good breakfast, and then we started off to see if we could find an officer of the *etat-major*, and get a permission to go nearer the front behind the last line of trenches, and distribute some clothes and food to the poor people. Many of the peasants went back to their ruined villages once the Germans were out of them, and were encamped there in absolute misery, living in wagons or sheds—any sort of shelter they had been able to find We wanted very much to get to them, but the officer whom we interviewed wouldn't hear of it. He was much surprised at seeing us at Villers-Cotterets, and thought that we should not have been given a *sauf-conduit*. "It was no place for *civils*. nor women and children." "Had we come from Paris?"

"No, by road from Mareuil."

That surprised him still more.

"Did we meet any *civils* on the road?"

"No, not one."

He again repeated that it was no place for women, and advised us to get back at once before nightfall; said there was no possibility of getting any nearer the front, these days, with fighting going on all around us.

We meant to go to the hospital to see what they wanted there (we had already sent several boxes of bandages and hospital shirts from the *ouvroir*), but were advised not to, as there were several cases of typhus, and it was very hot. We loitered a little in the town, hearing the cannon much nearer and louder than at Mareuil.

The people say they are accustomed to it now; don't mind it. What they don't like are the shells. We talked to some of the shop people, and bought pens and *briquets* made by the soldiers in the trenches out of pieces of German shells. As a rule the people did not complain of the Germans; said they behaved well when people remained in their houses; but it was a reign of terror; all the mothers terrified to have their boys playing about, as they made short work with boys if they got in their way, or didn't instantly guide them to any place they wanted to go to, or answer their questions—they shot so many in Belgium— boys of eight to ten years, who certainly did them no harm.

The drive home was lovely. The country looks beautiful, but one felt so strongly the tragic stillness and absence of life and movement. We stopped at La Ferté, and had tea with the *abbé* in his garden, which was green and quiet and peaceful, such a contrast to the street, quite choked up with lorries and heavy carts and wagons, and all the paraphernalia of war.

Our *curé* came to dinner—a, most frugal meal. We sat until 10 o'clock in the garden, and our *militaires* came and talked to us. They were interesting, telling their experiences and the horrors they had seen. One young man, son of a rich *bourgeois*, was much impressed by the war; said he could never forget the first dead he saw after the Battle of the Marne, in a village near us; fifty Germans lying dead in the fields—and that was nothing to what he felt when he came a little later upon forty or fifty Frenchmen lying in heaps, some with such expressions of suffering on their faces. He said he could hardly get past the bodies; as he turned into a courtyard of an old *château*, he suddenly came upon a German soldier who was terror-stricken, unarmed, throwing up his hands, begging for life. "I couldn't kill him, *Madame*, there in cold blood, a perfectly helpless, unarmed man—though I suppose I should have done it with the bodies of my comrades lying so near. But I couldn't. I took him prisoner and handed him over to the authorities."

They all said what we often do, that no one who had been through this war could ever be the same again; the entire mentality must change.

The boys listened with rapt attention, and later, when he was going to bed, the eldest one, Willy, said to me: "Why didn't he kill the wicked German, Danny, who had killed so many Frenchmen?"

This morning we hear the cannon distinctly, about twenty miles away, the *militaires* say. They went off early, at 4 this morning, to take food to the men in the trenches near Soissons, and said it was infernal—the sky a blaze of fire, and the steady roar of the big guns. And here it is the *Fête-Dieu*; the children came early to the garden and carried off as many roses as they could find, and one or two *reposoirs* dressed with flowers have been arranged on the road on the route of the procession; and the girls in their white frocks will scatter roses before the sacrament. "*Le Bon Dieu qui passé*," as they say in the country, and all ought to be peaceful and smiling.

During the mass every time there was a silence in the church, we heard the long, steady growl of the cannon, and we wonder who will be missing at the roll-call.

We are taking the last train this evening for Paris. It would be impossible to travel in the daytime in this heat.

I am writing in my room, leaving *written* instructions to Mme. G. and the mayor as to what rooms I will give. I hear voices and laughter in the garden, and see the boys having a fine game of ball with Pinto, and Charlotte being photographed under the little "*pergola* C." by one of the young men. It has been curious and interesting living there three or four days with the army. It has brought us into such direct contact with the soldiers. We have thought and talked of nothing but the war. The autos and motorcycles came in and out of the courtyard all day, and we always heard the rumble of the big *autobuses* as they went backward and forward.

We sent our letters off by the military autos. They passed twice a day and took our letters, if we left them at the *poste*. The postal service is very irregular, the telephone cut entirely, and the telegraph reserved for the army. It was Mareuil under a very different aspect.

Our soldiers told us they expected and hoped to remain still ten days or a fortnight at Mareuil, and they would certainly take care of the property. We begged them to use the dining-room when we had gone. As long as we were there they dined outside in the courtyard under the office windows; but it didn't disturb us at all as they dined much earlier than we did. Mme, G. and the chauffeur did their cooking, and I imagine the chauffeur did ours, too. They were all on the best of terms.

I wonder what the next turn of the wheel will bring, and when and how we shall see Mareuil again!

Tuesday, June 15th,
Rue de la Pompe.

I was busy in the morning, looking over and putting into boxes Willy's papers—finished with the *Congrès de Berlin* and the Coronation of the Emperor Alexander. It all seems another life so far away.

All the *Aisne* letters and newspapers were most interesting. I found some *sauf-conduits* (passes) from German officers, written in German, in 1870, and various letters about prisoners, wounded soldiers, and *francs-tireurs*, of whom the Germans were always afraid—some letters from mayors and farmers, all about Bourneville, from where W. had sent soldiers to join Bourbaki's army.

I have put all the papers of that time together, and when the war is over and Francis comes bade, we will arrange a book with the reminiscences of the father and the son, of the two wars.

It is warm this evening. C. and I sat in the small salon with open windows and no lights, trying to make some sort of plans for the summer. We give up this apartment on the 15th, and are literally *dans la rue*. The doctor says we mustn't establish ourselves at Mareuil; there are so many dead men and horses buried near us, in the fields, that it would not be possible. We must let a winter and cold weather pass before settling there again.

The street is perfectly quiet and empty; we might be in any small provincial town—only the searchlights from the Tour Eiffel sweep over it from time to time.

Wednesday, June 26th, '15.

Many soldiers came to be dressed before going back, and some of them brought wives and children; but the greater part of them were from the *pays évacués*, hadn't heard anything of their families since the beginning of the war, in August. It is very difficult to get any news from the departments that are occupied by the Germans.

We had one or two people to dinner. Dr. and Mrs. Watson who have been untiring in their work and sympathy for the fighting nations, Mr. H., the novelist, and Comte H. de P. The last two men stayed on a little while, talking after the others left.

Mr. Herrick was just from Venice; said the enthusiasm there when war was declared and the troops left was extraordinary, and the old hatred of the Austrians flared out like fire. He was much interested, too, in all Portes told him of the feeling in the country, in France, which so few foreigners ever get really to know—that curious, respectful intimacy that exists in the country, between the *grand seigneur*, the owner of the *château*, and the village people, the butcher, the farmer, the *cantonnier*, all with their opinions, and all delighted to talk politics and agriculture with the *chatelaine*.

Thursday, June 17th

Another lovely summer day. H. and I went late to the Bois; had tea at the Châlet des Gauffres, close to Paillard's. It was lovely sitting there under the shade of the big trees, but so quiet and empty. One would almost forget the war except that every now and then a wounded soldier would pass, sometimes head bandaged and arm in a sling, and often a poor fellow limping along on crutches, the trouser hanging loose from the knee, a nurse in uniform walking with him. Everybody had a "*Bon jour, mon ami!*" for the soldiers, and they seemed pleased at the sympathy. Mme. de G. and Bella V. dined, and Bella was most interesting. She had been to Nancy and Lunéville to see her husband, who commands a cavalry regiment in those regions.

It was the first time she had seen any of the horrors of war, as she was in England when the war broke out, and couldn't get back to her home in Cambrai, which is occupied by the Germans. She was horror-stricken at the sights—ruined villages—nothing but heaps of ashes—desolated fields, with every now and then a small mound and a rustic cross of sticks, showing somebody was buried there; one or two *châteaux* completely destroyed, no roof, no windows, nothing but the four walls standing, and great holes in them. The I.'s have lost everything—all the inside of their beautiful old *château* burned, and everything of value taken away—accumulations of centuries, pictures, tapestries, books, nothing left. I wonder how many more will be in the same condition before the end of the war. The Germans will certainly burn and plunder all the country behind them when they begin their retreat—when! . . .

Saturday, June 19th.

We have been very much taken up with patterns of masks at the *ouvroir* today. Something must be found to protect the soldiers from the terrible asphyxiating gas used by the Germans. The nurses who have taken care of some of the poor fellows who were caught in those vapours, said it was awful to see them gasping and choking their lives away. Our doctor says *we* ought to have masks. If there should be a great Zeppelin raid with poisoned bombs, and our windows got broken, we should certainly need masks to protect ourselves. I wonder if we would ever put them on. I don't think there is much danger for us *au 1ᵉʳ*, but the maids on the sixth floor would feel happier—so we will procure them for all the household.

Today has been a day of rumours, street rumours, which all the maids hear and believe. The *métro* (underground railway)—a tunnel pierced through from Soissons to Paris—Paris blown up! I think there should be a severe punishment for the spreading of such reports. Some people are easily frightened, and a panic in the civil population might have had a bad effect at the front.

I don't like the Zeppelin alarms myself, the *pompiers* dashing through the streets with that sinister "*garde à vous*," gets on my nerves.

Monday, June 21st, 1915.

I went with Anne B. this afternoon to help her tea at the American Ambulance. Among the many good things the Americans have done since the war broke out, is their voluntary service at the Ambulance, not only as nurses—many women can't nurse, have no vocation, and are not young enough, nor strong enough—but in many other departments: bandage-room, lingerie, etc Every afternoon from 3 to 5 there is a tea provided by American ladies for all the *employés* of the Ambulance—nurses, doctors, orderlies, chauffeurs, boy scouts. The ladies serve the tea themselves, and it is no *sinecure*, as everybody takes two cups of tea, some three. There are cakes and buns unlimited.

It was interesting to see the different types of nurses, some ladies, some professionals, of every age and nationality, though, of course, most of them are Americans. Some of the young ones (and very young some of them were), looked very nice in their short skirts, long, white blouse *d'infirmière,* and a pretty little cap of tulle or muslin on their heads; some middle-aged, serious-looking women, simply dressed in black or dark blue with the white apron, who were extremely glad to have a cup of tea, looked like good, steady workers. It was amusing to see tall, broad-shouldered chauffeurs asking for tea not too strong. One young fellow asked to have his very strong. I said to him: "It is very bad for your nerves to drink such strong tea."

"I've done it for over twenty-eight years, *Madame*, and it has done me no harm yet."

We talked a little (he was English), and he told me he was the eldest of six brothers, all soldiers at the front.

"How old is the youngest?"

"Just eighteen, *Madame*."

"It was wicked to let him go—a child!"

"Couldn't keep him, *Madame*; all his friends went!"

He had just come back from the front where he had spent twenty-four hours with four of his brothers, and they had been photographed in the trenches.

"Have you got a father or mother in England to send them the picture?"

"Oh, yes, *Madame*; they have got the picture of the five of us, all well."

Thursday, June 24th.

It is very warm. Agnes Welsh and I went to the concert for the English Catholic church of St. Joseph. It was well done: girl and boy scouts sold programmes, and made a background with the flags of the Allies, when all their national airs were sung. An Englishman with a pretty voice sang "God Save the King." He sang two verses, then requested the public to sing the last one with him, and very well it sounded—ever one singing, including some wounded soldiers, French and British, of whom there were a good many in the *salle*. They ended by the "*Marseillaise*," very well sung by Mme. H. of the Opéra; and then, too, all the public joined in at the last verse, and the enthusiasm was frantic.

The "Star-Spangled Banner," under the heading of "National Airs of the Allies," was also very well sung by Miss M. (Let us hope it is a good presage, and that the sympathies of the United States are with the Allies, *en attendant* something more tangible.)

Saturday, June 26th, '15.

It was lovely this afternoon, though warm; and H. and I went across the Champs Elysées to have tea at Laurent's. Charlotte and Frank met us, and we had a pleasant hour sitting under the trees. It was quite a new aspect of the well-known *café* to me. I have lunched and dined there so often in the old days. I remember a dinner there only last June, the garden filled with pretty women, very much dressed or undressed, in that extraordinary fashion of last year, just before the war, when all the women wore transparent, clinging garments—*Tziganes* playing, *jeunesse dorée* smoking expensive cigars and discussing the winner of the Grand Prix. Paris at its gayest at the end of a brilliant season. All those men have gone now, some in the ranks as simple privates, facing the awful days in the trenches, and all sorts of privations, without a murmur. Many have fallen, many come back crippled for life, and many more must fall before this awful war is over!

There were few people in the garden—women and children—some nurses in their uniform, with soldiers and officers, all taking tea.

We asked a young officer, evidently on the staff, if the news, was good (there is so much camaraderie now, everybody speaks to everybody). "*Mais oui, Madame, nous les repoussons lentement, bien lentement, mais ils reculent!*"

Sunday, June 27th, '15.

Again a lovely summer day. I met Comtesse de Franqueville (*née* Lady Sophia Palmer) coming out of the English church, and we walked home together. She was funny over her own people; says the English are just waking up to facts after eleven months of war, and realising that they have a terrible fight before them, and a cruel, vindictive enemy who must be crushed. She also said all her people couldn't say enough about the French, not only of their fighting qualities (they are a fighting race), but of their quiet, steady determination to go on to the bitter end.

Monday, June 28th,
Rue de la Pompe.

Anything so perfectly uncomfortable as my apartment can't be imagined. One *salon* is crammed with furniture, chairs standing on tables—trunks and boxes everywhere; the large salon and the smoking-room filled with garments, blankets, etc., for the refugees.

Charlotte has done very well with the *ouvioir pour la vallée de l'Aisne*. People have sent most generous contributions from England and America, and the ladies themselves have made a great many things. The young women of the U. S. Embassy have worked with her, and they have a very good collection of clothes, from babies' shirts to men's waistcoats and trousers, also sheets and blankets. She has filled several strong linen bags, also made at the *ouvroir*, with clothes, and is sending off a large *envoi* to the bishop of Soissons, who has made an appeal for help for the unfortunate peasants in his *diocèse*, where hundreds of villages have disappeared entirely, nothing left but a black, charred plain.

The bishop remained at Soissons through many bombardments, living in a cellar with his parishioners. He only came away when the bombardment ceased a little, as he felt he could do more for his people if he could move about and tell of their wretched situation.

July to December 1915

Friday, July 2nd, 1915.

It was very warm this morning. I lunched with Mme. de G. and Bella; Arthur and Charlotte were there. Arthur was very interesting, telling us about his *usines* (factories). He was asked to remain at his place. (He had a brother, brother-in-law, a nephew, and three cousins at the front—five Waddingtons "*sous le drapeau*") and keep his factories going to make as much material as he could for the army. But how? with whom? All his best workmen had gone to the front. It is in such cases that one realises what mobilisation means in France—all the nation in arms. He decided to risk it with some of the old workmen and women, and is doing very well, the women working perfectly.

The women have been up to the mark everywhere, working in the fields, driving cabs and ambulances, and now there are several woman conductors on the big tramways. They look very well in a long, black blouse, which completely covers their dresses, the regulation *sacoche* (black leather bag) slung over the shoulder, with a leather strap, and a *bonnet de police* on their heads.

The other day, when I was going by the tram to the Rue de la Pompe, a man in the tram was very rude to the woman conductor, who was young, evidently quite new to her work, and who wasn't quite sure of the stops at the street corners. He spoke very roughly and rather jostled her, so that she nearly fell out of the car. The men in the train remonstrated vigorously, and the man had to get out.

July 4th.

A very hot day. C. and I and the boys went up to the Bois to lunch at the "Racing Club" with the M.'s. There were not many people; the breakfast good, though the service was slow. There were only two waiters for about half a dozen tables. We had ours outside, under the trees, and were quite cool and comfortable. The club is in the middle of the Bois, quite shut in by big trees. No one was playing tennis except some Japanese, who were playing extremely well, as they do everything. They were correctly dressed in white flannels, used all the English terms, but looked perfectly exotic. It was curious to see their yellow faces, with keen, narrow eyes and yellow hands coming out of the white flannel shirt.

We had the papers, but they are not interesting, the war news very brief, each day's *communiqué* exactly like its predecessor, and will be, I suppose, until some great battle or the defection of one of the Middle Empires gives a real result.

Friday, July 9th.

Charlotte took the little gold she still had to the *Banque de France* this morning. The country has called upon everyone to take their gold to the bank, where it will be exchanged for notes. We hadn't much, as we had given all ours to Francis. In the beginning of the war people said all the men must have gold on them, as in case they were made prisoners, the gold would be useful; so they all had *louis* sewn in a belt, which they always wear. Now they say just the contrary, that they must have no gold, and as little money as possible, as the Germans take everything. One didn't realise until the war had really tasted some time, what a large part lying and stealing play in the Teuton's idea of a glorious and wonderful war.

C. said it was most interesting at the bank. Quantities of people, a great many *guichets* open, and everything done quickly and with the greatest order. One man next to her, brought a little chamois bag, out of which he shook ten thousand *francs* in gold. Next to him was a boy with a ten-*franc* gold piece—his last *étrenne* (New Year's gift). A great many women bringing twenty to forty *francs*. Everybody received notes in exchange and a ticket:

Banque de France
Versement pour la Défense Nationale
La Banque de France constate que Madame Waddington a versé ce jour en or, la somme de . . . . en échange de billets de banque. Le 12 juillet 1915.

We will keep the ticket as a souvenir of the war.

Saturday, July 10th, '15.

A nice-looking young Belgian officer came to see me this morning, to collect some money which friends in America had sent me for an Englishman who is organising a field-kitchen at the Belgian front. He says what America has done in Belgium is superb. Thousands of people would have starved to death if America hadn't come to the front so liberally. She is now extending her work, to the north of France, where the misery is appalling.

Charlotte and I did some shopping for Francis in the afternoon. He asked for a big cake, *iced*, for their 14th July banquet, to be sent to a Champagne merchant in whose house they are living, and who was going down to Rheims. We made him a fine *paquet* of cakes, cigars, bonbons, jam, etc. They are so pleased at the front to have a few *douceurs*.

As we had gone to Colombin's for the cakes, we stayed to tea. I hadn't been there since last summer. There were a few people, among others Mrs. Bacon, whom I was delighted to see again; everyone liked them so much when they were at the embassy here.

Tuesday, July 13th.

It has poured, a regular downfall all day, but we are all delighted as the country was drying up for want of rain. When I was starting to meet Bessie Talleyrand, with whom I had made an appointment to go to go to the Italian Hospital, H. said: "I suppose you will take your waterproof?" I wished I could, but some German *frau* is probably walking about very happily in it, as all the cloaks and rugs that were in the hall at Mareuil were stolen.

I found Bessie at the Gate des Invalides, Josephine with her, just arrived from Rome. Both her sons are at the front with the Italian Army, and she has passed her examination as nurse, and is enrolled at the Italian Red Cross, but there are no wounded yet in Rome, so she asked for a week's leave to come up and see us all here.

We found Palma, Princess di Poggio, Theresa, Bessie and daughter, Comtesse Siméon, at the hospital, which is very well arranged—large, clean rooms opening on a garden. The men looked well cared for and as comfortable as they could be. One poor young fellow, with a refined artist's face, a sculptor, had his leg off. Bessie had arranged to give him an artificial leg, one of the good ones, light and articulated, and he was so grateful

He and two others were in the same room, all moving about convalescent. Two had been at the Battle of the Marne, and couldn't say enough about General Maunoury, who was in command.

My nephew, a colonel of dragoons, said the other day the Battle of the Marne was a miracle, ... a miracle that saved Paris.

We went all over the hospital, ending at the two upper floors which the Duchesse de C. directs and runs entirely at her own expense. The rooms are quite beautiful, high and light and white; not a hospital smell of any kind, and even on this dismal afternoon they looked bright. Eight or ten men, all convalescent (one with his left arm amputated), were sitting at a table in the big window at one end of the gallery—an *infirmière*—and M. C, who is devoted and so kind to the men, teaching them to make artificial flowers out of *mie de pain* (bread-crumb). The *infirmière*, who turned out to be Mme. Boni, the famous *danseuse* from the Opéra (Italian-born), was dressing them, and talking so easily and nicely to the men. It seems they all adore her, and sometimes she dances for them.

It is curious how all professions, dancers, singers, lecturers, find work among the soldiers.

We had tea in the officers' and *infirmières'* dining-room—no one there but ourselves.

Wednesday, July 14th.

Such a quiet *fête*; no illuminations, no flags, no dancing in the streets at the principal *carrefours*. There was quite a display of military. To mark the day in some way, they had transported the body of Rouget de Lisle (author of *La Marseillaise*) to the Invalides. A fine regiment of *cuirassiers* passed and were wildly cheered by the crowd. Some of the women saluted the flag by the military salute. It looked rather pretty. It is difficult for the *infirmières* to return the salute. All the officers and soldiers salute an *infirmière* in Red Cross uniform, and I think it would be pretty if all the women could answer in the same way.

A great many wounded soldiers were walking about the Champs Elysées, and many people gave them cigarettes and tobacco. I was so sorry I hadn't any with me. One hardly likes to give money.

Friday.

I was at the *ouvroir* all the afternoon. Professor Hall with his wife and daughter came in. They are so interested in France and the war, and appreciate so thoroughly how splendidly France has come out since the war (nearly a year now) that it is a pleasure to see them.

Saturday, July 17th, '15.

I had a nice afternoon at Versailles. C. met me at the station. We went first to see the rooms at the *hôtel*, which are charming, large and airy, giving on the *Boulevard de la Reine.* Then we found the boys in the park and sat there for some time. It rained at intervals, little summer showers, but one is completely sheltered under the big trees or little recesses cut out in the high, stiff box-hedges. Soldiers in uniform were doing the gardening, clipping, watering, etc. We had tea at "At Home," one of the numerous new tea places on the *place d'Armes,* which have developed since two or three years. Mrs. Bliss and Mrs. Hall came in. They had been to see a colony of French and Belgian children, orphans. It seems that there are thirty or forty babies of two years of whom no one—not even the two Belgian nuns who brought them—knows anything—neither their names nor parents. They were found in *cellars* with a lot of miserable children.

Sunday.

I went to the Gare du Nord this morning to send off some packages to Soissons, and to ask about some that had been announced to me from England. (They, of course, hadn't come. I wonder who gets all the packages that I don't.)

I wanted, too, to see the *cantine* where Charlotte works. She was just starting for the English train. She is one of the *quêteuses,* which is rather hard work, as they go into all the carriages, just a few minutes before the train starts, and have to scramble out in a hurry when they are told. Occasionally the ladies don't get off in time, and are carried off to the next station.

She looked very nice in her white dress and *coiffe,* and absurdly young. She has had some funny experiences. She heard two young men saying in English: "We must give ten *francs* to that pretty girl," and when she thanked them in English, they were much surprised. "Oh, we didn't know you were English," and much more, when she said: "I am not English, I am French!"

She generally gets a very good *collecte.*

I went over the *cantine* with her afterward, which is very well arranged. Two long wooden tables spotlessly clean—and an excellent meal—all served by ladies, who wipe the table each time a plate or dish that has been used is taken off . At the end of the hall there are about fifty beds, where the poor men who are too ill or too tired to go on can rest.

I talked to some of the men. As a rule they looked well. Almost all, as they went out, put a *sou* in the box that was at the door, marked: "*Pour les repas du soldat.*" I said to our men: "*C'est bien ça?*"

147

"Oh, yes, *Madame*, we have had a good meal; we must leave something for our comrades who, perhaps, will need it more."

Versailles, Monday, July 19th.

I came out yesterday for Frank's birthday. We spent all the afternoon in the park, down by the canal, where there is a very good little restaurant. We brought out the birthday cake, which the *pâtissière* explained she could not make as she would like, with his name and age in beautiful coloured letters on the white icing—as she was so short of hands. But she did put a bow of ribbon and a flower.

There were a great many people at the restaurant, French and British officers with pretty, well-dressed women under the red umbrellas which made charming Little niches under the trees.

There were boats of every description on the canal, and autos waiting on the road. All the warriors are enjoying themselves immensely. We stayed in the park until 7 o'clock. There was nothing but uniforms to be seen. The soldiers come out from 6 to 8, and every one had a girl hanging on his arm. They foretell an extraordinary increase of population. I would certainly prefer English babies to German, if we are to have a great infusion of foreign blood.

The *château* looked beautiful as we walked up to the terrace, all its great *façade* of windows a blaze of light from the setting sun; and in the distance, over the trees and canal, that soft blue mist that one sees so often in Versailles at the end of the day.

As it was a birthday we made a great exception and dined at the Reservoirs. There were a good many people, pretty women and officers dining. We walked back to our Hôtel Vatel, and it rather reminded me of Marienbad—people dining outside at all the *cafés*, and women walking about alone, quite independent.

It is C's *ouvroir* day. I am sorry to leave. It was so cool and fresh this morning, and so resting to the eyes after the pavement of Paris. Our rooms are on the third floor, and we look straight into the big trees of the *boulevard de la Reine*.

Thursday, July 29th.

I went with Agnes Welsh this morning to see Charlotte at the *cantine* of the Gare du Nord. Mr. Washburn met us there. He is very keen about everything connected with the war, and wants to see everything and help where he can.

There were a great many people on the *quais*, and I left Agnes to look for Charlotte while I went to the *cantine* to see if she was there.

She wasn't. The old man who presides told me she was making her *quête*. The room was full of soldiers; every table taken, and there were a great many waiting outside—all their hats and rifles piled up, and on each knapsack a big loaf of *pain du soldat*—such nice-looking rye bread, *pain de seigle*, they call it here. I went back to the *quai*, where I found Charlotte. She was on the best of terms with all the railway officials, who were all smiling at her. She still had two more trains to make, and we waited on the *quai*.

The crowd was interesting, quantities of soldiers of all kinds—*permissionnaires*, who were met and embraced by wives, mothers, and sisters; squads of fresh young men starting off to the front, and melancholy groups of one-armed, one-legged men, cheerful in spite of their mutilation, and so proud still of the uniform. When they are finally out of the hospitals and unfit for active service, they must, of course, give up the uniform, which is a great blow to them. Even those who have only worn it a few months, who were wounded early, hold to their *pantalon rouge*. I think the government must give a badge or medal of some kind to the men who were wounded in the war.

When C. had finished, we went back to the *cantine*, and Agnes gave medals and tobacco to the soldiers. There was an interesting man there, just from Arras, with one shoulder badly hurt. He had seen horrors. Germans packed into a Red Cross ambulance, calling for help. When the French soldiers went forward to open the door, a *mitrailleuse* hidden inside, mowed them down like grass.

They give the men an excellent meal: soup, very good, a dish of meat and vegetables, cheese, fruit, coffee, and wine or beer.

Charlotte came back to breakfast and went off immediately to Versailles.

August 5th.

We are having beautiful summer days, and usually at this season are established either at the seashore or else at one of our favourite summer resorts, at Marienbad—but this year it is difficult to know where to go. All the hotels at the seaside are used as military ambulances, or else closed altogether, and besides we are all so busy that it doesn't seem right to leave Paris.

It isn't very warm. I go up to the Bois sometimes in the morning. It is empty, a few old gentlemen sitting on the benches reading the papers—nurses and children—not many.

Warsaw has fallen, but I don't think it is a very brilliant victory for the Germans. The Russians stripped the town of everything before leaving, and retreated in perfect order. I fancy we shall hear no more of the grand triumphal entrance the *Kaiser* was to make with the empress, who was said to be waiting at Hindenburg's headquarters, with splendid robes and jewels for the *grande rentrée*. . . . .

Monday, August 9th.

It has been grey and warm. I went to the *cantine* of the Gare St. Lazare after dinner to get Charlotte who was *de service* there—had been there since 4 o'clock. Both she and Mme. d'A., who was working with her, seemed rather exhausted with the heat and fatigue. However, both ladies were carrying about trays with bowls of hot *bouillon*, and huge pieces of bread and sausage.

They don't give an entire hot meal at the *cantine* after 7.30 (dinner), but they have hot bouillon, coffee, bread, cheese and cold meat at night. The military trains arrive at all hours and always after the appointed time.

There were quite a number of soldiers; some of them looked too tired to eat. Two young ones with fever could hardly stand. They were given beds to have a good rest for their early start the next morning.

They have ten beds and a bath in a room alongside of the dining-room. An *infirmière* is always there, day and night. The *cantine* is supported by the quotes (collections) the ladies make in the trains. They go in couples to all the outgoing trains, at the last moment, when the passengers are all seated. Madeleine got twenty *francs* the other day from a lady in the English train, who was very frightened and nervous about the crossing, and hoped the *louis* would bring her good luck with all the mines and submarines.

It certainly isn't a pleasant moment to cross the Channel with the danger of being sunk—and always the interminable waits at the *douane* and passport *bureaux*.

All the service at the *cantine* is voluntary. No one is paid except the cook and a boy who washes the dishes. They give a very good meal—soup; meat, vegetables, cheese, as much bread as they like, and beer, wine, or coffee—whichever they prefer, all *gratis*, of course. The meals cost the *cantine* fifty *centimes* a head. I can't imagine how they can do it so cheaply, but Mme. de B., who runs it, is an excellent manager. She is there every day, sometimes twice a day.

The *quête* entirely covers the expenses, in fact more than covers them, as they have a fair sum in reserve.

I stood at the door some little time, watching the crowd of soldiers of all arms, ages, and colours. There were some Senegalese, black as ink, and yellow Moroccans who passed. Many looked wistfully at the open door and the two long tables filled with soldiers, and all were told to come in. They deposited their kits outside, waiting their turn and were so pleased to talk a little and smoke a cigarette. I had a provision with me. They respond instantly to any mark of interest. Even the black *Sénégalais* who couldn't speak French, broke into a broad smile when C. appeared in her *infirmière* dress, and said: "*Merci, ma soeur; moi manger!*" So she installed him at one of the tables and brought him his soup.

We came away about 10.30; soldiers were still coming. The *infirmière* in the medical room and her two young fellows were asleep couldn't eat anything, but they would have a good breakfast in the morning.

I left C. at her hotel, where she had some difficulty in getting in. The staff of servants is considerably reduced. The hall porter is a child twelve years old, who naturally was fast asleep in a big chair, and didn't hear anything.

Saturday, August 14th.

I went down again to Mareuil for twenty-four hours on Thursday. We still have French soldiers in the house, some of the officers very exacting; and Mme. G. felt unable to cope with them.

It was dark when we arrived, at 9 o'clock, and we had to grope our way across the track and into the little *salle*, where everyone was obliged to show their *sauf-conduits*; eight or ten unfortunate people were not *en règle*, hadn't the necessary papers and were sadly preparing to spend the night at the station in the dark. One woman, well dressed and speaking in an educated voice, came to ask me if I was also kept, and did I know Mareuil; was there any hotel or *auberge* of any kind where she could go for the night. Mme. G., who had come to meet us with her lantern, said she thought there were good clean rooms at the only hotel in the village.

We all walked off together in the dark, and the poor woman looked so forlorn, I told her she had much better stop at my house. I could give her a bed and a meal. She was very shy, and when I named myself, that seemed to make matters worse. She couldn't think of intruding. I insisted a little, but she evidently couldn't make up her mind to come. I couldn't see her very well in the dark, but I think she was a *boutiquière*

151

of a good class, or the wife of a small farmer. Her voice and language were perfectly good, like so many women of that class, who express themselves well and have very good manners.

One of the railway men was walking behind us, so I told him to take the lady to the hotel and see that she got a good room. We parted at our gate. I told her if she couldn't find a decent room, to come back, but she didn't, and I suppose found what she wanted,

I found no officers at the house except a *corporal de gendarmerie* who is always there, and whom we are glad to have, as it is a certain protection.

Mme. G. was very eloquent over her last band of soldiers: the officer most disagreeable, wanting to make various changes in the room— among other things, to knock down a *cloison* (partition). When she protested, he answered: "*Cest la guerre! Mme. Waddington a bien donné sa maison aux Allemands; elle ne peut pas la refuser aux Français!*" "*Donné*" is perhaps not exactly the term to use, as the Germans took forcible possession of an empty house.

Naturally, I shouldn't dream of refusing the house to French soldiers, and wouldn't want to!

Francis is very comfortably lodged in a small *château* with a good library and plenty of books, and a large airy room.

However, that unwelcome officer didn't stay very long, though he told Mme. G. the place suited him, and he should stay a month; but he was sent on after two or three days.

The *curé* came to dinner, and we sat out afterward. I tried not to see the potatoes and only smell the roses, which are beautiful. I have never seen them so lovely, climbing ones, of course. The whole side of the house is covered with such lovely white roses, but only the climbers. All the flower-beds were trampled over by the German horses, also the herbaceous border around the boys' lawn.

I told Mme. G. to lock certain rooms, and left a note for the mayor, who didn't come to see me, asking him to insist upon the soldiers occupying only the rooms I indicated in the old house.

We heard the cannon distinctly all the afternoon. The *curé* says the passage of the troops is awfully hard on the poor people, as they carry off everything—blankets, mattresses, etc. Of course one can understand the poor fellows, cold and wet, not being able to resist taking a blanket when they can get one. And I imagine all soldiers do the same, but it is awfully hard on the village people, who have not yet replaced all the Germans took. Many of them are still sleeping on straw, covered with sacks.

He says, too, that the troops of refugees are melancholy. The big *salle* at the *mairie* is never empty. They put down fresh straw every day, and the village takes bread and milk to the unfortunate women and children, who rest a day or two, then start off on their long, weary tramp to find homes that have ceased to exist.

Paris, August 18th (Wednesday).

I was at the *ouvroir* early, then stopped to see Charlotte, who was starting for the Gare de l'Est with the boys and a camp-stool, to meet Francis. The train was due at 6, but there was sure to be a delay. She had already been there Tuesday, thinking he might perhaps come, and said it was interesting to see the long file of women—mothers, wives, and children, waiting for their men. The line stretched out nearly across the great courtyard; some had brought camp-stools, but most of them sat on the ground. She said it was pretty to see how each *permissionnaire* was welcomed as he arrived, his whole family embracing him, children clinging to his coat-tails, and carrying his bag.

Our soldier got here about 8.30, looking very well and gay, so pleased to be with us all again.

Mme. Sallandrouze and Madeleine dined, and we were a very happy family party.

He wears his uniform very well, quite as if he had been accustomed to it all his life. The boys couldn't keep off of him. They all went off early, as he had had a long night's journey. He stays until next Wednesday, a short week; but one is grateful for very small favours in wartime, and it is everything to have him back, well and gay, and confident that things are going well with us.

Thursday, August 29th, '15.

We all lunched with Mme. Sallandrouze, who was delighted to have her two military *ménages*, as the R.'s are here too. He is on sick leave, having had trouble with his heart. Both men were most cheerful, telling us all sorts of experiences.

Francis went off directly after luncheon with Charlotte, to order himself shirts and a new tunic. I insisted on the whole party coming to have tea with me at Laurent's in the Champs Elysées.

I met Norah G., who wanted very much to see Francis, and told her to come too, and we had a very pleasant afternoon, sitting under the trees—the two men making quite a pretty bit of colour in their *bleu horizon*. Every *garçon* in the place was around our table, fascinated by the stories both men were telling.

Francis, Charlotte and the boys dined with us, and he played a little after dinner. It seemed quite the old times, except for the talk and the change in him. He has grown older, graver, with a curious steady look in his eyes. The conversation was exclusively war. He said such curious things happened with so many men of all kinds serving in the ranks, particularly in the Territorials. His *commandant* (major) said to him one day that he had just done such a stupid thing. He was superintending the unloading of a camion filled with heavy rough planks. He thought some of the soldiers were slow, lazy, and called out to them rather sharply: "*Voyons, voyons, il faut que cela finisse; un peu plus d'énergie!*" Still there were one or two who seemed awkward, didn't know how to handle the heavy planks, one particularly, a man about thirty-five years old. Finally he apostrophised him directly, saying: "Don't you know how to work? You look strong enough! What did you do before the war?"

"*Mon Commandant*, I was *professeur au Collège de France.*"

One of Francis' comrades, who ranks him, is the son of a well-known big Paris grocer, like Potin—a very nice fellow. They were very good friends. One day he came in looking rather glum, didn't seem disposed to talk. Francis couldn't understand what the matter was. At last the young fellow said: "I hear you are the cousin of the smart colonel of *cuirassiers* who was stationed here, with the same name."

"Yes, he is my first cousin."

"Oh, I hear, too, that you are the son of an ambassador!"

"Yes, my father was ten years ambassador in London."

Still silence; then:

"I suppose that after the war you won't want to see me anymore; we shall never meet; you won't know me."

"That is not at all nice of you to say. I shall always be delighted to see you, and after the war is over, if we both come out of it, I hope you will come to see me often, and we will talk over war-times and life in the trenches, and all the days of close *camaraderie* we spent together." He was rather mollified, but it was some time before he could quite get back to the old footing.

Sunday, August 22nd, '15.

Today was lovely, a bright sun, but cool. Francis, Charlotte, and the Tiffanys dined. Francis had been to the club where his friends (the old gentlemen) were delighted to see him. There are no young ones left in town, and the *embusqués* who work at the *ministères* or *etat-major* don't show themselves at the dub.

We had very good champagne which Francis' friends had sent for him to drink while he was *en permission*. When he is at Rheims he lives with these Champagne people, who are devoted to him. *Madame*, who has had six sons, took care of him when he was ill.

We drank "*France, et les Allie*s" standing, and sang all the national airs after dinner. We tried to be gay, but with such heavy hearts, not daring to face the future.

Tuesday, August 24th, '15.

It has been warm all day. Francis came up to Charlotte's *ouvroir* for the *vallée de l'Aisne*. He was much pleased at the way she had managed the thing, and decidedly impressed with all the trunks and wardrobes full of clothes.

The Welshes came to dinner for his last evening and were so interested in all he told them. The two boys are on his back all day, and Charlotte looks radiant, her eyes like stars.

Wednesday, August 25th, '15.

I went to the hotel before breakfast to see if Francis had all he wanted, and to decide upon a small apartment for Charlotte, and another school for the boys. They came to breakfast, then went off for last commissions. Everybody gave him things—a pipe, cigars, two bottles of old brandy, books, Kodak. He went off at 5. Charlotte went with him to the station. I took the boys for a turn in the Bois. They were rather tearful when he bade them goodbye and told them they were big boys now, and must take care of their mother and "Danny." For me there was nothing more to do, only a kiss and "God bless you, Mother!" and he was gone. The partings are hard when the last moment really comes.

Saturday, August 28th, '15.

Charlotte said that the scene at the Gare de l'Est on Wednesday night, when Francis left, was wonderful. Hundreds of women and children saying goodbye to their sons and husbands, and all so courageous, smiling, and making all sorts of plans for *après la guerre*; not a tear, as long as the train was there. When it moved off, the soldiers cheering and singing, and all the people on the *quais* cheering, some of them broke down.

I always think of the poor little girl in the first days of the mobilisation, trying to be brave, when the *gars* told her not to cry: "*Nous reviendrons!*"—looking up at me through her tears: "*Tous ne reviendront pas, Madame!*"

We are all delighted with the Russian naval victory at Riga; it seems as if the tide was turning. The Germans may find a winter campaign in Russia as fatal as Napoleon did.

We have just heard of d'Agoult's death—such a charming fellow. He was for some time naval *attaché* at London with us, and we liked him and his wife both so much. They have had so much trouble, have lost three sons.

Friday, September 3rd, '15.

A letter from Francis today, saying the order has come from General Headquarters for him to pass his examination of interpreter at last; that looks as if he would be named. He is so anxious for it, is tired of carrying despatches. I wonder where he will go.

It has been very cool today. Some people had fires.

Saturday, September 4th '15.

It is still cold today. I went late to see Comtesse d'Agoult Poor thing, she looks miserable; heard the news from a friend of d'Agoult's, a naval officer sent from the *Ministère de la Marine*, to tell her. She thought he had come to see her about a bicycle, welcomed him most cheerfully until she saw his face. "*Madame*, I have not come to speak to you about the bicycle. I have bad news for you. M. d'Agoult is wounded, severely wounded."

She said his face told her the truth. She merely asked: "When was he killed? How?"

"By a shell. He died in two hours; never regained consciousness."

It was a melancholy visit. We went back to the old days when he was naval *attaché* in London, and we were all so fond of him. They had a fine little family, three boys and one girl. All the boys are dead, and now he, the last of his name. He needn't have gone to the front, was over fifty; but he said he had no sons to fight for France; he must go himself.

As I was walking across the bridge I met Mrs. Watson, who picked me up and we went for a turn to the lakes. The Bois was almost deserted; but the Champs *Elysées* looked fairly alive with some lights in the avenue and the various hospitals.

I hope Charlotte and the boys are enjoying the seashore. The children have been so long in Paris and were pining for a beach where they could run all day, and not be told all the time not to make a noise and break furniture and gallop over people's heads in a hotel. Town is no place for strong, cheerful boys, country-bred.

Sunday, September 5th.

A beautiful warm day. I went with Bessie to Bagatelle to see the Russian Field-Ambulance they have just sent to France, and which starts for the front tomorrow morning. It looked most complete—the operating-room on wheels. There were a great many people there, in fact all over the Bois, and uniforms and languages of every description.

Wednesday, September 8th.

The days are so exactly alike that one loses all count of time. Many of the Americans here are very hard on Wilson and the ridiculous position in which he has placed the country: "America, the laughing-stock of the world!" I should think D. must go (and Bernstorff long ago)! When one remembers how Sackville-West was given his passports for so much less important reasons!

Friday, September 10th.

Still lovely warm weather. We had a great many soldiers and soldiers' wives at the *ouvroir* today. Some of the women look so absolutely miserable All want work, but we can't give to all. Our funds are getting exhausted. The *ouvroir* has been working since the beginning of the war (August, 1914). People have been most generous. There was a magnificent *élan* at first, but of course no one thought the war would last so long. The *Kaiser* said he should sleep in Paris on the 21st August, 1914. Apparently he changed his mind!. . . .

Tuesday, September 14th.

There is no especial war news. The Russians seem doing better. We see a good many people at the *ouvroir*, but no one really knows anything of what is going on.

I have decided to go to Petites Dalles for ten days. Outrey will take me down. He told me I could not go with an ordinary *sauf-conduit*, as it was a watering-place on the coast, and the whole coast was infested with spies. I must have two witnesses to say they know all about me, and to certify that I was a respectable woman, not a femme *légère*! He could be one witness, and I asked my friend the *restaurateur* at the corner of the street to be the other. He looked so respectable and well-dressed when I picked him up at the *café*, and was beaming at the idea of testifying to the respectability of "*Son Excellence Madame l'Ambassadrice."* The *Commissaire de Police* knows me perfectly well, as I have to get a *saif-conduit* every time I go down to Mareuil. The officer looked at all my papers, then remarked: "*Madame*, you are not a Frenchwoman born?"

"*Monsieur*, you can see that on my *certificat de mariage.*"

"Were my American parents living?" Then: "How tall are you?"

"I should think you could see that as I am standing before you."

But it wasn't enough. I had to stand up under a measuring board (like a criminal), and he took down my exact height. It was really too stupid. But all French people love red tape, and the smaller officials revel in their authority.

My two witnesses were also subjected to a strict examination, though their papers were *en règle.*

I had an interesting visit after breakfast from a Chicago man, Mr. K., a friend of Ambassador Herrick, who gave him a letter to me. As it was my day at the *ouvroir*, I was obliged to go out at once, and suggested to him that he should come with me and see our work. He was interested in all he saw, and promised to try and help us when he got back to America. It was quite interesting to hear an impartial, intelligent American man discuss the war. Some of the Americans here, particularly the women, are quite hysterical when they talk about Wilson's policy, and war in the United States between Americans and Germans; they say they are ashamed of being Americans. He laughed at the idea of any revolution in America; said the Germans talked very sentimentally about their *Kaiser* and their "*Vaterland*," but that, if it came to the point, not one of them would leave their good solid business, bankers and brewers, and throw in their lot with Germany.

Paris Dalles, September 23rd.

We have had some lovely bright summer days in this pretty little Norman village. It consists of one street running down to the beach, a small stretch of *galets* (pebbles), very little sand, and shut in by high cliffs at each side. There are a few shops and houses in the street, but most people take one of the villas on the cliff, or else a little back in the country, which is lovely—broad roads with splendid old trees.

There is a hotel on the beach which has been turned into a hospital. No one in it now, but they are expecting wounded and refugees every day. The other hotel, where we are, is at a little distance from the beach, up a hill, has a nice terrace where we sit and have our coffee after lunch, and get a view of the sea.

It was curious to be in a place where there was no sign of war; no sick or wounded soldiers, no Red Cross flags anywhere, no nurses in uniform, no men except old ones, quantities of nurses and children. The only thing that made one think of war was the crowd of people (the whole village) waiting at the little fruit-stall for the papers, everybody talking to his neighbour and discussing the *communiqué*.

There is no especial news these days; the Russians have evacuated Vilna—always the same tactics—removing everything of value and retreating in good order.

Bulgaria is *inquiétante*; she is mobilising, and no one knows what that crafty Ferdinand means to do. It all seemed unreal when we were talking on the beach, watching the sun dip down into the sea, and the lovely sunset clouds that threw a soft, beautiful light over everything.

The weather got much cooler about the end of the month, and we were glad to leave. We were the only people left in the hotel. The big dining-room looked forlorn with no table but ours.

We had a beautiful day to leave—a big omnibus with three Norman posters with high red collars and bells came over from Ivetot to get us. We went through lovely country, sometimes passing *châteaux* with great wide avenues with the double border of trees one sees so often in Normandy; sometimes little farmhouses, with gardens and orchards, a few cows grazing placidly in the fields. Scarcely any horses and no men. Everywhere the women were working in the fields.

Our horses took us at a very good pace, trotted steadily up and down hill, so that we really made our journey quite rapidly. It was a pleasant change to be in a horse-vehicle, and not to dash through everything in clouds of dust in a motorcar.

At Ivetot there was a complete change. The little town and the station were filled with soldiers, "Tommies," most of them evidently fresh arrivals, their uniforms quite smart and new, showing no signs of campaign.

There were several pretty young English nurses, evidently on the best of terms with the warriors.

While we were waiting on the platform for the Paris Express, a train drew in with German prisoners. We saw the officers quite distinctly, in a lighted carriage, smoking and playing cards. The men were in luggage-trucks. No one said anything or made any hostile demonstrations of any kind—except a few of the soldier railway porters, who scowled (so did the Germans), and muttered "*Sales Boches!*" under their breath.

Sunday, October 3rd, 1915.

A lovely warm day. I walked up to the avenue Malakoff after lunch, to see Mme. de Laumont, whose husband and son were buried yesterday (at least the husband was); the boy, twenty-four, killed in action, was buried where he fell. They had got with difficulty a permission the son to come to Paris for forty-eight hours to go to his father's funeral. When the *estafette* arrived with the permission, the boy was killed. He wrote a charming letter to his sister, just before the attack, saying, "If this reaches you, I shall be dead. We attack tomorrow morning. I am in the first line," and telling her to do all she could for his mother and father. The father was already dead.

I didn't see Mme. de Laumont, but her mother, who adored her grandson. Mme. de Laumont had gone to see a friend, Mme. de P., whose son, eighteen years old, has also been killed. Is this cruel war going to take all our loved ones away?

We had a good many visitors at tea-time. No especial news; Russians holding on well.

Tuesday, October 5th, '15.

I had an interesting morning which changed my ideas a little. They revolve in a circle—the men at the front and the work of the *ouvroir*. I seem always to be calculating how many shirts, how many *caleçons*, two-thousand metres of flannel will make, and how and where to get the woollen stuffs. Everything has more than doubled in price, and besides, the government buys everything for the army.

I went with Mr. B., a charming American who knows Paris well (and all the rest of the world—has been everywhere), to see a little bit of old Paris. The *rue de l'Ancienne Comédie*, the famous Café Procope, where Voltaire, Mirabeau, and dozens of other well-known writers and *grands politiques* used to meet and discuss questions and proclaim theories which inflamed the minds of the young generation and upset the civilised world. We went into a little back room and saw the painted ceilings, and the Voltaire and Mirabeau tables. We really had a delightful hour in the past, standing under an archway where Danton, Marat, Desmoulins, and Charlotte Corday had passed, with hearts beating high with patriotism and ambition, scarcely realising the power that was in their hands.

We walked through the *cour de Rohan*, a beautiful little square, very old-fashioned court with wonderful doorways and iron gratings. One could hardly believe one was in modern Paris with the busy, crowded *boulevard St. Germain* five minutes off.

We lunched at the *Palais de Justice*. I was the only woman, and it was interesting to see all the *avocats* coming in with their gowns and square caps. The *café* was lower than the street, and we walked up the three broad worn steps that Marie Antoinette walked up to get into the fatal tumbrel that carried her to the scaffold. I don't know why, but the old, worn stone steps say so much to me. I seem to see the thousands of weary feet that have tramped over them.

Wednesday, October 6th.

I was at the *ouvroir* all the afternoon. We didn't have as many soldiers as usual, and only a few visitors. One lady had been to St. Sulpice, where there is an enormous colony of refugees, French and Belgian—all most comfortably installed. Where there are families, they have two rooms and can do their own cooking and washing. The nuns look after them and beg for clothes—no matter what kind; they can always disinfect and clean, mend and find good pieces in any quite worn garments. It seems that some of the children's frocks are a curiosity, all patchwork. They get a great deal as we all send them things that we can't use. I have had one or two cases of old clothes that I had unpacked in the courtyard, and even then the smell was something awful.

Mme. W. arrived there just as a large party was being sent off to the country. She said it was a wonderful sight. They were dressed evidently in all the second-hand garments that had been given to them. Some of the men had top hats and dress coats and redingotes of black broadcloth—poor things!

We are sending troops to Salonica, which seems rather hard with so many Germans still in France. It is extraordinary how the Balkan states embroil the whole of Europe.

Friday, October 8th.

We are all much delighted with the first result of the Allies' offensive, but a little nervous over Bulgaria. I wonder if Ferdinand really believes in Germany's promises and the readiness with which she disposes of other nations' property.

Sunday, October 10th.

Our visitors today were rather blue over the Bulgarian attitude. The Duc de L. and Sir H. L. very nervous, say there is no use of sending a small force . . . that was the mistake of the Dardanelles; and yet the Allies, if they mean to follow up their dash at the German trenches, can't weaken their front in France.

Monday, October 11th.

I lunched with Comtesse D. at Ritz, where there were quite a number of people. We heard of Casteya's death—severely wounded and died in the hospital—another of Francis' friends, one of those who danced at the house. He leaves a young wife and child.

The loss of *young* lives is something awful, and for what? There must come a heavy reckoning some day to the *Kaiser*, but that won't give us back all those who are gone!

After lunch we went to see the German cannon at the Invalides. There were quantities of people, many soldiers of all grades. To the uninitiated, one cannon looks very like another, but they all showed traces of battle. Some of the air-guns, with their muzzles pointed up in the clouds, were curious. What interested me much more than the cannon were the people looking at them. There was no boasting, no expressions of triumph, but a quiet steady look on all the faces. One felt the determination to go on to the end. "*Nous les aurons!*" I heard several men say.

Sunday, October 17th.

Everyone was much excited this afternoon over the Zeppelin raid in London. Mr. B. read us a letter from a friend who was coming out of a theatre, when one near was struck by a bomb. They had been warned at the Savoy Hotel, half an hour before the Zeppelin arrived, but didn't heed the warning, didn't think it was possible. A great deal of harm was done, quite two hundred people killed and wounded. No details have been in the papers.

It seems incredible that the British *avions* can't get at them. A strict guard is kept over Paris. Several Zeppelins have been announced, but so far none have come. It is much easier for them to get to London, as the Channel fog prevents their being seen.

October 19th.

I went to the atelier in the rue de Chateaubriand this afternoon, where our *Comité International de Pansements Chirurgicaux* is temporarily installed. Mr. W. was there, very busy unpacking cases, and making big parcels to be sent off to the hospitals. It is entirely an American work. All the *pansements*, blankets, old linen, etc., are sent direct from America. They send splendid things, which are most appreciated. All that I sent to some of my hospitals were very acceptable.

The Paris hospitals are well supplied, but those nearer the front—

even in big towns like Dunkerque and Calais—are in great need.

There is always friction between the *Croix Rouge* and the *autorités militaires*.

I went to see the Comte de B. afterward, who has come up ill from the country. He was so depressed, saw everything so dark, that I was quite unhappy. Not only the actual moment with this awful fighting going on, but the *après la guerre* France with no men left, no money, and no credit. Of course he criticised the government, and still more the diplomatists. (He is an ambassador's son.) They ought to have foreseen what was going to happen, and made suitable provision—as if anyone could foresee what that mad *Kaiser* was going to do.

Friday, October 22nd.

The Mygatts leave this morning for America, *via* Bordeaux. They are not at all nervous. I must say I should be, and would certainly not take a French or English steamer if I was obliged to go to America. I hope they will send a wireless as soon as they are out of the danger zone.

Several people came in to tea at the *ouvroir*—all much excited over the murder of Miss Cavell, the English nurse.[1] I wonder how even the Germans dared to cover themselves with such obloquy. The details are too awful. She behaved magnificently; knew all the time she was helping the men away that she was risking her life.

The Balkan news is bad. It doesn't look as if the Allies could arrive in time to save Servia. It is awful to think of our young men giving their blood and their lives for those savages. I am afraid our diplomacy has not been very brilliant in the Balkan negotiations. "Someone has blundered."

Sunday, October 24th.

Things don't look cheerful in the Balkans. Greece declines Britain's offer of Cyprus. I suppose she couldn't accept such a palpable bribe.

We had a nice letter from Francis, the first since several days. He was in the thick of the last offensive in Champagne; says the noise of the cannon and the quick-firing guns was awful. He had to *piloter des convois de munitions* in his brigade (show the way to munition-lorries), and was thanked by his colonel for his coolness and promptitude.

Their regiment lost a great many men, and a great many *hors de*

---

1. *Nurse Edith* Cavell: Two accounts of a notable British nurse of the First World War—*The Martyrdom of Nurse Cav*ell by William Thomson Hill & *With Edith Cavell in Belgium* by Jacqueline Van Til also published by Leonaur.

combat from the asphyxiating gases.

He writes at night, says:

> I am writing at the window. It is a beautiful moonlight night. The noise of the cannon has ceased for the present. We don't hear a sound except the rumble of the motor-ambulances bringing in the wounded; except for that and a few columns of smoke and sparks going up over Rheims, at which the enemy are still throwing incendiary bombs, we should never dream a war was going on.

> I suppose one gets accustomed to everything, and in a way we lead a normal life—eat, drink, and go out to see our friends. But at night, when the streets are perfectly dark, not a creature passing, no sound of life anywhere, a great sadness and terror of the future comes upon us.

Tuesday, October 26th, '15.

Today we have had a thick yellow fog. Shops and trams lighted, quite like London, except for the blacks. I walked over to the temporary installation of a new "Surgical Dressing Committee" in a rather dark, cold studio in the rue Chateaubriand. I found three or four of the ladies, Princesse R., Comtesse S., Mrs. P., working very hard, the rooms filled with cases, some of them not unpacked. The ladies were sitting on boxes and working at tables (a plank put across boxes) and looked very businesslike and very cold in their white *infirmière* blouses. There is a small stove, but it doesn't heat enough; the place is really not comfortable, and not nearly large enough for all the boxes that are arriving all the time from America.

Mr. W., our secretary, tells us many cases have arrived at Bordeaux. How long they will stay there I don't know. It seems that several consignments of cases and packages have crossed the Atlantic once or twice. Of course they are very short of hands at Bordeaux, and the unloading is a very long affair. When the vessel has to start back and not all the cases have been unloaded, they remain on board, go back to America, and hope for better luck next time.

The Clearing-House does very good work; and the government takes a great deal of trouble to see that the parcels are properly distributed.

I went late to tea with Mrs. P. to meet Mr. Powell, the war correspondent. I think his book. *Fighting in Flanders*,[2] the best of the quan-

---

2. *Fighting In Flanders* By E. Alexander Powell also published by Leonaur.

tity of war books that have been written. It is so natural and tells all his adventures so simply and frankly. He has been everywhere and seen everything since the beginning of the war. It was most interesting to listen to him. Of course his point of view was absolutely American, but I think his sympathies are quite with us. He says the French are fine fighters. He was all through the last Balkan War, and didn't think another one would have come so soon, though he felt the smallest spark would start mischief there.

Sunday, October 31st, '15.

We had a good many people at tea-time, all talking of two things: the new ministry and King George's accident. I imagine Galliéni is a very good appointment. It must be better to have *un homme du métier* at the War Office. Still I fancy Millerand will be regretted in the army. The soldiers liked him very much. I should think, too, the continuation of Jules Cambon and Briand at the Foreign Office was excellent. Cambon is very clever, not easily humbugged, not even by the *Kaiser*, who made a great fuss over him when he was ambassador in Berlin.

Sir H. L. came in late; said the king was doing well, no bones broken; but it was a narrow escape. His horse slipped and rolled on him, bruising him terribly. For one awful moment the officers thought he was dead. It is too unfortunate, as his visit to the front has been such a success. The soldiers were delighted with him. He was so simple and kind. Several people told me he reminded them so much of his father—so interested in everything. Certainly King Edward had an extraordinary gift of sympathy, and knew exactly what to say to people and how to say it. I wonder what he in his wisdom would have thought of this war. He understood his nephew perfectly. I don't think any insanity on the part of the "War-Lord" would have surprised him; but for a whole nation to go suddenly mad and fancy themselves chosen by God to chastise the civilised world would have astonished him.

Tuesday, November and, '15.

These have been melancholy days, though there were quite a number of people in the streets carrying bunches of flowers, and the churches were crowded. A good many men, a good many soldiers. I got a chair for one poor one-legged young fellow. He was so glad to get it; said he wasn't accustomed yet to walking with crutches, was so afraid of slipping on the wet crossings. We are getting quite used to seeing the *mutilés* at work again. All the big shops have taken back their *employés* who have been wounded but are still able to work.

At the *Trois-Quartiers* there is such a good-looking young man at the *ascenseur* (lift). He has lost his right arm, and limps a little, but he looks very smiling; has two crosses, the *Croix de Guerre* and the *Légion d'Honneur*. Everyone knows him, and I fancy he has to tell his battles over again many times.

The papers are full of the new Ministry. I think Galliéni's appointment gives great satisfaction.

The Servians are making a gallant fight, but I am afraid the poor little country is doomed.

ANNEL

Château-Ambulance d'Annel
(8 kilometres from the from),
Saturday, November 6th, '15.

We got down here last night. I decided quite suddenly late Thursday evening to come. Mrs. Depew had breakfasted and would bring me down in her motor if she could get me a *sauf-conduit*. She couldn't, but I asked the U. S. ambassador, Mr. Sharp, where I was lunching Friday, if he could do anything for me. He couldn't give me an official passport as I am not an American subject, but gave a letter with the embassy seal. Mme. D. was rather doubtful if I could get through, but I thought I would risk it, and I had, too, my *pièces d'identité*.

We started at 4 o'clock, Mrs. D. and I and her English chauffeur, the motor filled with packages of all kinds, from hospital dressings to a *"quetch"* pie, which we stopped for at Henri's, and which was very difficult to transport. It slipped off the seat once or twice. However, it arrived safe.

It was a beautiful evening, still and bright, the road as usual, deserted except for military autos and ambulances. It was quite dark before we arrived at P., our first halt, and we were getting a little nervous. Suddenly we saw a bright light; a blue-coated soldier sprang up before us, his musket held up horizontally, barring the way. The chauffeur showed his pass, also Mrs. D. The man asked no questions and we passed. It was a relief as it would have been a bore to have been obliged to stay the night in a little village. I don't know if the ambassador's letter would have helped me; but as no questions were asked, I didn't show any papers.

We passed the other sentry in the same way, and were quite pleased when we turned into the great courtyard of Annel.

We passed through one village where *spahis* are quartered. It looked weird to see the tall figures in their white turbans and long scarlet cloaks, emerge from the shadows and disappear again in the darkness as the auto dashed past.

We were quite a large party at dinner: Mrs. D., her daughter, and the daughter's governess, and the medical staff, very cosmopolitan. The head surgeon was English, the second American, and a French *médecin en chef*; also a young English chauffeur with his ambulance, and a Frenchman who knows English well, as a sort of *surveillant*.

The Englishmen don't speak much French, but enough to get on. We had a quiet evening.

Today it has been beautiful, the sun shining in at all the windows, and the park lovely with the changing autumn tints, the poplars too beautiful, the long avenues like a wall of gold.

I walked about a little in the courtyard in the sun. It was most animated, soldiers, motors, orderlies coming and going. Mrs. D. and I went for a stroll in the park, heard an *avion* over our heads, but didn't pay much attention, so many pass all the time. Suddenly we heard our batteries at O. and the villages near firing hard, and little white puffs of smoke, like clouds in the sky. The men came running out. It was a German *avion* making for Compiègne, and passing directly over the *château*. We stood a few minutes under an *abri* (there are several in the park), but thought we might as well go back to the house. We didn't run, but we walked fast. One or two bombs were dropped in a field, but didn't do any harm.

The cannonading has been incessant all day, the windows shaking and the house trembling when one of the big guns roared. Before tea we walked to the end of the park to see the trenches and barbed-wire entanglements they are making there. We are so close to the front here that they are taking every possible precaution in case the Germans should advance in this direction. Of course one gets accustomed to everything, but it is unusual to live in an atmosphere of *avions* and trenches.

Tuesday, November 9th.

It has been beautiful again today. There was to have been a concert this evening, but late last night there came a telegram saying it must be postponed:

Impossible d'avoir sauf-conduits pour les artistes!

It was a great disappointment and a great bore for Mrs. D., as she had invited all the officers of the neighbouring *cantonnements* (who don't get much distraction down here). In the course of the afternoon we heard laughing and singing in the courtyard. We went out to see what was going on. A piano which Mrs. D. had sent for, for her concert, had arrived in an ambulance; a big *zouave* was playing, and four or five soldiers inside were singing.

As the concert was postponed Mr. D. suggested some music in the convalescent ward, which used to be the music-room, where there is a fine organ. She played the organ. Frances the cello, and the men sang solos and choruses. Some of them had very pretty voices. They finished, of course, with the "*Marseillaise.*" One poor fellow, an officer, who could hardly stand on his crutches, helped in and settled in an armchair, making a great effort for the "*Marseillaise,*" dragged himself up and stood as straight as he could, while the famous *chant de guerre* was being sung.

Frances was charming with the men, so simple and gay. I can't think it is a good thing for a girl of her age to be in such an atmosphere of suffering and misery, but all the conditions of life are so changed by this awful war that ordinary rules don't exist.

We had several officers to dinner (among others, the Duc de R.), just out of the trenches, not having had their clothes off for nine days and nights, and all so *en train* and confident. Yet it is for these men between thirty and forty that the life is so difficult, brought up in every comfort and luxury, thrown suddenly into such a rough, dangerous life. Many of the best names in France are serving as privates in line regiments. It is different for the peasants, the young ones especially, who don't know what war means, and go off full of illusions.

I am thinking of a little shepherd, eighteen years old, who went off from my village—a child who knew nothing of life but fields and animals and sun and air, and who slept every night on a heap of straw in a warm grange alongside of his beasts. He was so proud to handle a gun and be a soldier. His regiment was in Flanders, he was rushed at once to the front, was struck by a shell fragment the very first days, died in agony, poor child, and begging for his mother; and there are hundreds in the same case. The nurses tell me there are so many of the young ones who call for their mothers. One poor boy, half out of his head with pain and fever, called always for "*Maman.*" She said to him, putting her hand on his head: "*Mais oui, mon petit, maman est là!*" and the boy was quite satisfied and went off to sleep.

It is a beautiful morning. Many of the convalescent soldiers ate walking about in the park with canes and crutches and bandaged arms and legs. Every day I stop and speak to such a sad little couple—father and sister of a poor young fellow who is dying—wounded in the spine, paralysed. The old man is a type, small with red cheeks, many wrinkles, and white whiskers. He is dressed in stiff, black broadcloth; the clothes hang loosely on him. I should think he had borrowed them to come. The sister looks a little more modern. It seems that the boy wanted to be a Capucin monk. The doctor says there is no chance for him. They know it quite well, and are waiting here for the end.

After breakfast, Mrs. D. and I went in to Compiègne in the auto. It looked melancholy enough. Half the shops shut; nobody in the streets. Usually at this season Compiègne is full of people, hunting and shouting, and the famous *pâtissier* jammed. I would hardly have believed it was Compiègne,

We went to see the house knocked to bits by a bomb from a German *avion*, which also killed three nurses.

We had some French officers to tea: the Duc de Rohan, Noailles, and one other. They were interesting enough. Rohan was at the Battle of the Marne, gave a most graphic account of it; said their orders were categorical: "*Mourir sur place, résister jusqu'à la fin.*" He never thought he would get out alive, nor that Paris could be saved.

Paris, Thursday, November 11th.

We came in this morning. A lovely day. The woods looked beautiful, but the country is dead; nobody in the fields or in the woods. They are making trenches everywhere. I don't know why. Perhaps they think the Germans may still make a last desperate dash on Paris.

Paris, Monday, November 15th.

I have taken up my regular Paris work again. We have had such miserable-looking soldiers these days at the *ouvroir*—men just out of the hospital and going back to the front. Some didn't look fit to go back, but they were all quite ready to begin again.

Friday, November 19th.

It was lovely yesterday. Charlotte, Willy, and I walked about a little and went to Emile Paul to have some books sent to Francis. He writes he hardly has time to finish them. The colonel and all his comrades clamour for them.

We had a nice musical evening last night, almost the old times. The Wolffs and Mr. B. dined and we played all the evening. I was delighted to accompany Wolff again, though I was rather nervous as I never touch the piano now except to make the boys sing the "*Chant du départ*" and the "*Marseillaise.*" Wolff played divinely. It was a real pleastire, almost made me forget the war and the haunting terror always in my heart of what may come to us.

Saturday, November 20th.

We had a meeting of our committee of bandages and hospital dressings this afternoon at Mrs. W.'s, an American lady who kindly put her apartment at our disposal. An interesting English nurse was there, who was very practical in her suggestions. She said what we all realise, that the American dressings were not *all* such as are used here. Evidently not only each country has its own special dressings and habits, but each surgeon as well.

However, the things from America are excellent, arrive in perfect condition, and as everything is given, it is a fine thing to offer to the French hospitals. Some of the poor ones in the country need everything, and even some of the military hospitals—they have just the *stricte nécessaire*—are grateful for anything.

Monday, November 22nd, '15.

Poor Admiral Boggs died this morning. He was a fine type of a sailor and a gentleman. I went to the house before breakfast, just saw Anna a moment. She looks badly. It has been a long strain for her.

After breakfast I went with Fanny de M. to a meeting of the French-American Committee for the Belgian *Croix Rouge.* There were quite a number of ladies. Comtesse Greffuhle presided. Mrs. Sharp, American ambassadress, was there. They decided to have a *gala matinée* at the Grand Opera, the first time it has been opened since the war. A Belgian deputy made a short speech, very grateful for everything that was being done for Belgium, but so sad. He spoke with much emotion. It is awful to think that there are children whom no one knows about, not even what their names are; a lot of them were picked out of cellars in the Belgian towns and villages that were burned and destroyed— huddled together like little animals.

Friday, November 26th, '15.

I went to the *Crédit Lyonnais* this morning, but couldn't cash my small cheque. There were long lines of people subscribing to the government bonds. The *employés*, mostly women, some mere girls, perfectly bewildered with all they had to do. The cashier told me they would not close as usual at 4 o'clock, would go on all the evening. There were all sorts and kinds—poor, bent old women buying one bond, soldiers of all grades—one young sergeant, good-looking, evidently a gentleman, making a big investment, and three or four very dressy young ladies, that is to say, dressy for war time: very short skirts, leather gaiters, short coats like the soldiers, with big pockets, and all carrying a fairly big leather bag. We all carry bags with *papiers d'identité, permis de séjour, Crois Rouge* medals, etc. At any moment one is liable to be stopped by a policeman and asked for papers—particularly all English-speaking people, as the very zealous French official can't always see the difference between English and German spoken fast.

Monday, November 29th.

An awful day—cold rain. Charlotte and I went to tea with M. H., a bachelor friend and country neighbour. There were only twelve to fourteen people, and lovely music. It was a real pleasure to be distracted for an hour from all the anxieties and misery of these awful days.

There was a man there just back from Servia who told us horrors of the miserable peasants flying in cold and snow from the terrors of the Bulgarian invasion—women carrying babies, one on each arm, smaller children tugging at their skirts and dropping off to fall down and die on the roadside, in the snow. We were haunted all night by the awful pictures he gave us.

We are all working hard here for the Servians, but the little we can do seems nothing when a whole people has to be cried for. I ask myself sometimes why such suffering is allowed. We are taught always to believe in a God of mercy, who does not willingly afflict nor grieve the children of men! Surely if the whole world has sinned grievously, it is expiating now.

Abbé D., my Catholic *curé* and friend, says we mustn't question the decrees of Providence— but we can't help thinking. . . .

The news from Francis is good. He hopes we are thinking of Christmas and plum puddings for himself and his men. He also wants warm waistcoats—as many as we can send; says the men from the *pays envahis* are in desperate need, as of course their families can send them nothing.

Wednesday, December 1st, 1915.

It has rained hard all day. Bessie G. and I went to a meeting of the Belgian-American Committee. Mr. Allen is going back soon to

America, and thinks it might be a good thing to take over some films, and start some Allied cinematographs over there, and counteract the wonderful propaganda the Germans are making with theirs. It seems they have splendid ones; all sorts of pictures, showing the *Kaiser* in full uniform, the "War-Lord" speeding his generals on their way; taking patriotic leave of his children and grandchildren. Certainly we could send some terrible records of havoc and murder, whole villages destroyed, both in Belgium and France, and bands of unhappy refugees tramping along the deserted roads, trying to carry some of their household goods, but obliged to throw them away as the heavy march went on. All of them needn't be tragic.

I often think of the description of the Queen of the Belgians going to parliament the day of the mobilisation—very pale, very quiet, her sons on each side of her. When she appeared in the royal box, there was a dead silence for a moment (she is a Bavarian princess, a Wittelsbach), and she grew visibly agitated, her hands trembling. Suddenly there were bursts of cheers, all the deputies standing, waving hats and handkerchiefs, shouting: "*Vive la Reine!*" It would make a pretty picture.

Thursday, December 2nd.

Charlotte, Frank, and I went out to a military hospital at Drancy, near Le Bourget. It rained all the time, which was a pity, as the hospital is established in the old *château*, which stands in a large park. There are fifteen men, all very well taken care of by French doctors, and the *Soeurs de St. Vincent de Paul*, but no luxuries nor little refinements. The good sister who took us through the wards, said the men were not spoiled by visits or presents—was much pleased that we had brought cigarettes and chocolates.

Some poor fellows were too badly hurt to care about anything, but they tried to smile. One followed Frank with his eyes. I said to him: "You have children?"

"I don't know, *Madame*, I had two, but I have heard nothing since the first days of the war. We come from a village close to the Belgian frontier. Had a little farm which we worked, and which gave us all we needed—but now!" And the poor fellow's voice broke. "If I could only know they had a roof over their heads and were not starving!" We took his name and address, and will try to get some information, but it is very difficult.

Sunday, December 5th, '15.

We had a good many people at tea-time, all discussing Kitchener's journey east. B. says he hears the troops are coming back from Salonica. I can't believe it; having made the effort, I think they ought to stay.

Monday. December 6th.

Charlotte and I went shopping this morning, getting a Christmas dinner for Francis and his comrades. They are ten at the mess; we wanted to send a turkey, but the man at Potin's advised us not to. It would certainly spoil in the eight or ten days it takes to arrive at the front; so we did what we could with *pâtés de foie gras*, hams, conserves and plum puddings. The puddings are made in tins expressly for the soldiers, and were as heavy as lead to pack. I hope they will get there.

Francis, now being at some distance from Rheims, will not have the Christmas dinner with turkey and champagne he would have had with his friends the Champagne people.

This afternoon we had a meeting of our Bandage Committee, and then went to look at rooms which someone told us the American Radiator Company would let us have for our *ouvroirs*. They are beautiful big rooms, quite unfurnished. The company is doing very little business, so I hope they will let us have them. Everybody talking Salonica. Say the French and British troops will leave.

Friday, December 10th.

I went up late to see Charlotte who has a soldier staying with her—a man from St. Quentin (*pays occupé*), who has arrived in Paris with a permission of six days—knowing no one, no friends nor family here. Charlotte heard of him through his brother, a young fellow badly wounded, whom she had known at the B. hospital. The man, a gunner, looked very nice. Frank seized my hand as soon as I got into the house, and dragged me to the *lingerie*, saying: "*Viens, Danny, viens voir le poilu de Maman!*"

He looked rather sad, having just seen his twenty-two-year-old brother at the hospital badly wounded in the arm. They hope they can save it, not amputate; but it will always be paralysed. He can never use it.

December 12th.

Charlotte, the boys, their little friend Alice Dodge, and the *poilu* came to breakfast. The *poilu* looked very nice; had had a bath, been shaved and all new underclothes, and the maids had cleaned and mended his uniform. He was a very good-looking young gunner, and the children were delighted to have him. C. took the whole party, including the wounded brother (whom they picked up at the Biget), to the circus.

Monday, December 13th.

I dined at the Crillon with Mr. D. Mr. Bacon came and sat with us. He rather reassured me about America and the German element. He doesn't think the government's policy very spirited, and does consider the situation grave, but laughed at the idea of civil war, or the Germans giving any real trouble in America. Says the Germans couldn't stand for a moment against the Americans if it came to a crisis.

One or two English officers came and sat with us. I asked them what Kitchener had come over for. They replied, naturally, that they didn't know—and wouldn't have told us if they did. Someone said he looked very grave, but he always has a stern face.

Wednesday, December 15th.

I went to tea with the Watsons, to meet an American nurse who has just come back from Servia. She says the misery there is too awful for words. The flight of the wretched women and children in the cold and snow, over the mountains is something not to be imagined. Old people and little children too big to be carried, too small to struggle through the snow and cold, left to die on the roadside.

She is going home to rest, but wants to come out again in the early spring.

Dr. Watson read us a charming letter from a French *curé de campagne*—so large-minded, and so convinced that the religious feeling is coming back in France.

Thursday, December 16th (1915).

I went to tea at the Ritz, where Mrs. Depew had organised a sale of *pelotes fleuries*, to give a Christmas present to the soldiers in the trenches. They were very pretty little cushions of velvet and satin, with a wreath of artificial flowers around them, and a fall of lace like an old-fashioned bouquet. They were very well arranged in the hall at the Ritz, and I should think a great many were sold. Mrs. D. and some of her friends had invited people to tea, and it was a very gay scene. I hadn't seen so many pearls and velvet dresses for a long time. The company was mostly foreign, which explains the dressing. None of the Frenchwomen here wear anything but black or dark tailor suits.

Sunday, December 19th.

We had an interesting breakfast. Mrs. and Mr. Willard (no relation to each other) and Charlotte came. Mrs. Willard, who is connected with every important and international working committee in America, has just come over, and is going to organise the French branch of the "Surgical Dressing" Committee. She was amusing over the trousers she had brought over for me. In one of the cases sent us from America, were twenty dozen woollen waistcoats, but no coats nor trousers. It seemed impossible to get any, though my men friends were very generous. One or two, instead of sending me flowers, sent me several pairs of trousers. I said one day at the *ouvroir*, that if I didn't get any more soon, I should put a notice in the papers in big headlines:

Madame Waddington Wants Trousers

Mr. Willard said if I would write him a letter saying exactly what I wanted, he was sure he could get me some from America.

The result was most gratifying. Some began to come at once, and Mrs. W. brought me over one big bag full of trousers. She said she was pursued by them. Some packages arrived on the steamer the day she left.

Thursday, December 23rd.

I breakfasted with the Ségurs. He was rather blue about the war news, and we were all unhappy about Salonica. It seems so awful to have our soldiers sacrificed for those brigands in the Balkans. We have no *interest* there, nor in Egypt either. I wish the French could have stayed at home and driven the enemy from our soil, and not risked themselves in the East.

Ségur also criticised America and Wilson's policy very severely. I couldn't say she was playing a very spirited part. Of course it isn't her fight; but she might have protested in the name of Humanity, and made herself a fine position as the generous young neutral power across the sea.

Charlotte and Mrs. Dodge came for me there at 2 o'clock, and we went out in Mrs. D.'s motor to the Military Hospital at Drancy. The two ladies had been there once or twice taking *douceurs* to the wounded men, and they decided to make them a Christmas tree. The *supérieure*, the Soeur Récamier, a charming woman, was delighted when they told her what they wanted to do. Though it was pouring, she insisted upon going at once into the park to choose a tree, put on her black knitted shawl and *sabots*, and chose a very good one, and promised to have it put up and ready for them today.

The motor was so full of packages of all kinds that it was rather difficult for us three women to get in, but we didn't mind. We found the tree very well installed in a corner of the big *réfectoire*. The good sisters were in quite a flutter of excitement. One or two convalescent soldiers and a soldier priest, the Père Lausan, just from the front, were waiting to help us. The *père* mounted on a ladder to put the star quite at the top of the tree. It was very high, and as he had been badly wounded in the stomach, the Soeur Récamier was most unwilling he should go up; but he assured her his legs and arms were solid, and two tall soldiers held the ladder.

The tree was quickly dressed with so many willing hands; but they hadn't brought enough candles. While they were dressing the tree, I inspected the harmonium, as Charlotte thought I could, perhaps, accompany the soldiers if they sang anything, or play a march when they came in. I could do nothing with it, no matter what stop I pulled out, it always responded *grand jeu*, and roared through the hall.

The sister who plays in the chapel came down and managed it better, though she said it was old and out of order. She was a charming, refined-looking woman, seemed hardly to touch the notes, and brought such a prettier sound out of the old instrument. The *supérieure* told me she was a beautiful musician—*premier prix piano Conservatoire*—but that she had given up her music. It was a sacrifice she was obliged to make to the *Bon Dieu*.

"But why, *ma soeur*? Surely music is a beautiful and elevating thing!"

"Yes, but it was too much of a pleasure for her, and took time which should be devoted to other things. They must all make that sacrifice when they give themselves to God. We have also a young violinist—*premier prix Conservatoire*. She, too, never touches her violin. It was difficult for her at first."

The *père* asked Charlotte if she would like the men to sing something—a *Noël quelconque*—which she, of course, agreed to with pleasure.

We had a quiet evening. The news seems good. Everything quiet at Salonica.

Friday, December 24th, '15.

I did a little Christmas shopping after we came out of the *ouvroir*. I had thought I would go, perhaps, to Potin's and get some chocolate and little things for the boys' stockings, but there was such a crowd even outside the shop, a long line stretching out into the street—one or two soldiers *permissionnaires*, with their babies on their shoulders, while the mother held the bag for the provisions—that I instantly gave up that idea, and got my things at another place. It looked quite like Christmas. The shops were open and well lighted. Some of the *fleuristes* had a beautiful show of flowers. People were apparently buying. One lost for one evening the impression of the dark, empty streets we have lived in so long.

The *patronne* of the confectioner's shop, which was quite full, told me they were doing a fairly good business—much better than last year.

I took the things up to the boys. They wanted me to stay to dinner and go to midnight mass with them, but that was not easy to arrange, with no carriage, nor even servant—so H. and I had a quiet dinner at home.

Saturday, December 25th, '15.

I went to the American church and was disappointed not to hear "Hark the herald angels sing." C. and the boys stopped to say "Merry Christmas" on their way to breakfast with the *Bonne-maman*. Outrey appeared about a o'clock with a taxi, and we went over to get Mme. Sallandrouze and one boy. Charlotte and the other one went with Mrs. Dodge in her auto. It was a cold, drizzling rain, but we didn't mind, and it didn't take more than an hour to get to D.

We found the hospital under arms, sisters, nurses, and various women employed in the *lingerie* and kitchen waiting in the hall. We lighted the tree at once, the two big convalescent soldiers helping—all the others had been kept carefully away, so as to have a surprise.

The tree was really lovely, all white, nothing on it but white candles and shining silver ornaments. The packages, one for each soldier (120) were piled up on a table. Each package contained a pair of woollen socks, a knife, tobacco, chocolate, a pipe and pencil with a long chain to go in their pockets, which they all like, two handkerchiefs, and a notebook, agenda, with a picture of Joffre; oranges, cakes, and an enormous cheese were also spread out on tables.

When the last candle was lighted the doors were opened and the men came in, the *grands blessés* first, on crutches, with canes—heads and arms bandaged. Three or four carried by their comrades on their backs, putting them down so gently on the long cane chairs provided for them. A soldier-priest (they have been wonderful in this war) just from the front, with his vestment over his uniform, made a short prayer, and blessed the tree. The men sang very well the old Noël of Adam, Then Charlotte's youngest boy, Frank, recited very prettily the Noël of Théophile Gauthier, and Willy, holding the flag taller than he was, sang the verses of the "*Marseillaise*," the whole assembly joining in the chorus. Willy was a little timid at first, but the men encouraged him.

Then the distribution began. The boys had two of their girl friends to help them—Alice Dodge and Mrs. Fairman's granddaughter. The packages were all numbered, and it was pretty to hear the little childish voices calling out the numbers, 15, 20, 50. Each man (that could) stood up when his number was called and saluted, saying: "*Présent*." It was funny to see all the big men eating cakes and chocolate like schoolboys.

The good sisters hovered over them all, taking such good care of the wounded men, lest they should slip or fall.

When all the candles were burning low, the Père Lausan made a short address, thanking the ladies in the name of the men for the pleasure they had given them—not only the material part, the packages—but also for the thought in making the *fête* for them, sick and wounded, spending their second "war Christmas" in a hospital. The tree would always remain a bright spot in their hearts and memories.

Charlotte and Mrs. Dodge were very pleased; they had taken a great deal of trouble, and were quite repaid by the smile on the men's faces, as they all filed out. Poor fellows! I wonder where they will all be next Christmas?

We had a quiet family dinner with the Sallandrouzes and Henry Outrey. Drank the health of all our soldiers at the front, and tried not to miss Francis too awfully, nor to think of the other Christmases when we were all happy, and war never crossed our brains.

Wednesday, December 29th, '15.

I *flanéd* a little on the *boulevards* this afternoon. The poor little *boutiques* were not doing a very brilliant business; but the *boulevards* looked gay. A good many soldiers, *permissionnaires*, with their families, were walking about; some blind ones—such a sad sight, were being led through the crowd, and the *patronnes* of the *boutiques* tried to explain the toys to them. A good many people gave them flowers, violets, and Christmas roses, and that they seemed to like. They look very sad; but the people who take care of them say they are cheerful.

Someone told me a pretty story the other day—a lady who is

a beautiful musician plays quite often for the blind soldiers at one of their hospitals—the other day she had played all sorts of things, marches, popular songs, national airs. Almost unconsciously she started a waltz, and in a moment they were all dancing.

December 31st, 1915.

Paris is certainly looking up a little. There was such a crowd again at Potin's this morning that it was useless to attempt getting in, and in the afternoon some of the famous chocolate shops, the Coupe d'Or and, I think, Marquis, put up their shutters. They had nothing left; were quite unprepared for such a demand.

I dined at Mme. Sallandrouze's with Charlotte and the boys. We have dined there for years on New Year's Eve, and as usual, the boys helped us through the evening, as we played games with them. I came home early to finish the evening with H., taking Charlotte and the boys home first. The streets were perfectly dark. No sounds of activity anywhere. It is just after midnight. I hear no bells but some clocks striking the hour. This tragic year has finished with anguish and mourning for so many! I don't know what 1916 may have in store for us. Hardly dare to hope. But if a great sorrow comes to us, we must bear it, as so many women have in France—proud to give their sons and husbands to the country, but always carrying the ache in their hearts.

Paris, January 1916

January 8th.

Another tragic year is beginning with not many changes. Thousands of homes desolate, thousands of young lives sacrificed. Germans still in all our most prosperous northern provinces; still in their trenches at Soissons near Compiègne, eighty miles from Paris. In spite of that we lead an almost normal life, and have got accustomed to the horrors of war. Of course, one is busy and absorbed. I really only see the people who work with me at my different *ouvroirs*. I went to tea one afternoon in my *ouvroir* dress at the Swedish legation. There were not many people there. Countess Granville, of the British Embassy, also in her plain working dress. It seemed curious to see lights and men-servants, and a pretty tea-table. One has got so entirely out of any social life of any kind. M. de Stuers, Dutch Minister, was there. He had just seen Reinach, one of our clever political men, arrived from Salonica. and much pleased with all he had seen. The Allies' camp splendid. They will never be attacked. He also spoke most admiringly of Sarrail, the French general in command, a dashing, independent officer.

January 14th.

There are all sorts of reports today about the *Kaiser's* illness. One doesn't know exactly what to wish. If his death would end the war sooner, one would welcome the news. But will it? To us the crown prince seems absolutely incompetent, but some people say he is strongly supported by the "War Party" and "*Junkers*" (young noblemen).

January 20th.

I went to the *ouvroir* this afternoon—found our *caissière* (cashier) rather nervous at being late, having just arrived. I thought she had had bad news of her husband, who is at the front, but she explained why she was late. She was standing at the door of her house, with only a shawl on her shoulders, no hat, when she saw a hearse pass, with a small coffin, evidently a child, and a soldier walking behind it quite alone, crying. She said something, she didn't know what, moved her, her feet carried her out into the street. She ran out, slipped her arm in the soldier's, and walked along with him. A fat old *concierge* next door did the same thing, stopping and buying a few pennies' worth of flowers from a cart as she hurried on, to put them on the coffin.

Several other people joined them, and by the time they got to the cemetery, there were about a dozen people walking behind the hearse. The poor man was too dazed at first to speak, but finally told them it was his only child, his wife was ill, and he had twenty-four hours' leave to come and bury the child. He gave his name and address, would be so grateful if someone would look after his wife. He was going back to the front that night. Jeanne went over the next day, found the poor woman in a miserable little room, ill and depressed. A neighbour looked after her. Of course the *ouvroir* will see that she is properly cared for, and try and find some work for her when she gets stronger.

January 24th.

The Duchesse de Vendôme, sister of the King of the Belgians, came to the *ouvroir* today with the Infanta Eulalie of Spain. She was much interested in our work. Thought the sleeping-bags very good. They were designed by Mrs. Mygatt herself, and are much better and more solid than those one finds in the shops. She was very interested in all the soldiers who came for clothes, talked to them, and shook hands with them all. Was much amused with a little *Zouave*, who looked about fifteen years old, with his open collar and fresh young face. He had been detailed to guard some German prisoners. Had protested, saying he wouldn't keep them—would kill them all. No one paid any attention to his protestations, and he was sent off with a squad of men to look after the Germans. In the night, he and one of his comrades got up and cut off the ears of six of them. "Would *Madame* like to see the ears? I have some in my pocket," diving down into his pocket and producing a brown paper parcel.

That the *duchesse* hastily declined, telling him it was wrong and unsoldierly to mutilate unarmed men. "Yes, I know that, *Madame*; they have all told me so, and I have been punished; but I shall do it again. I will always hurt and kill a Boche when I can. Ah, if *Madame* could have seen the things I have seen," the colour all coming into his face

181

like an angry child while he was talking, and keeping tight hold of his grim parcel. I think he got a very good package. We heard him still talking to our women as we went back to the big room, and his last words were: "*Au revoir, Mesdames. Je ferai mon devoir, mais je tuerai tous les Boches que je rencontrerai.*" ("Goodbye, *Mesdames*; I will do my duty, but I will kill all the Boches I meet.")

Francis came for a short leave last night. He looks very well. Was too much taken up the first twenty-four hours with the pleasure of seeing his wife and boys again, and being in his own house (with a bathroom), to tell us many of his experiences at the front. However, that will come later. I think, too, it is a trait of the Waddington men, perhaps of all men, never to tell anything when they are asked questions. When they fed like it they will talk easily enough. We had a Zeppelin *alerte* last night about 10 o'clock, just as we were leaving the *salon*. The firemen dashed through our street sounding the "*garde à vous*," but it didn't seem to trouble the people very much. All lights in the street (there were only two very dim ones) and houses went out, but the people came out on the balconies.

Marie and I did the same, but we couldn't see anything, and no one seemed at all excited. Our *concierge* and our humble friend, proprietor of the restaurant at the corner of the street told us there was no danger in our quarter. We might go to bed. The *restaurateur* (proprietor) has occupied himself with us ever since the beginning of the war, when the first Taube flew over Paris. Had his cellar well arranged with rugs and lamps, and always told us not to be afraid, he would come and take us to his cellar, where we would be perfectly safe if there should be any real danger from Taube or Zeppelins. I always meant to go and see his installation, but never seemed to find time.

January 31st.

The days go on regularly and monotonously. I went this afternoon with Mrs. Boggs to the Ambulance Américaine. She with three or four other ladies gives tea there every Monday. Every day some ladies give tea, which is evidently much appreciated as they sometimes give three or four hundred cups. They give tea, bread, butter, and cakes. There are no invitations. Any one employed at the Ambulance is welcome. It is a curious mixed crowd. Doctors, nurses (ladies and professionals), chauffeurs, ambulance-drivers, orderlies—no wounded—their tea is taken up to them. There is every variety of type from the young, pretty American girl in a spotlessly white dress, bright-coloured silk jersey, and a little lace butterfly doing duty for a cap, on her head, to the comfortable middle-aged nurse in the ordinary Red Cross uniform, sitting down for a few minutes to have her tea, and then going directly back to her work.

They are almost all English and American nurses, volunteers, though there are some Swiss, and I saw one or two Dutch women. The men, too, are of all classes. Yesterday Abbé Klein was there. He is the chaplain of the Ambulance, and a charming man, clever, cultivated, refined, devoted to the soldiers. The doctors come sometimes, the orderlies often in their white jackets, and always drivers and stretcher-bearers. We stayed there until 5 o'clock, when there were no more people, happily, as there were no more cakes or bread. We passed through one of the big wards on our way out. It looked beautifully fresh and clean, and there seemed to be plenty of people to attend to the wounded. But, oh, the pitiful sight of those long rows of beds, and the pale drawn faces that one passed, the men trying to smile or say something if one stopped a moment!

The Francis, all four, came to dinner—the boys sitting on each side of their father. He had been shopping all day, renewing all his clothes from socks to cap. He says they wear their uniform so constantly, night and day, that they never have time to get anything washed or mended. Francis told us all sorts of things of life in the trenches, up to his knees in water, or carrying despatches along bad country roads at night, with shells bursting all around him. He says it is melancholy to go back to some of the villages that have been shelled. The Germans always seem to pick out the churches, which stand there roofless, all windows gone, merely the four walls remaining. A ghastly souvenir of this horrible war. Can we ever give back to them a tenth part of the harm they have done us?

February, 1916

It seems natural to have Francis at home, coming in and out, and always bringing some friend for a meal. Last night we had a banquet. We began with a small dinner, which grew until I wondered how we ever could serve so many people. It is impossible to get an extra man to serve; there are none left; but the two parlour-maids did very well, and of course the meal was of the simplest description—*menu de guerre*. We had Francis, Charlotte, and the two boys; Comte and Comtesse Louis de Ségur, very old friends (he was one of Francis' witnesses when he married); Comte and Comtesse Bernard de Gontaut, with their son, a lieutenant of dragoons, also home on leave; Marquise de Talleyrand, who gave Francis his first rocking-horse when he was about four days old; and Baron de Grotestin, of the Dutch Legation, an old friend. Ségur has fifteen nephews and great-nephews fighting; one is killed, two badly wounded. Francis and Guy de Gontaut told us all sorts of things about their trench experiences.

It is astounding how men brought up as they have been in every comfort can stand the life—take it quite as a matter of course. We made music, of course, winding up with all the national airs and patriotic songs. Poor Madame de Gontaut was reduced to tears. She is very sad since the war—Guy, her youngest child and only son is the apple of her eye. They stayed very late, and the two little boys were so tired that they went sound asleep on a sofa in the ante-room, and we had great difficulty in rousing them, and getting them into hats and coats to go home.

★★★★★★

Francis has gone back to the front. He and Charlotte dined at a hotel not far from the Gare de l'Est, and I took the boys for a run in the Bois. Poor little things, they are always upset when their father goes off and it is pretty to hear them promise to be good and take care of mother when the last goodbyes are said. The partings are hard. I wonder how many more we shall have. Now the long days of waiting begin again. We hear so little—are days without letters. Just now all our hopes and prayers are centred at Verdun, where the fighting is terrific.

All the great chiefs, Joffre, Castelnau, are there, and we have seen one or two officers who have come back wounded. They say the slaughter of the Germans is terrible; they go down in masses under the great French guns, but come steadily on, marching over the bodies of their comrades. Our men think they are given ether or alcohol of some kind, which goes to their heads and makes them crazy—they come on laughing and singing like madmen. Our losses, too, are very heavy, but we don't see any lists of killed or wounded. Very few Verdun wounded have come to Paris.

Charlotte looked rather white when she came back from the *gare*. However, she is a soldier's daughter, her whole heart is with "Fighting France," and she wouldn't have her husband anywhere but at the front. She said the trains were crowded, hundreds of soldiers going back and saying goodbye to their womankind, and that all the women were brave, no fear, no murmurs. The French women have been wonderful ever since the first awful days of mobilisation, when suddenly in a few hours their lives were completely changed—all their men called to arms—but after the first shock all accepted the inevitable, and set to work to replace the men in farms, gardens, mills, shops, and in small trades of every kind.

Sunday, 23rd.

I went over to lunch with Bessie Talleyrand today. The Seine looked bright and dancing as I crossed it. A few flowers are coming up in the garden. The sun streaming through the big windows of her *salon*. A young Belgian officer, Prince de C, lunched and was most interesting, telling us of much that happened in Belgium in the beginning of the war. Their *château* is almost in Germany, so close to the frontier. He joined the army at once, but his sister remained at the *château* with a younger brother, where she established an ambulance with French, English, and German wounded. She also had a few French and English soldiers hidden in a tower at the bottom of the garden. She and her young brother were in the hall one afternoon when three or four German motorcars, filled with officers, drove up.

They all got out, came into the hall, and one of them, a tall, good-looking man, introduced himself as the Duke of W. (a royal title), said they would like to dine, had their own food, but would like the use of the kitchen and dining-room; also that they must search the house as they knew English soldiers were hidden there. She said there were none in the house, trembling at the thought of the four or five who were in the tower. They insisted upon searching the whole house, and left a guard at the door of the hall, forbidding his sister and brother to leave it. However, they found no one, and she heard nothing more of them until late in the afternoon a young officer appeared with a message from the duke, inviting her and her brother to dine with them. This she refused curtly, without giving any excuse, which rather surprised and disconcerted the young officer, who retired. In a few minutes the duke appeared, already in a temper. Why had she refused his invitation to dine with them?

"It is quite impossible," she answered, "which you will surely understand when you think about it."

He wouldn't listen to her, insisted upon a reason—so then she replied that it would be impossible for her to break bread with people whom she despised, soldiers who burned churches and villages, and killed helpless women and children. He flew into a rage, told her to hold her tongue, and banged out of the hall. Her young brother was frightened, thought they would do something awful to her, so a little later when one of the younger officers asked him to dinner, he thought he had better go. The Germans all behaved perfectly well at dinner, said nothing about the war, talked weather, roads, and farming prospects. He said the dinner was very good. They drank a great deal of wine. They left directly after dinner, with a great noise of clanking sabres, spurs, and snorting autos. Some days later they were warned that they were being watched, and the young man was advised to get out of the country. He succeeded in getting across the frontier, having all sorts of adventures. He ended by swimming across the canal.

Soon after the sister was carried off to Brussels by the German military authorities, who told her she was only wanted to give evidence in the case of Miss Cavell, that unfortunate English nurse who was murdered; would be brought back at once to her *château*. She never got back, was sent to prison in Germany, shut up in a cell, and obliged to wear prison uniform, allowed to go out for half an hour every day in the courtyard, and she is still there, (as at time of first publication). She writes occasionally to her brother. Lately, thanks to one of the cardinals, she has obtained certain mitigations of the strict prison discipline, can receive books—no papers—and material for working. One of her greatest deprivations was the want of light. All lights were put out in the cells at 8 o'clock, and those long hours of darkness were almost unbearable. What a life for a refined delicate woman! However, those brutes didn't murder her as they did the poor English nurse. One must be thankful for small mercies in times like these.

February 28th.

Our only idea is Verdun, where the French are fighting magnificently, the crown prince still hurling masses of his best troops on the French guns.

We have letters from the *curé* at Mareuil begging us for food, clothes, *everything* for refugees, from some of the villages near Soissons, and asking us to come down for a day or two. We can't—we have no motor, and all passenger-trains are stopped on the Chemin de Fer de l'Est, as they are rushing troops to Verdun.

These are the last pages of my War Diary. There is so little to say. Even the splendid defence of Verdun doesn't mean the end of the war, and so many books about the great war have been written and will be written that the simple details of a family life are hardly worth recording.

When my grandsons come to manhood and have sons of their own, when the world is at peace and the cannon hushed, and women are busy and smiling in the little hamlets where their mothers spent long months and years of suspense and anguish and mourning, they perhaps would like to read "Granny's" remembrances of the Great War.

With the British Expeditionary Force

Hazebrouck. October, 1916

Sitting at my window, in a rather dark provincial hotel, looking out on a courtyard where one tree stands up against the grey northern sky, the wind always howling dismally, and the tree swaying in a perfect tempest—I ask myself if I am the same person who, a few days ago, was spending long happy hours at a lovely island just off the coast of Vendée. I used to lie out on the warm dry sand, my head on a heap of seaweed, seeing nothing but the blue sky overhead, the sea at my feet, a few pleasure-boats drifting leisurely along. There were no fishing-boats, for the men are mobilised, and now the women do a great deal and replace their husbands in many ways. I have not heard of any who have ventured forth on a fishing cruise, which was the great occupation and resource of the island.

Except for the total absence of men (save very very old ones), there is nothing to indicate that a great war is going on. There are no soldiers, no wounded, no hospitals. The women all knit, trudging alongside of their donkeys; and life in all classes flows as easily and placidly as possible.

I left suddenly, called away by the illness of a grandson, to this place in the extreme north of France. Even now, it all seems a dream. The long, weary journey with so many changes of vehicles that I think a balloon would not have seemed unnatural, the long wait at Nantes, in the dark station, the only lights being at the office of the *chef de gare* and the ticket-office, for a crowded train so taken by assault at once by travellers and above all soldiers returning from their leave, that it seemed useless even to think of getting in. However, thanks to Mr. P., whom we met at the station, and who really pushed us on to the platform, we did manage to find our two places, the only unoccupied ones.

The *couloir* was crowded with people sitting up all night on bags, rugs, the bare floor. We rather remonstrated with the railway official who came for the tickets and who looked harassed and depressed. He said they could do nothing; everything was in the hands of the military; everything for the army came first, men, munitions, and that it was not a time for civilians to travel. He was quite right. It is not! But when we suggested that they might put on another carriage, or at least not sell tickets, when he knew there were no more places, he jeered at us; said they had no "extra carriages," and if, when the train arrived at Nantes, it was *réquisitionné* by the military authorities, all the civilians would be put out and left on the quay—at 10 o'clock at night.

I had two hurried days in Paris trying to get a passport and *sauf-conduit* for Hazebrouck (which I didn't get), but they were very kind at the Foreign Office, and gave me a *laissez-passer*, which I think would have carried me through even without the famous blue paper of the *Grand Quartier général*.

Mr. Cambon said he would telephone at once to one of his friends at the *Grand Quartier*, to tell the military authorities at Calais to let me pass. It was a long journey; takes five hours in ordinary times, but I was en route for thirteen hours; left Paris at 9.30 and got to Hazebrouck at 10.30 next day.

The train, a very long one, was crowded with British soldiers. After Amiens, we really went through an enormous British camp, thousands of tents and *barraques*. It was a fine day, and we saw every variety of English life; nurses walking about in couples, officers playing tennis, soldiers at football. Long lines of cavalry with very good horses. A military funeral; men marching with arms reversed; endless *fourgons* with munitions and food and cannon. The men generally very fine-looking, very smart in their short jackets (so unlike our long French tunics), which give them an extraordinary length of limb.

They were principally young men; I don't think they had done much fighting yet. Their uniforms and boots looked clean.

We got to Calais about 5, and had two hours' wait there. The station was a curiosity—a solid mass of khaki-dressed men coming and going, whistling gaily, making all sorts of jokes with everyone. I didn't hear "Tipperary." That seems to have passed for the moment.

We had to go at once to the room where papers were examined by the military authorities, who were very stiff and curt. I was a little uncomfortable, knowing mine were not *en règle*.

There were two trains, just one for Dunkerque and later Hazebrouck. A nice-looking woman, a lady, who was going to Dunkerque, was not allowed to pass; her papers not right. She protested vigorously; said *the commissaire de police* had told her everything was quite *en règle*. But the officer was inexorable. "We have our orders, *Madame*; we cannot let you pass!"

The poor thing was bitterly disappointed; didn't know where to go in Calais for the night. She asked me if I was going to Dunkerque.

"No, to Hazebrouck."

"You will never be allowed to pass, *Madame*;" but I told her I thought I was all right.

I gave the maid, who had her *sauf-conduit*, my *laissez-passer* and *papiers d'iden*tité, but I didn't feel quite happy until I heard the officer say: "*C'est très bien; nous avons reçu des ordres de faire passer Mme. Waddington.*"

We had two hours to wait; couldn't go out of the *gare*; but the buffet at Calais is very good, and we had a very nice simple dinner.

When I asked for cold chicken, the man was much taken aback, saying they hadn't had any chickens for weeks.

There was a big *table d'hôte* for British officers.

I started again about 7. Again a very long crowded train, stopping at all the little stations. None of them were lighted. People scrambled out in the dark as well as they could, carrying bags and bundles.

One poor woman with a wounded son with her, who was going to St. Omer, thought they had arrived at their destination, and got out at one of the small stations; was much put out that "Jean," whom she called, was not there to meet her; and had just time before the train started to climb in again. St. Omer was two stations farther on. The poor boy looked so weak and tired, as if he couldn't stand much more. However, at St. Omer, Jean with a lantern and quite a group of friends were waiting, and he seemed all right.

We didn't move as we had been told the train didn't go any further than Hazebrouck. It was not quite so dark there, but it was such a long train that we had some little distance to walk before we were hailed by Francis (whose voice told me at once that the boy was better, before I could ask any questions), and one or two officers, who took our papers and passed us at once, without making the long wait at the *bureau* where the *sauf-conduits* and other papers are examined.

The hotel was just opposite the station, and we walked across.

Mme. S. was waiting for me. My room was next to hers; we all talked together for a few minutes. Then Francis came into my room and we talked until midnight. The child has been desperately ill with infantile paralysis, but his life is saved now. The great question is how he will get over it. The left arm is paralysed; the neck and shoulders, too, quite stiff; but the brain is quite clear. The poor children have had a terribly anxious ten days. They say nothing can describe the kindness of the British doctors and nurses, of everybody, in fact. The *infirmières* and *religieuses* of the *Croix Rouge* have been very good to them.

My first visit to the hospital was sad enough. The French *Croix Rouge* have their *salles* on the first floor of the Collège St. Jacques, and on the story above, up a very steep flight of steps, our little Frank and his mother are installed in two bare, high, comfortless rooms, with windows so high that we had to get a chair to look out. However, they were very glad to have even them, as it was very difficult to find anything. The town is crowded with British troops and refugees.

I found the poor little boy much changed, so thin, and his face drawn, but not suffering, and his head quite right. It was pathetic to see the quiet little figure so helpless and unlike himself.

He has nice English nurses, day and night, and likes them very much with their helpful ways and gentle voices.

Dr. S., the English doctor, is perfectly devoted to him, comes three times a day, and is so gentle with him. His room opens into a *dortoir* (awful), with its rows of beds and stools without any backs, at the side of each bed. A long table runs down the middle of the room.

They had cleared off one end, and there Charlotte made her tea, and the English nurses the little soups and jellies which the boy likes.

The first few days were bewildering. I saw so many people. It is still a confused memory. The doctors, the *infirmières*, the *abbé*, *directeur* of the Collège St. Jacques, the *religieuses*, the *infirmières-majors*. One of them, a tall, fine-looking woman, one of the important ladies of the place, in the white nursing dress and *coiffe* and beautiful diamonds in her ears—the day-nurse, Sister P., passing backward and forward in her grey dress, the little cape bound in red. The *directress* of all the British nurses (some Red Cross, some Territorial, some Military) is Sister S. R., an absolute *femme du monde*, with a charming manner and most energetic and capable.

One or two visitors from the town who came to see Charlotte. The visitors always remained in the *dortoir*, some sitting on the stools, some on the beds. And the wonderful cooking creatures—a *femme de manage*, a *réfugiée* from Armentières. She looked like a savage; had no particular features—lumps all over her face, and a gruff voice like a man's.

We are in the firing-line, but are not bombarded. The place is not important enough, but from Armentières and the neighbouring village, which are bombarded all the time, groups of refugees come almost every day, and they tell us the misery is appalling—the town overcrowded with frightened, helpless women and children.

We left the hospital generally a little before 6; and I think I shall never forget those first walks back to the hotel. Quite dark; the great place just lighted enough to see how dark it was, and always autos and big lorries dashing about.

As the days went on and I felt happier about the child, I found much that was interesting. It was curious to live in this quaint little northern French town, really more Flemish than French, with its narrow, pointed houses, red roofs, and canal wandering through low green meadows—and yet to feel oneself in an English garrison. The town is under British martial law. They control everything. Big soldiers with M. P. ("Military Police") on their caps, stand in all the main streets to direct the traffic; and it is funny to see them standing absolutely calm and imperturbable when torrents of invectives are hurled at them by indignant natives in their country carts, in an absolutely unintelligible jargon.

I asked one of them the other day if he had learned any French. "Not much, but it doesn't matter, *Madame*. We make them understand; and we don't mind their talking; we are accustomed to it."

The shops are what one would find in any English provincial town—food (jam, of course, of all kinds), clothes, beds, illustrated papers. The "Tommies" seem on the best of terms with the townspeople. They pay well for everything they take; and the doctors are very kind to the refugees, sick and wounded.

There are a great many Anzacs (Australians and New Zealanders) in the streets. They are not so military-looking as the correct, well set up "Tommy"—but they are a fine lot of men, generally tall, broad-shouldered and young. They swing along at an easy pace, their big hats turned up on one side, their jackets rather loose, high boots, and enormous spurs. They say they are splendid fighters. Their record is a fine one; but they are pretty hard to manage, with no idea of military *étiquette* or "difference of rank."

One of the officers (they are generally English, the higher ones), remonstrated with a soldier the other day for not saluting a colonel. The man promptly replied: "He would not salute any more colonels; he had saluted two the other day *who had not returned it, and he was going to salute no more!*"

I was amused with some of them I met the other day in a shop. I and several other people were buying fruit, grapes, pears. The *patronne* showed us a fine bunch of white grapes. They looked very good, firm and yellow where the sun had touched them.

"How much?" said one of the men.

"Three *francs* fifty," replied the woman.

Upon which the man broke into a loud peal of incredulous laughter, saying: "You won't sell any at that price. In my country, we get a big basket full for one shilling," and he and his companions went off whistling and laughing, but declining absolutely any purchases.

Our hotel is opposite to the *gare*. Every day we see troops coming and going. The other day quite a large contingent of British and Australians arrived. The British waited quite still—a long khaki line just outside the station, while their officers *parleyed* with the railway men. The Australians, hardly a second; they jumped over the barriers, pushed aside the *employé*, and were in the middle of the street and in all the cafés like lightning. They are as agile as monkeys; vaulted over the fences and slipped in and out of the quantities of motors and big carts without slackening their pace. They ran as hard as they could out of the station.

The *gare* is always crowded all day and all night, as there is a constant passage of troops. When they stop for three or four hours only to rest and eat, the streets are most animated, and the shops, *pâtissier*, tobacco, postal-cards and picture-papers do a roaring business. But it is quite different when the trains with wounded arrive. The grey Red Cross ambulances are drawn up close to the station, and one sees the ghastly burdens that the big "Tommies" bring out so gently.

One day the station was shut all day. No passenger-trains (there is only one, morning and evening) were allowed to start. Someone told us afterward that "tanks" were passing. I don't suppose we should understand much if we did see some—still one likes to have an idea of all the new infernal war engines, and these seem terrible.

When one remembers the old days when one spoke of a possible great continental war, everybody said all would be over in a few months. The new killing inventions were so awful that in a few weeks there would be no men left on either side. And now, in October, 1916, we are getting ready for a third winter in the trenches, making warm clothes and trying to keep up our courage. But at night, when we are comfortable in bed, and the rain and wind are beating against the window-panes, we wonder how much more our poor men can stand!

Today, it is bright and mild, the sun not too pale, really shining, and Hazebrouck appeared quite different. It is market-day, and the great place is covered with stalls and vehicles; and the British and Anzacs are wandering about and buying.

It is certainly the great day here. Our *patronne* asked us last night if we would please breakfast somewhere else this morning, at one of the *café* on the *place*, or perhaps with M. *l'Abbé* at the College St. Jacques (Charlotte took all her meals in the réfectoire of the *collège* as long as they were living there, at the *abbé's* table, on a platform from which he could dominate the classes when the boys were there), as she couldn't give us the private dining-room we always had.

For years, twenty I think she said, certain clients had always breakfasted in that room on market-days. The poor lady was quite worried in her mind; but we compromised by saying that we would breakfast early, at eleven.

We stopped at the *pâtissière's*, a very good one, to order some *brioches* for tea, and she showed us, with much pride, a table in the inner room covered with most appetising cakes. She said she was always very busy on market-days, and made a great many cakes and tarts. But that now, since the English were here, she made twice as many, and often had to shut her shop at 6 o'clock when she had nothing left.

She advised us to take our cakes at once as she knew she could not keep them: "*Ces messieurs prennent tout et ne raisonnent pas*" ("These gentlemen take everything without discussing").

We thought her advice good, and carried off our cakes.

As usual, the English impose their habits wherever they are: their church services, 5 o'clock tea in *all* classes, their tennis, their football, quite simply, with an absolute disregard of the customs of the country.

I suppose there are no two nations so unlike as the French and the British; but I think this war will bring about a better understanding between the two countries, each one recognising the other's qualities, the splendid fighting and endurance on both sides. But they fight differently, as they do everything else.

★★★★★★

We have finally found charming rooms for Charlotte and her boy.

She couldn't remain any longer in her garret at St. Jacques, as the holi-days were over and the boys are coming back to school (poor little wretches, to sleep in that awful *dortoir*). We all, including Mme. de L., who came in from her place two or three times to see C. before she went off to Paris, saw all the houses and lodgings that were left in the town, but nothing was at all tempting. One clean little *bourgeois* house down by the canal, well exposed (when there was any sun, it would come there), we had almost decided upon, but Dr. S. objected so vig-orously that we didn't like to go against his opinion.

There are some very nice houses with a long, low *façade* on the street, and very big gardens running off at a great distance behind; but, of course, they were all occupied by British officers. However, Dr. S. had one in his head, where Major D., the British "Town Major" lives. Francis and Charlotte went to see it, and were delighted. A good large house, with a lovely garden, but they didn't think they would be able to get it. Finally after many negotiations, the thing was arranged. C. saw the town major and the *propriétaire*, a nice woman—and she has four good rooms. Major L. most kindly gave up his bureau, a large high room opening on the veranda and the garden; said his things should be taken away at once.

There is a sort of a *serre*, or winter garden all closed in with glass on one side of the *bureau*, and two good bedrooms upstairs.

The English officers, staff, interpreter, etc., occupy the rest of the house. It is very well situated in an open part of the town; and today, as I am sitting writing in C.'s *salon*, one couldn't want anything prettier. The garden is full of flowers, all in bloom, roses, begonias, geraniums, with a very good stretch of lawn and a tennis-court. It is really a very sheltered spot. They call it in the town "*La petite Nice.*"

It was a little difficult at first making the winter garden comfort-able, but people lent some tables and screens, the major a *chaise longue* and we added small tables and chairs; and with some Turkey-red table-covers, photographs, and a writing-table it really looks quite nice.

C. has made friends with the gardener, who keeps her well sup-plied with flowers and a few vegetables.

It is interesting to live, so to speak, with the army. All day, soldiers and civilians pour into the courtyard and veranda. The English *bureaux* are quite at the other end of the veranda, and the men and visitors don't get near our end. We only see tall soldiers moving about and don't hear anything. One can hardly believe one is in a house full of men. C. feels very well guarded. The gas burns all night in the corridor, and there are always people about. Francis, who is twenty miles away, nearer the front, comes about once a week for twenty-four hours, sometimes on horseback, sometimes on a bicycle. But he is very busy: all sorts of local questions come up all the time, and of course his Anzacs don't speak one word of French. There is a stable in the courtyard where he puts his horse.

The first time he came without letting us know, so, naturally, nothing was ready. However, some of the English orderlies brought straw and water, and C.'s beautiful *femme de ménage* went out for oats and hay.

He always dines at the British mess, as the cooking arrangements in the villa are of the most elementary character.

One end of the winter garden (it is a very long room), is cut off with a high wooden screen, and behind that C. has a gas-stove (which the *proprietress* of the villa left here when she went away) and a big petroleum-lamp. Two long tables and a variety of kettles and saucepans.

Her woman and Sister D. make all the little jellies, and cook an occasional chop which the boy wants.

She has also made great friends with the *bouchère* across the street, who told her one day she would make her dinner and send it over to her. She had been a cook herself, knew all about it. Would *Madame* come and see her kitchen? C. said it was beautifully clean, so she accepted, and the woman sends her over very good soup, chops, filet, anything she wants.

Francis dined one night (for a wonder didn't ask any one) and said he hadn't had such a good dinner since the war.

There is a large old-fashioned Flemish kitchen opening into the courtyard, as they all do here, with a fireplace big enough to roast an ox. But the English have it. *Enfin, à la guerre comme à la guerre!* They are camping and not at all badly off. The boy is very happy in his big room. His bed is drawn up to the open window, and he loves to see the flowers and the gardener at work. When it gets too dark to see anything, he knows all the steps; the doctor who is very good to him, his father's horse in the courtyard, and above all the quick light step of Sister D., his English nurse.

I can't say enough about the English nurses, particularly the military nurses. In fact, the whole English equipment is wonderful; all the details so well carried out. What they have done since the beginning of the war is admirable. When one thinks that they had practically no army, and that everything had to be organised!

Francis had great difficulty in getting a nurse. He telegraphed to Lord Bertie, the British ambassador, and to various people in Paris, but the formalities were endless. It seems the British are very strict about having their lines entered. Finally one of the high officers here telegraphed for a military nurse from London. She was told one afternoon she must leave the next morning for France to nurse a serious case at Hazebrouck. She crossed to Boulogne in a troop-ship, stood all the way over—they were packed like sardines—found an ambulance waiting for her at Boulogne, and came straight off to Hazebrouck—three hours' run. Francis was standing at the door of the hospital; saw the nurse arrive; couldn't believe it was his nurse—as she had only been telegraphed for the day before, but went to see if he could help her as she seemed to have some difficulty in making herself understood in French.

She told him she was Sister D., had left London that morning, and was told to come to Hazebrouck to nurse a serious case in Mr. Waddington's family. "I'm Mr. Waddington," he said; "and you are to nurse my boy." He took her directly upstairs—said in half an hour she was installed—didn't mind apparently the very primitive, uncomfortable surroundings, hardly wanted a cup of tea.

They are mobilised like soldiers. She came with her rations and her kit-bed; had no idea if she was coming to a camp or a tent or a hospital.

She hadn't been half an hour in the room when a soldier appeared bringing her her *billet de logement* for the next day. She is a night-nurse. She got all her instructions from the doctor, arranged herself on the table in the *dortoir* all she might need for the night, made friends with the child; and his poor mother went to bed with a feeling of comfort and security she hadn't known for days.

The day-nurse too (she is a Territorial, not Red Cross) is most competent, and they are both so cheerful. They have all passed an examination for simple cooking, and can make the soups and jellies that an invalid wants.

I wish we had such an organisation in our military hospitals; but those schools of trained nurses don't exist in France. Of late years it has been rather the fashion for the *femmes du monde* to pass examinations for the *Croix Rouge*, and I believe there are some excellent nurses; but they are not numerous and all voluntary. The Frenchwoman ought to be a good nurse. She occupies herself so much with her household and her children, going into every detail.

It was pouring the other day. I believe it always rains in these northern towns. The big place was like a lake. I tried in vain to get a pair of india-rubbers but couldn't, and was very uncomfortable in my wet shoes.

Sister S. R., the head of the British nurses, came to see us—wonderfully equipped. She had on a long black mackintosh (tarpaulin, like what the sailors wear), with big pockets and a hood, and high rubber boots. She left her mackintosh outside, and came in in her white clothes, looking as clean and dry as if it were a sunshiny June day. She told us she had done all the campaign of the Yser in a field-hospital, at the front, and that she never could have done it without the rubber coat and particularly the boots. The soft black mud was something awful; they really went in up to their knees. They lived in tents and had to go backward and forward to the hospital and the sanitary trains.

She said she never could have imagined anything so awful as the wounded men who were brought in. Bundles of mud, their clothes stiff with blood and dirt of all descriptions. Those who had been only lying out one night in the battlefield, in good condition compared to those who had remained sometimes forty-eight hours.

She was most interesting, and I couldn't help thinking as she sat there on a bed, or a stool, in the *dortoir*, with her fine profile and "grand air," that, after all, blood tells, and that the gently-born lady accommodates herself better than the ordinary woman to all the discomforts and dangers that a field-nurse is exposed to. Of course there must be the vocation, or else the strong faith that one's life is not one's own at such a time, but in God's hands, to be sacrificed when the time comes.

I am thinking of a nurse we were all so fond of, who left Paris to go and take charge of a hospital at Mosch, where shells were falling freely. She had a young *religieuse* with her who was nervous, frightened of the shells, couldn't make up her mind to leave the shelter of the house and venture out into the open. Our good sister encouraged her, and one afternoon they left the house together. Our sister was struck instantly, killed at once by a passing shell. They gave her a soldier's funeral, with the flag covering the coffin. Her memory lives in many hearts.

Sunday.

I almost felt as if I was really in England. I stepped in at the church of St. Eloi on my way to see the children. It is a fine old church, standing in a green dose like so many of the English cathedrals. There were a good many men in church, two Scottish soldiers in kilts kneeling on the stone pavement, most devout. I was surprised. One doesn't think of Scotsmen as a rule as Catholics.

When I came out I met a squad of English soldiers coming from church, their sergeants walking alongside swinging their canes. And at 6.30, when I came home, I heard English hymns being sung. I stopped under the *voûte* of the Hôtel de Ville to listen. The English have a room there, and service twice a day for their soldiers and nurses. The men's voices sounded very well in the perfectly still, dark night.

We never go out at night. No civilians are allowed in the streets after 9.30 o'clock. I stopped at the *pâtissière's* one morning to order some cakes for tea, and found there three young Tommies trying to get something to drink. They couldn't understand the woman, and the woman couldn't understand them. But she divined that they were hungry, and gave them each a small *brioche* which they didn't want. I came to the rescue, asking what they wanted: "Something to drink, *Madame*; we have been travelling since 12 o'clock yesterday, and have had nothing to eat or drink."

"What do you want? Beer, whisky?"

"Oh, no, *Madame*, tea; but we can't get it."

I asked the woman if she couldn't give them some tea and bread and butter, but she hadn't any tea, only chocolate and cakes, and was, besides, expecting British officers to breakfast; had an elaborate table spread with cakes and jam.

They looked so disappointed that I thought I would carry them off to the *café* of our hotel, where they would surely get something; so I told them to come with me, and we all walked off together. "I think you must be an English lady, *Madame*, as you are wearing the English Red Cross medal."

"No, I am not English, but I love the soldiers, and all my men are fighting."

We walked on very amicably; one or two passers-by looked rather amused at the party, and they tried to tell me where they had come from, but their British pronunciation of French names made it impossible for me to understand.

When we got to the *café* I told the *patronne* to give them a good breakfast, saying to them: "But don't you want more than bread and butter? Would you like some ham and eggs?"

"Oh, yes, Mum," with a broad smile on each young face. They thanked me very nicely and respectfully, and I left them in Mme. M.'s hands.

I found Francis and Captain S. having tea with Charlotte when I got to the villa, Francis was very hungry and rather tired, having ridden I don't know how many miles with some of his officers, inspecting *cabarets* (taverns). It seems there have been one or two cases of diphtheria in their *cantonnement*, which the doctors thought might come from drinking out of dirty glasses; so they visited all the *cabarets* in the neighbourhood, inspecting mugs and glasses, and threatening the old women who kept them with all sorts of punishments if they weren't cleaner and more careful. Some of the ladies were so irritated and so voluble that even Francis found it difficult to deal with them: such a flow of *patois*, half French, half Flemish, that he couldn't always understand them. However, the great point was that they should understand him.

His life is not always very interesting, but it is a change from the trenches and carrying despatches, and I think it is just as well to see every side of the war.

He is astounded at the British equipment; such wonderful organisation, and such abundance of everything. They had had a "church parade" on Sunday, which he said was most impressive, in a half-ruined church—almost the whole roof off, windows gone, floor too, in places. The *padre* (as they call all the priests and clergymen) brought a small harmonium with him, which Francis played. They gave him a book, as of course he doesn't know the English hymns; and he said the men sang very well. They finished with "God Save the King." He was in a deadly terror lest he and the harmonium should topple over, the floor was so rickety; but they got through all right.

He and Captain L. brought me home. It is about twelve minutes' walk to the hotel, and he went back with S. to dine at the mess. There were a great many British officers dining at the hotel that night, and three or four enterprising spirits burst into our little private diningroom, possibly in search of an adventure of some kind, hearing women's voices—and one couldn't blame them for that at Hazebrouck. I think the sight of the two grandmothers rather quieted them, and they beat a hasty retreat, without having had time to get a glimpse of the young aunt.

The hotel is just opposite the *gare*, and is always full. It is a typical provincial hotel, with fairly good rooms, high and light, with wonderful furniture. Mme. S. has a remarkable *couvre-lit*, a sort of snuffy brown, on her bed, but the beds are perfectly clean and comfortable, and the wooden floor is washed once a week. The staircase is perfectly dark, but when we come down to dinner at 7 o'clock, a small bedroom candlestick is placed on the flat end of the banisters, which gives a faint twinkle of light. The courtyard is covered, and at one end there is a double washstand, with one or two towels hanging from a peg, and always before meals there are two or three Tommies in shirtsleeves having a good wash. I should think no one ever stayed in the *hôtel* but *commis voyageurs*. They have certainly never had people of our class before, and our ways and wants are very wonderful to them. It is kept by two women, and all the service is done by women. There is one old *maître d'hôtel*, but he doesn't sleep in the house, so at 10.30 they take off the bell and don't answer the door.

We hear violent knocking sometimes between 10.30 and 13, and very strong language in unmistakable Anglo-Saxon tones, but no one takes any notice. The *hôtel* slumbers peacefully on until the next morning.

Every now and then we see two motorcars dashing through the town at break-neck speed, the one behind with a red *fanion* means a general's car, his *aide-de-camp* in front. The Tommies all range themselves on one side and stand at attention.

C. and I made a most unsuccessful shopping expedition the other day, couldn't get any of the ntumerous things we wanted; a screen, a bathtub, a pair of thick boots for Willy, a waterproof also for Willy. As usual, the English came to our help, and a bathtub was sent up from Boulogne or one of their military bases.

The townspeople are very civil and most serviceable, but they are a little bewildered by the British occupation and all the things the English want which the French soldier knows nothing of.

Everybody knows us as we are the only strangers in the place.

I had a visit the other day from Mlle. de B., the type of the good old French *bourgeoise*, with a very polite, old-fashioned manner. She has a charming house in the Rue de l'Eglise, one of the best streets in the town, with a beautiful garden at the back, and pretty, heavy, old-fashioned furniture in her rooms. Almost all her house is taken by British officers. She is *Présidente de la Croix Rouge* for this part of the country, and also of the Belgian Relief Committee. She had seen my name on one of the Franco-American Belgian committees, and came to see if I could put her in touch with the Paris committee. They have quantities of refugees here, and among them civilian wounded, women and children.

I thought I had seen every stage of refugee misery at Mareuil, with those first miserable bands that passed through our villages the first year of the war, but there were no wounded. I saw a group of refugees, women and children from Armentières, the other day—six women, young, strong, not over thirty, and a little girl of eight—each with a leg off, hit by a fragment of shell. They had no crutches, not even canes, merely sticks, like what the boys cut in the woods, with a notch at one end to prevent them from slipping! They looked utterly miserable, huddled together in a corner of the place. It made one ill to see them. Happily it was not cold, nor raining.

I said to one of the women: "Why did you stay? You were warned to leave as any day Armentières would be bombarded."

"But, *Madame*, where can we go? It is our home, our only home; no one wants us here or anywhere. We have no clothes, no food, no shelter!"

It is perfectly true. They don't want them in the towns. They have already more than they can take care of.

Another woman said: "I don't complain, *Madame*, I have *only lost a leg*. I am a washerwoman and can still stand at my tub and use my arms. There are others worse off than me—but I would like a pair of crutches."

Mile. D. says the town is doing all it can, but they must have some help.

Happily the British occupation is pouring money into Haze-brouck. The soldiers of all ranks don't deprive themselves of anything, and pay well for all they want. One of the girls at the *bazaar* in the *Place*, a sort of general shop where you can get anything, from tennis-rackets to fine Flemish lace, told us she had learned English quite well, so as to be able to understand what the soldiers wanted. Said she liked the Australians very much—"*de beaux gars*." They all had money, all wanted to spend it, and buy presents for their girls at home.

We assisted at one of the purchases which was most amusing. A very good-looking young Australian was buying a handkerchief edged with lace. He was very particular about the lace, that it should be good, *pas* imitation, and wanted it put in a white box tied with a ribbon. He paid for it, and carried it off under his arm. The girl told us they had sold dozens of fine handkerchiefs and cravats trimmed with lace.

These warriors from over the sea are evidently most amiably dis-posed toward all the *jeunesse féminine*. When I came into the *hôtel* one after noon, five or six soldiers—Tommies and Anzacs—were sitting on benches outside the *café*. Quite a pretty girl came along, carrying rather a heavy basket. The soldiers all smiled up at her, crowded nearer together on the bench making a place for her to sit down, saying, "*Bon jour, Mamzelle, asseoir!*" But the girl laughed and nodded and passed on. I had the impression though that she had sometimes accepted invitations to *asseoir*.

They are a cheerful lot, always whistling and singing, and so pleased to talk to anyone who will talk to them. I fancy they are like the American cowboys—perhaps not quite so rough in their language. They are generally tall, fair, clean-shaven, with nice blue eyes. They are all volunteers as there is no compulsory service yet in Australia, though I suppose it will come, as I think it will come in all countries after this dreadful war. There are all sorts and conditions of men, just as there are in our Territorials. One of Francis' colonels is a leading lawyer in Melbourne.

We talked one day to some of the men who had been fighting on the Somme. They said it was awful. They don't like the trenches and the long-distance guns where the man fires mechanically at something he doesn't see. The shells, at least, they can see and protect themselves sometimes!

They don't like the Germans and their way of fighting. An angry look comes into their bearish blue eyes when they tell you of some of the German atrocities.

We hear the cannon very regularly, but not so distinctly as at Mareuil. No one minds. They say they don't mind even when an enemy *avion* appears; all run out into the middle of the street.

I think it is the windiest place I ever was in. We get a fierce blast every time we cross the *place*. We are quite sheltered in our villa. The garden is really charming, so well arranged that one sees a great distance over green meadows and what they call here *forests*. To us, accustomed to the splendid forests near us, Villers-Cotterets, Compiègne, etc., it seems a very ambitious name for the few clumps of trees that dot the horizon.

We often have visitors at tea-time; and the men tell Charlotte her *salon* looks very inviting with its lamps and red table-cloth.

Sometimes we have unexpected visitors. Reggie Hunt and a brother officer appeared the other day and thought we looked quite comfortable. He had inquired at the station if Mme. Waddington was in Hazebrouck. (He had seen me in the street one day when he was passing through—couldn't believe it was me; hadn't time then to stop.)

They told him, certainly, Mme. Waddington was here, living with the "Town-Major," which sounds queer. They both had very large newspaper parcels; had been shopping. They are stationed, I think, at St. Omer.

Another day we had Henry Outrey, looking very well. He is just named interpreter with an English brigade; says the officers are charming. He was going somewhere; he didn't know where, the next day. It was nice to see him and go back to old happy October days in Mareuil, when no war nor rumours of wars darkened the horizon.

Everybody stops and talks to the child when his bed is drawn close to the window. His gramophone (awful things, I think) is a great joy to him and his friends. We went for a drive one day, but we couldn't go more than a mile out of town without a *sauf-conduit*. What we saw of the country was not very pretty—low meadows, a long, straight road with the usual line of poplars on each side. Our driver didn't seem to find it very pretty either, as he brought us back into the town and showed us the beauties of Hazebrouck. A camp—near one of the hospitals with tents and flags, and always a little patch of flowers, looked rather pretty. Every building of any importance is occupied by the British, with a large Union Jack; British soldiers at the door and all sorts of mysterious letters which I couldn't understand. The boys know them all. I think I did master R. F. C. (Royal Flying Corps).

The aviators looked a fine energetic lot of young men. The Francises have seen some rather interesting air chases; British *avions* chasing Germans, only they fly so high it is rather difficult to follow an the movements.

I am thinking of going back to Paris, and have sent in my demand with all my papers to get out of Hazebrouck, which seems almost as difficult as to get in. I rather dread the long journey, but it is not very cold yet, and Mme. S. and Madeleine will come too, as they are obliged to be in Paris a few days on business.

We have decided to leave on Monday the 17th. The child is getting on well, and I feel I leave him in very good hands. I shall miss the tea in the winter garden, and the coming and going of tall British soldiers at the other end of the veranda.

Willy went hare-hunting the other day with some of the British officers, and had a blissful afternoon. His young eyes saw the hare first always, and he and the dogs went mad with excitement until they were allowed to start in pursuit. They ran through ploughed fields, over ditches and fences, but didn't get the hare. He was covered with mud up to his eyes when he came in.

We have said goodbye to all our friends (I think they will miss us in the shops) and taken our last dark walk across the *place*. I wonder if I shall ever see Hazebrouck again? I suppose not, and with time it will be confounded with the other war memories. They are not all sad and grey. The sun breaks through the clouds sometimes, when one hears of splendid acts of bravery and endurance in the trenches—and the hand-to-hand struggles. Or among the civilians in the villages in the war zone, where the women and children are doing men's work in the fields and the farms, helping each other, and sending all they can to their men at the front.

In a village near ours a girl of thirteen is running the farm. At the beginning of the war it was a thriving farm with a man and his wife, six sons and one daughter. Then the blow fell, and all the men in France were mobilised; the father and his two eldest boys went off at once—four hours after the decree of mobilisation was received in the village. The farmer had no time to put his house in order, but left the farm in the hands of his wife and the two big boys, aged fifteen and sixteen. The man and his two eldest sons are killed—the two next are in the army—the poor mother a wreck physically and mentally, can do nothing, cries all day. The whole work of the farm is done by the girl and the two little boys. The little one can't do much, is only ten years old, but he can keep the cows and carry cans of milk or baskets of butter.

I see the girl sometimes; she looks and is perfectly well; never complains; never asks for anything, except occasionally a warm petticoat or a hood to keep her head and neck warm and dry when she is working in the fields.

There are hundreds of girls doing that work all over France.

We made our home journey quite comfortably, once we got started, but there was a great crowd and confusion at the *gare*. We went early, and one of the officers took us to a small room or *bureau* of some kind where we could wait quietly until our papers were examined. There were a great many people in the room talking and asking for information of all kinds, principally English, but they didn't really talk loud or make much noise.

A blue-coated French sergeant, seated at a table rather peremptorily told people to be quiet, *not* to talk. I was rather astonished, and said to the man: "Why mustn't they talk? They are not noisy!"

"On account of the English, *Madame*, this is their *bureau*, and they don't like anyone to talk."

Our carriage as far as Boulogne was full of young British, Australian, and Canadian officers going on leave to England. Some of the Australians had never seen London, and were most excited at the idea, and so afraid they would miss the boat at Boulogne, as we were late, of course. They were all very gay, telling all sorts of stories. They had a great deal to say about the *padres*, for whom they seemed to have a great respect; said some of them were so human. One had preached a splendid sermon one day, and remained afterward talking to the men, still reminding them that at any time their lives might be asked of them, and they must give them willingly for their country. They all agreed, and one young fellow said: "All right, *padre*, we'll all play the game when the times comes; but it isn't for tonight. Come and have a drink!"

"Yes, I will with pleasure," said the *padre*, and a good long drink he took, and then they all sang "God Save the King," and felt very happy and cheerful.

We passed again through the long lines of *barraques* and tents that reach almost to Amiens. At every station there were British soldiers and nurses. It seemed almost strange at Amiens to go out of the British atmosphere.

The Gare du Nord was crowded with blue-coated soldiers coming home on a *permission de huit jours*, all smiling and pleased to be back, looking out so eagerly for their womankind, who, they knew, were waiting for them at the station—wives and children standing for hours in the long line to catch their first glimpse of their hero from the Somme; the children crowding around "papa," and carrying his bag or his bundle.

It is tragic to think how many "papas" will never come back, and that we can do nothing for any of our men at the front. All our prayers and tears are unavailing if the decree has gone forth and their lives must be given for their country.

www.ingramcontent.com/pod-product-compliance
Lightning Source LLC
Chambersburg PA
CBHW032057080426
42733CB00006B/311